BREAKING
GRIDLOCK

BREAKING GRIDLOCK

Moving Toward Transportation That Works

JIM MOTAVALLI

Sierra Club Books
San Francisco

The Sierra Club, founded in 1892 by John Muir, has devoted itself to the study and protection of the Earth's scenic and ecological resources—mountains, wetlands, woodlands, wild shores and rivers, deserts and plains. The publishing program of the Sierra Club offers books to the public as a nonprofit educational service in the hope that they may enlarge the public's understanding of the Club's basic concerns. The point of view expressed in each book, however, does not necessarily represent that of the Club. The Sierra Club has some sixty chapters coast to coast, in Canada, Hawaii, and Alaska. For information about how you may participate in its programs to preserve wilderness and the quality of life, please address inquiries to Sierra Club, 85 Second Street, San Francisco, CA 94105.

Sierra Club Books
85 Second Street
San Francisco, California 94105
www.sierraclub.org/books

Published in conjunction with Crown Publishers,
New York, New York. Member of the Crown Publishing Group.
Random House, Inc. New York, Toronto, London, Sydney, Auckland
www.randomhouse.com

SIERRA CLUB, SIERRA CLUB BOOKS, and the Sierra Club design
logos are registered trademarks of the Sierra Club.

Library of Congress Cataloging-in-Publication Data
Motavalli, Jim.
    Breaking gridlock : moving toward transportation that works /
by Jim Motavalli.
        Includes bibliographical references and index.
        1. Transportation and state—United States.   2. Urban transportation policy—
United States.   3. Transportation—United States—Planning.   4. Urban
transportation—United States—Planning.   5. Infrastructure (Economics)—
United States.   6. Traffic congestion—United States. I. Title.
HE206.2 .M67 2001
388.4'0973—dc21   2001020258
ISBN 1-57805-039-1
10 9 8 7 6 5 4 3 2 1
First Edition

To Mary Ann, Maya, and Delia, who rode with me

Acknowledgments

I WISH I COULD personally thank every train conductor, bus driver, and pilot who helped me on the long journey that became this book. Instead, I'd like to express my sincere appreciation to the people who operate American mass-transit systems for carrying on against overwhelming automotive odds and for helping to relieve congestion that would otherwise completely suffocate urban and rural life. Along the way, I had help from Linda Baker, who showed me Portland and let me borrow some of her ideas about sprawl; Amanda Presley, who got me the goods on bullet trains; Hillary Young, who conducted some of the more interesting Big Dig interviews; Sharon Boddy, who put me in touch with the carless world; Leslie Pardue, for a contribution on national parks; Jennifer Bogo, who held the fort at *E;* and Doug Moss, who reluctantly indulges peripatetic editors. My editor, Linda Gunnarson, was a pleasure to work with on my first book, *Forward Drive,* so I made sure she was available before setting forth on this one. My agent, Sabine Hrechdakian, continues to be an ideal combination of hardheaded businessperson and very sympathetic literary judge. Thanks are also due to Katie Alvord, G. B. Arrington, Dick Bauer, Janine Bauer, Rachel Bauer, Milton Beach, Dan Becker, Robert Beinenfeld, Dave Burwell, Reeves Callaway, James Cannon, Jim Cobb, Robert Cotter, Dr. Joseph Coughlin, John DeCicco, Hank Dittmar, Robert Edison Fulton Jr., Randy Ghent, Deborah Gordon, Scott Harris, Lesley Hazleton, Elizabeth Hilts, Laura Hitchcock, Kevin Hoover, Roland Hwang, Orna Izakson, John Kaehny, Jane Holtz Kay,

Charles Komanoff, Hans and Kate Koning, Fred Krupp, Ty Lasky, Jan Lundberg, Paul MacCready, Charles and Diane Mark-Walker, Paul Moller, Bill Moore, Jack Nilles, Sean O'Neill, Grant Parker, Lynn Ann Peterson, Anthony Rizos, David Rothenberg, Robert Silver, Gar Smith, Maren Souders, Daniel Sperling, Robert Stempel, Dick Thompson, and Watts Wacker.

Contents

Carriages without horses shall go,
And accidents fill the world with woe.
Around the world, thoughts shall fly,
In the twinkling of an eye.

—Martha "Mother" Shipton
(1488–1561), from *Prophecy*

Introduction

IN 1965, when I was thirteen years old, my parents sent me to stay at a Christian boarding school in the far north of India, where the world's second most populous nation borders Tibet and Nepal. It was wild country, there in the foothills of the Himalayas, and Woodstock School was almost unreachable by road. Only the odd Jeep or Land Rover made it to our mountaintop aerie, where the evening quiet was broken only by birdcalls, monkeys crashing through the trees, and the occasional cry of a jaguar. Life at school was still very much as it had been in the nineteenth century, and the graves of British officers and their families kept the colonial heritage alive.

It was five miles to the little village of Mussoorie, along a five-foot-wide path regularly knocked out entirely by rock slides. I happened to be visiting the bazaar there one Saturday morning when a well-known Indian film star, delivering his son to Woodstock, arrived to great fanfare. The car made an indelible impression: in a country where the few people with private automobiles drove putt-putting Hindustan Ambassadors (very bad knockoffs of an early 1950s Morris) and the roads were filled with oxcarts and bicycles, the film star had shown up in a brand-new Cadillac convertible. It was like Proust's madeleine, a delegate from the world I had left behind when I'd come to India the year before, a world of fast V-8-powered cars running on spacious interstate highways dotted with drive-ins, billboards, and bright green exit signs. Far from being repulsed by the sight of that Cadillac, I was filled with intense longing. I ran a finger along its dusty tail fin, earning a warning gesture from the chauffeur.

Within a year I was back in Connecticut, living in the shadow of the Merritt Parkway, a scenic route that, when it opened in 1938, had been considered the last word in fast transit. "More than any 'futurama' at the World's Fair, more than any dream of the futuristic designers, it shows what the highway of the future should really look like—a highway where the eye is filled with beauty and the mind with peace as the car purrs safely along," wrote the *Bridgeport Post* at the time.[1] (Recently I found an old hand-tinted postcard from 1940 entitled "Along the Merritt Parkway." The smooth-as-glass highway looks wide enough for four cars, but only three are visible in what looks like about a mile-long stretch.)

The state I was returning to was now served by two major highways. The Merritt had been complemented by I-95, the north-south federal highway stretching from Maine to Florida. President John F. Kennedy had opened the toll road with a ribbon-cutting ceremony on November 14, 1963, just eight days before he was assassinated, calling the new six-lane artery "the most modern interstate highway system in the world." In a burst of optimism, highway planners dubbed Connecticut's section of I-95 a "Ribbon of Hope" because of the economic opportunity it would bring. When I was little, my parents would take me to view this beacon of progress under construction. They said the sight of all that big earth-moving equipment always calmed me down.

And as soon as I was sixteen, I had a car of my own, commuting to high school and later to work along that same corridor. It was the best of times for the American automobile, buoyed by postwar prosperity, thirty-cents-a-gallon gasoline, and a brand-new interstate system that connected everyone to everything, just as the railroads and trolley cars had once done.

I-95's unwanted passenger was urban sprawl, known positively at the time as affordable developments for urban exiles in search of their half acre—and the cocktail parties, good schools, and backyard barbecues that came with the territory. The highways worked in tandem with the corridor's commuter railway, Metro-North, to make the good life possible. Hollywood paid tribute with postwar films such as *The Man in the Grey Flannel Suit* and *Mr. Blandings Builds His Dream House,* satirizing suburbia while celebrating it, too.

Fairfield County, like most American suburbs, kept right on growing, crowding out farmland and often leaving only the name behind. Where were the big shade trees at Twin Oaks Estates and the wildlife at Deer Run Apartments? The highways, dissuaded by rocketing land values and not-in-my-backyard opposition, couldn't begin to keep pace. I-95 today is pretty much the I-95 of 1963, but traffic on it has tripled. Mass transit is in no position to help out. Only 4 percent of state commuters use it. The trolleys that once carried passengers from New York City to Maine are now only a memory. The fuming diesel buses that have taken their place are a nightmare of missed connections and competing jurisdictions, with most transit lines ending at town borders. Metro-North, despite its loyal commuter base, sags under an aging infrastructure and seems ill-suited to meet the needs of the new information worker, who travels not to New York but to an office tower in another suburb.

A majority of Fairfield County's commuters, a group that most definitely includes me, now spend about a fifth of their time on the road stuck in bumper-to-bumper jams, wasting thirty-three hours a year and sixty gallons of gas. The highways aren't growing, but use of them climbs a steady 1.5 percent a year. The coastal corridor of I-95 was designed forty years ago for 50,000 cars a day; today it carries 150,000, and 172,000 is the projected figure for 2020. Driving habits are a big part of the problem. The number of car trips on major highways has increased 96 percent since 1968. Of the 166,566 workers counted in the region during the 1990 census, 74 percent drive their cars to work solo, say the state Departments of Motor Vehicles and Transportation.

The traffic problem in Fairfield County isn't just an inconvenience. All those idling cars have put the county and its surrounding region into the Environmental Protection Agency's air-pollution top ten. My fellow commuters and I breathe what staff attorney Karyl Lee Hall of the Connecticut Fund for the Environment describes as "the worst, absolutely the worst, air quality in the state." She adds that air pollution is only part of the problem: dirt and contaminants from the roads also wash into rivers, lakes, and Long Island Sound, endangering aquatic life by starving it of oxygen.

In addition, those idled commuters, frantically dialing out on their cell phones and even trying to send faxes, collectively represent hundreds of thousands of hours of lost productivity. In 1996, the Road Information Program estimated that congested roads in the largest twenty-five urban centers cost commuters $43 billion annually in wasted time and fuel costs.

In 1997, after years and years of watching the daily commute sink back to sub-nineteenth-century levels of frustration and elapsed time, Governor John Rowland nailed a fifteen-point traffic-reducing program on the door of the sometimes-somnambulant Connecticut Department of Transportation. If fully implemented, Rowland said, the plan would cut congestion in the corridor by 5 percent by 2002—all without building any new roads. Instead of pouring more concrete, the state would try to get commuters out of their cars with a series of incentives designed to bolster rail and bus travel, as well as encourage vanpooling, ferry services, flexible work hours, and telecommuting. To achieve that 5 percent reduction of cars on I-95, congestion will actually need to be cut by 12.5 percent, since traffic builds at a relentless 1.5 percent a year.

In 1997, there were high hopes that a fast-ferry commuter service would be running by 2000, but plans were shelved by local zoning and parking squabbles. No fewer than three companies had announced that they would launch ferries, with runs to Manhattan's financial district and La Guardia Airport in Queens, but starting dates were repeatedly pushed back. The plan to reduce traffic on the main strip road, Route 1, had met only 18 percent of its goals by 2000, the Department of Transportation said. But it added quickly that it had successfully removed 1,504 cars from I-95 and the Merritt Parkway. "Where's the beef?" critics asked.[2]

An ambitious $58 million railway improvement plan to add parking, make improvements, and survey passengers made absolutely no progress in its first two years. Most railroad stations in Fairfield County (far from the "intermodal" ideal of linked transportation systems) are isolated and have long waiting lines for parking spaces, deferring the dream of adding train commuters. Would-be rail passengers also chafe at the slow, delay-plagued schedules in an era when European trains routinely zip along at more than 150 miles per hour. (In 1849, Fairfield County commuters on the New York, New Haven, and Hartford Railroad could get to the city in an hour—the same amount of time it takes today.)

Carpooling, never that strong in Fairfield County, has almost disappeared, mirroring a national drop from 19.7 percent of the commuting public in 1980 (when memories of the fuel crisis were still fresh) to 13.4 percent in 1990. Highway planners now contemplate an era of permanent tie-ups, when traffic levels at noon and three P.M. rival those of rush hour. There is talk—who knows how serious—of double-decking I-95, a monumental public works project that would cost billions and rival Boston's Big Dig Central Artery reconstruction in complexity and time frame. (A more modest proposal would simply turn the existing I-95 road shoulder into another traffic lane.)

Concern in the state reached such a crescendo that Governor Rowland was forced to convene Connecticut Transportation Summit 2000 in Hartford. Proposals totaling nearly $6 billion were put on the table, many of them transit-oriented. These included expanding train schedules, building up the state's airports, creating ferry routes, and offering cash rebates to employees who take mass transit to work.[3] I looked at my own auto-based commute, a straw on the camel's load, and began to realize I was part of the problem, too.

A BETTER WAY TO GO

To challenge my own car dependence, I recently decided to take public transportation to the office, along a perfectly workable route that involves the Metro-North commuter-rail system and two local buses. I live in an urban-suburban neighborhood that is close to the

Bridgeport, Connecticut, city line. My town isn't particularly transit-friendly, but for many of Bridgeport's car-free citizens, the bus and train are vital lifelines.

I set out walking to the bus stop at 8:08 A.M., about forty-five minutes before I routinely leave the house. I usually see the neighborhood rushing past through a car window, so it was a pleasure to be able to savor its sights and smells. The streets are from different eras, and the first thing I noticed was that the 1920s colonial houses were rarely built with attached garages; architects of the era preferred to hide them out back. The 1950s and 1960s split-levels, however, put their two-car garages out front, as an integral part of the house. By the postwar period, the automobile was a member of the family.

For the first time, I noticed the flower beds in the highway center divider near the bus stop. It may also have been the first time I noticed the bus stop, too. At 8:18, a bus arrived. The friendly driver noticed me fumbling with my change and told me I could put in $1.00 instead of $1.10. "I'll make you an honorary senior citizen," he said. I sat down and read the messages, one of which said, PLEASE OFFER SEATS FORWARD OF THIS SIGN TO THE ELDERLY AND HANDICAPPED. Unfortunately, the sign was posted on the front row of seats.

My fellow passengers were all black women, and most of them seemed to know each other. My neighbor, an older woman who carried a cane, explained to me that though she owned a car, the bus was more convenient. "And I like the drivers, too," she said. She was on her way to work at a mall department store.

At 8:30, the bus arrived at the central terminal in downtown Bridgeport. The city had shown some forward thinking many years ago, long before the word *intermodal* came into vogue, by building its bus station right next to its railroad station. I walked through the gritty bus station and onto the front steps of the newly rebuilt train depot, which offers both Metro-North commuter trains and Amtrak service.

A ticket to Norwalk, where I work, was $2.75. The clerk directed me to Track 4, which was through some doors, down an elevator, and up three flights of stairs, all with minimal signage. When I finally reached the platform, seemingly on the wrong side of the tracks, I found two out-of-breath women who'd just run over from the other side. They were shaking their heads over Metro-North's failure to provide coherent track information. "They don't volunteer any information unless you ask," said one, sitting down to flip open her laptop computer.

The train itself was about five minutes late. I sat next to two men in business suits bound for Manhattan, both with copies of the *Wall Street Journal*. For many New York commuters, the train is their one venture onto public transportation. It would be hard to imagine them on a bus.

The train car was aging, though tolerably clean. It never went above fifty miles per hour, crawling speed for Japanese and European express trains. An advertising placard near the automatic doors informed me that, on this week in 1892, Lizzie Borden had taken an ax to her parents. Just as I was settling in, the conductor told me that if I wanted to get off in East Norwalk, I'd have to move up a car. Shortly after I did that, the train stopped between stations. Although it was never explained, we were waiting for the relatively sleek Amtrak train to come roaring by, which it did ten minutes later.

The train paralleled I-95, and I could see the bunching traffic that would have been my fate had I driven that morning. Since the train has a dedicated route of way, it never gets caught in bumper-to-bumper congestion, though our slow progress made it hard to feel triumphant. I arrived at the East Norwalk station at 9:15, with no indication of how a weary traveler might find a local bus. I started walking in the general direction and, after half a mile, encountered a colorfully painted Norwalk bus. I waved my arms, and it stopped. The fare was an even dollar. As I again fumbled for change, a kindly older woman in the seat up front offered to make up any differential. She introduced herself as Dorothy Nagy, a medical supply worker who'd stopped driving seven years ago because of a stroke. "I like the buses just fine," she said. "And what with the price of gasoline . . ." She let the sentence trail off.

The bus stopped right at my office door. It was 9:25 A.M. It had taken me seventy-seven minutes to get to work, a fair bit longer than my usual twenty to thirty minutes, but a far more human and involving experience.

DRIVING OFF THE EDGE

Fairfield County's example and my own frustration with an increasingly arduous trek to work are microcosms in a country where traffic and auto-related pollution threaten to drive us off the edge. And the problem isn't just national; it's international: even Mussoorie, untouched by time well into the 1970s, has become a gaudy tourist mecca chockablock with cheap hotels and discos. Cars were a rarity in my day, but they're omnipresent now, and what was once bracing mountain air has been sullied by diesel exhaust from the tour buses.

To point all this out is nothing new, of course. A long shelf could be filled with books urging us to take a more sane approach to our transportation future. The problem is, they tend to offer prescriptions—fast magnetic-levitation trains, intermodal stations, clean hybrid buses, catamaran ferries, bicycles, fuel-cell cars—and leave it at that. But most of these new new technologies have been around for decades. A 1982 children's book called *The Kids' Whole Future Catalog* presented excited summaries of all these inventions and imagined that by 2000, surely, we'd be using all of them. What's holding them back is a national commitment like the one that built the hugely effective national rail link, which peaked in 1920, when there were 300,000 miles of federally regulated track. There's only half that now. The automobile has divided and conquered like no invention before it.

In April 2000, the *Washington Post* bannered an encouraging headline: "Mass Transit Popularity Surges in U.S." It seems that the number of people riding trains and buses is the highest it's been in forty years. Ridership is actually rising faster than automobile use. In Washington, D.C., for instance, the Red and Orange Lines are running at near capacity. That is good news, but it masks a grim little secret: all the forms of mass transit together, including trains, buses, bicycles, and that old standby the human leg, account for a tiny share of American transportation use. "Let's not break out the champagne," said William Fay, president of the American Highway Users Alliance, in the story. "Highway growth is the real success. By real numbers, far more people are driving cars than taking transit."

Unfortunately, Fay has a point. The transit numbers, although improving, look good only until they're compared with auto use. According to U.S. Department of Transportation data compiled in 1995 as part of the Nationwide Personal Transportation Survey, America's 100 million households make 1 billion trips a day. But of that, 900 million trips were by car, 65 million by foot or bicycle, and just 19 million by transit. (The rest are school-bus rides and "other.") Transit is not even 2 percent of the total.

Will those numbers shift dramatically as America becomes more transit-friendly? Dr. Joseph Coughlin, director of the MIT Center for Transportation Studies, is pessimistic that any dramatic change is in the offing. "I think the traffic stream in, say, 2050 will look very much like what I'm seeing out my office window right now," he told me. "Transportation policies are made every day as people put their car keys in the ignition. The independent variable is not technology but lifestyle. For transportation to change, the nature of home, work, and family has to change. There's no point in environmentalists and transit advocates preaching to people about where they should live and what form of transportation they should take. We'll continue to be car- and personal-mobility-dependent."

Reeves Callaway, a Connecticut-based auto industry insider whose company builds twin-turbo Corvettes and other ultrafast exotica, is nonetheless enthusiastic about the future of hydrogen power and other clean technologies for cars. Although he thinks it's probable that Americans will someday drive on automated highways, he doesn't think our enormous auto dependence is poised for a shift. "I'd be very surprised if there was a big change in the basic forms of transportation," he told me.

The satiric on-line publication the *Onion,* which specializes in news parodies, recently ran a story entitled "98 Percent of U.S. Commuters Favor Public Transportation for Others." Citing a fictitious American Public Transportation Association report, it concluded that four out of five Americans have recognized the need for "everyone else" to take the train or the bus.[4] That's funny, and it contains an uncomfortable grain of truth.

There's a rut in the middle of the road, and we're stuck in it. The work-bound traveler of 1950, even 1900, had more transportation options than does the ultramodern, cell-phone-equipped millennial commuter of today. Sure, that's grim, but we have some very viable options, and I'll examine them closely in this book.

Chapter 1 delves deep into the colorful literature of the nineteenth and twentieth centuries to critically examine the forward thinking of the time. It's interesting to note that nearly everyone got it wrong.

In chapter 2, the narrative zooms forward into an untenable present, where cities have sprawled and traffic has stalled. How, at a time when the pundits of the past thought we would be gliding effortlessly forward on rocket cars, have we become so decidedly earthbound? How are we going to get out of this trap of our own devising? Smart cars, smart tolls, and paratransit provide some glimmers of light.

A growing number of Americans live in "edge cities," business corridors between our traditional urban centers. Chapter 3 looks at how this peculiar land-use pattern, and the whole suburbanizing of the United States, has helped create gridlock. It also finds a few solutions in telecommuting and e-commerce.

Some urban centers are pointing to a better way. Chapter 4 goes on the road for an up-close look at five "transit cities"—New York; Boston; Los Angeles; Portland, Oregon; and Arcata, California—that are struggling to keep things livable as they go about the daunting task of delivering people to work and play.

Some European cities point the way forward, with their determined effort to limit the influence of the auto and encourage transit use. Through careful regional planning, Zurich, Copenhagen, and many other communities large and small have kept the car at bay. This approach contrasts sharply with the United States, where sustainable urban planning has taken a back seat to the auto industry's own vision of a workable future: high-tech cars to turn the long-distance commuter car into an extension of the living room, and looming ahead, the automated highway to take the driver out of the equation. Chapter 5 follows these divergent paths.

Chapter 6 looks at the prospects for reinventing the car as something cleaner and greener. If we're going to remain auto-dependent and "sprawled" for the foreseeable future, fuel cells and hybrid technologies at least point to a future where oil use can diminish and gradually reach a vanishing point.

The humble transit bus, which often gets neglected in transit planning, actually carries far more passengers than light rail and other popular modes. Chapter 7 gives the bus its due, and also looks at ways to reduce or eliminate the clouds of diesel exhaust issuing from its tailpipe.

Chapter 8 is a tour of the world's rail systems, including a look into the future as high-speed trains at last arrive in America, or at least the Northeast corridor.

Futurists invariably think personal transportation will head for the relatively uncrowded skies, but we're a long way from a private airplane in every garage. Chapter 9 looks at some answers to the deepening gridlock we've built around America's airports, and at some novel experiments that may really get off the ground.

The old-fashioned ferryboat is enjoying a long-overdue revival and may soon grow wings of its own, as chapter 10 explains. Are high-speed catamarans likely to make a difference in some of our more challenged transportation corridors?

And finally, in chapter 11, it's time to look beyond the automobile and to sum up the lessons learned from a handful of thoroughly punched train, subway, bus, and ferryboat tickets.

1

LOOKING FORWARD
FROM THE PAST

TO FIND A WORKABLE VISION of our transportation future, I decided to look into the past, beginning in the crumbling pages of some old books in the local library. Prognostications about the future have always been popular with the public, and never more so than in the nineteenth century, when H. G. Wells and Jules Verne were literary superstars. The fact that their predictions about transportation were both amazingly prescient and howlingly wrong provides us with insight into our own century, when we're once again casting about for something new.

Arthur C. Clarke, the author of *2001*, reports that science fiction as we know it today didn't exist until the seventeenth century and the invention of the telescope, which first made it possible to understand the scale of the universe.[1] From the beginning, these imagineers were far more interested in the idea of space travel than in moving around here on earth. Fanciful journeys to the moon were described as early as 1630. Cyrano de Bergerac was one enthusiast of that era, producing a book called *A Voyage to the Moon*. Jonathan Swift's *Gulliver's Travels*, published in 1726, was, among many other things, one of the first extended science fiction works. But it wasn't until the 1800s that the field truly flowered, attracting entries from writers as diverse as Robert Louis Stevenson, H. Rider Haggard, Mary Shelley, and Rudyard Kipling.

The acknowledged pioneer was Jules Verne, born in 1828 and probably the first true science fiction writer. It was Verne who anticipated the hydrogen economy by predicting that water would replace coal as the fuel of the future, and Verne, alone among his contemporaries, imagined a practical internal-combustion vehicle. Among the inventions anticipated by Verne, who gave the world such classics as *From the Earth to the Moon* and *The Tour of the World in Eighty Days* (later retitled), were the airplane, the helicopter, the submarine, the automobile, the computer, and even air-conditioning.

Verne was modest about his accomplishments. Shortly before he died, in 1905, he told a correspondent from the *London Daily News,* "It will perhaps surprise you to hear that I do not take especial pride in having written of the motor car, the submarine boat, and the navigable airship before they became actual realities. When I wrote about them . . . these things were already half discoveries. I simply made fiction out of what became ulterior fact."[2]

For Verne, born of middle-class parents in the seaport city of Nantes, writing was a way to escape the secure but boring legal career for which he'd been trained. Verne wrote his first novel when he was working part-time in the Paris stock market. "My friends," he told his colleagues there, "I bid you adieu. . . . I've just written a novel in a new style. . . . If it succeeds, it will be a gold mine."[3] He was right about that. The book was *Five Weeks in a Balloon,* and it launched a spectacular literary career that saw him writing two novels a year until he died, literally with pen in hand.

But *Five Weeks in a Balloon* wasn't the only book Verne wrote in 1863. He also produced the amazingly visionary *Paris in the Twentieth Century.* Never heard of it? It's not surprising, because the manuscript was locked in a safe for more than a hundred years.

Verne's publisher, Pierre-Jules Hetzel, didn't care for the new book. According to the introduction of the 1996 Random House edition, Hetzel turned down *Paris in the Twentieth Century,* proclaiming it "a hundred feet below *Five Weeks in a Balloon.*"[4] Nobody, Hetzel said, "would believe this prophecy."

Verne put his book away and went on to other things. The unpublished manuscript sat in a bronze safe until 1989, when the author's great-grandson sold the family home and disposed of its contents.

The keyless safe was believed to be empty, but when it was opened with a blowtorch, the manuscript was discovered inside.

What a world Verne imagined for 1960! The boulevards of Paris, brightly lit with electric light, were traversed by countless horseless carriages, "invisibly powered by a motor which operated by gas consumption." In Verne's motor, lighting gas "mixed with air was introduced into the piston and set off by a spark, producing forward movement"—an accurate description of today's internal-combustion engine. Verne's lighting gas was hydrogen, which drivers filled up on from curbside hydrants. BMW, among other companies, is currently exploring the idea of hydrogen-powered internal combustion and is working in partnership on similar hydrogen "hydrants." (The author also filled the wondrous balloon of his 1887 story "The Clipper of the Clouds" with hydrogen, inadvertently anticipating the *Hindenburg* disaster that occurred fifty years later.) Verne hedged his bets, though—he still imagined there would be a few horses pulling carriages in 1960, though they'd be kept off the streets after ten A.M.

Like most visionaries, however, Verne was a man of his times. He imagined the automobile, but not how completely it would eclipse the passenger train, which gets far more space in his book. Verne anticipated urban sprawl and imagined that Paris would grow well past its present limits, with neighborhoods arrayed along the new train tracks. The trains themselves had bid the Iron Age adieu; they were lightweight and ran on compressed air, so nearby residents suffered from neither steam nor smoke.

The young hero of Verne's novel eventually becomes disillusioned with the world of the future, but the author was nonetheless appreciative of its utopian transportation system. Verne wrote, "What would one of our ancestors have said upon seeing these boulevards lit as brightly as by the sun, these thousand carriages circulating noiselessly on the silent asphalt of the streets . . . these glittering trains, which seemed to furrow the air with fantastic speed?"[5]

Unlike Verne, H. G. Wells, born in 1866, was raised in near poverty. The family's circumstances meant that Wells was only sporadically educated, finally winning a scholarship to the Royal College of Science in Kensington. Before beginning his literary career, he worked as a tutor and journalist.

It was Wells's second book, *The Time Machine* (1895), that established his name, offering a depressing view of the far future in which humanity has split into two degenerated subspecies. Only a few years later, in 1901, Wells produced *Anticipations,* which was serialized in the English magazine *Fortnightly Review.* In that collection of stories, later published as a book, Wells foretold much of what the new century would bring, including prefabricated homes, airplanes, car-choked highways, and a triumphant suburbia. He even imagined the "Bos-Wash" corridor of uninterrupted development. Of course, he also predicted the end of capitalism in that book, but the free market has proven unexpectedly resilient.

Arthur C. Clarke believes that Wells was a better writer than Verne. "Perhaps he had too many gifts," Clarke writes in *Voices from the Sky.* "If he had not been so interested in politics, history and society, he might have written fewer but better books."[6] He was to write 150.

Some of the most remarkable passages Wells wrote are in "A Story of the Days to Come," a twenty-second-century vision collected in 1927 in *The Short Stories of H. G. Wells.*[7] Until the beginning of the nineteenth century, the author wrote, people seldom traveled more than sixty miles in a day and for the most part "dwelt in little towns and villages." But the machine age wrought many changes. Cities "darkened by smoky fogs, [un]sanitary and noisy" were the product of industrialization and a revolution in transportation, a process that had so accelerated by the year 2100 that conventional roads and railways had been abandoned. Replacing them were rubberized superhighways with slow and fast lanes, allowing speeds of up to two hundred miles per hour. In a quaint reflection of the times, the slow lane was reserved for bicyclists "and other conveyances travelling at a less speed than 25 miles per hour." The traffic moved along "with throbbing engines and noiseless wheels and a perpetual wild melody of horns and gongs." Pedestrians were, by then, a rare sight. Smog was banished too, thanks to electric heat, which replaced coal fires.

Neither Wells nor Verne could be called technological optimists.

For all the gleaming new inventions they predicted, they also foresaw quite a bit of human misery brought about by mechanization.

The visions of Wells and Verne reflected their times. There was a surprising amount of skepticism at the beginning of the twentieth century about the brave new world that was unfolding in front of everyone's eyes, and it's captured in the political cartoons of the period.[8] The pattern was to imagine a utopian future for inventions that had not yet appeared, then to deride them as calamitous once they actually arrived on the scene. That's the way they looked at the "bike craze" of the Gay Nineties, when every cyclist was seen as a speed demon.

In 1878 *Century Magazine* looked forward to the "aeronon of the twentieth century," which would be fish-shaped, made of light metal, supported by nonexplosive gas, and propelled by electric motors, moving at great speeds of up to eighty miles per hour. The author correctly predicted that such machines would "clip the claws" of the railway managers. By 1910, *Life* was imagining vast airships docking on the roofs of New York skyscrapers, the landscape disfigured by advertising that could be read only from the air. A year later, with airplanes dotting the landscape, *Judge* magazine imagined hordes of passengers parachuting from a derelict airbus.

The *Brooklyn Eagle,* in 1900, thought that bicycles and automobiles would "eliminate house flies and street noise." But by 1901 *Life* imagined chaos on the new fast expressways, especially if a horse and buggy happened to stray into the path of rushing traffic. Three years later, the magazine was even more pessimistic, depicting thrill-crazed motorists laying waste to the landscape, with belching smokestacks in the background as part and parcel. And *Life* anticipated the modern hot-rod craze in 1908, with a cartoon showing flaming youth taking its recess in a speeding automobile. The pedestrian of the future would have to carry bleating horns and blinking lights to avoid getting flattened, opined *Judge* in 1913.

Cities would, of course, be ruined. The coming of the car and other modern devices meant that hapless urbanites would be asphyxiated by fumes, strangled in electric and telegraph wires, and run over by hurtling traffic. The landscape of the late twentieth century, claimed *Life* in 1910, would be so filled with flying airships, elevated railway lines, and bridges going every which way that no one would be able to see the sky.

Much more optimistic was Edward Bellamy, a lawyer, novelist, and proponent of eccentric diets (milk, raw eggs, and whiskey) whose great work is *Looking Backward: 2000–1887*. Bellamy's book is fascinating because it looks forward from the nineteenth century precisely to our time.

Bellamy was a pretty turgid writer, though, and he only got worse after *Looking Backward,* which enjoyed a wide following (selling an incredible million copies before 1900). His stated purpose was to "reason out a method of economic organization by which the republic might guarantee the livelihood and material welfare of its citizens on a basis of equality corresponding to and supplementing their political equality." So his book is an economic and philosophical tome thinly disguised as a novel.

By 2000, Bellamy imagined, Boston would be a utopia: "Miles of broad streets, shaded by trees and lined with fine buildings. . . . Every quarter contained large open squares filled with trees, among which statues glistened and fountains flashed in the late afternoon sun. Public buildings of a colossal size and an architectural grandeur unparalleled in my day raised their stately piles on every side."[9]

Bellamy was no visionary when it came to transportation. His future folk walked everywhere. The closest he got to transit technology was the "pneumatic transmitter," which apparently moved goods as quickly as Federal Express.

Bellamy could perhaps be forgiven for not seeing the automobile coming. Most of the experts of the period didn't. The great 1892 World's Columbian Exposition in Chicago brought together sages from seventy-four countries, who gave their opinion on transportation in the 1990s.[10] Amazingly enough, though they predicted airplanes with great accuracy and believed that railroad trains would reach the heady speeds of one hundred miles per hour, they didn't see the car that was then just on the horizon. The transportation building at the big fair featured not an automobile of the future but a thirty-foot model of the British warship *Victory* and a specially built train of Pullman cars.

Special attention should be paid to "The Machine Stops," an amazingly visionary short story written by English author E. M. Forster in 1909. It anticipated not only the Internet, but also the human isolation it would foster. Forster's futurists have world-spanning airships, but use them only reluctantly.

In the years between the world wars, the need for escape during a global depression and the relatively new medium of film gave rise to some haunting futuristic visions. The most memorable was probably Fritz Lang's highly stylized 1926 *Metropolis,* set in the year 2000. In Lang's vision, an upper-class utopia (with tall skyscrapers and ultrafast airplanes) is kept in place by a vast toiling underclass, who sweat feverishly at underground machines and conveyer belts. Meanwhile, devilish bureaucrats devise robots to take the place of the trouble-prone workers. The coming of robots was also envisioned around this time by British prime minister Winston Churchill. Writing in *Popular Mechanics* in 1933, Churchill predicted, "Production of such beings may be possible within 50 years."[11] "Elektro," a Westinghouse robot prototype, was featured at the 1939 World's Fair in New York.

Things to Come, filmed in 1936 and taken from H. G. Wells's novel *The Shape of Things to Come,* was rather more optimistic than Lang's story of democracy for the few. In the film, a thirty-year-long world war has wreaked havoc, but the devastated "Everytown" is rebuilt as a glittering utopia (again with gleaming futuristic "skyships") by a benevolent class of "airmen."

The 1940s produced the gloomy prognostication of books like George Orwell's *1984,* reflecting the deepening Cold War. Technology was frequently seen as a weapon of mass control. But the 1950s were much more sanguine about the future. In a burst of postwar optimism, Americans imagined atomic cars running on power too cheap to meter, mechanical maids that would do all our work for us, food pills that would take care of hunger, and dissolving plates that would melt down the drain. By now, the pundits predicted, we should have routine ultrasonic flight (today limited to the troubled Concorde), electric cars in every garage, videophones (first depicted by French artist Albert Robida in 1889), cryonics, and the paperless office.

Modern science fiction, as opposed to the more stilted nineteenth-century version, has generally been so fascinated with space travel that it barely spares a thought for the more mundane surface transportation. Robert Heinlein's *The Past Through Tomorrow,* published in 1967, predicted that by 2000 a gasoline shortage would lead to the invention of one-hundred-mile-per-hour mechanized conveyer belts between cities. In Arthur C. Clarke's 1951 *Sands of Mars,* transport on the red planet is via "the famous Martian 'Sand Fleas,'" which are described as small, squat machines with wide balloon tires and pressurized driving cabs. It's hard to say what powered them in the thin Martian atmosphere. By the time he wrote *2061: Odyssey Three* in 1987, Clarke was predicting that a 2040 breakthrough in "stable muonium-hydrogen compounds" would lead to routine solar-system flights. The most convenient fuel was water.

The ever-imaginative Philip K. Dick spared little thought to getting around our woebegone planet, though he did have a character in the 1964 *Three Stigmata of Palmer Eldritch* driving a "Jaguar XXB sports ship with a flatout velocity of 15,000 miles per hour." Less-fortunate people made do with "thermosealed interbuilding commute cars." Isaac Asimov and Robert Silverberg devote many pages to the nuances of space flight in their 1992 *The Positronic Man,* but only one line to the "splendid robochauffeured limousine" that delivered a U.S. Robots executive to a Martian estate.

David Brin's visionary book *Earth,* written in 1990 and set in 2038, imagines transportation responding to a deepening environmental crisis. Writing before the consequences of global warming were generally known, Brin imagined an overcrowded world of ten billion people that had been inundated by rising sea levels. Holes in the ozone layer make any trip outside life-threatening, and even the livestock wear eye covers. Siberia is tropical, and Bangladesh's capital is under water. The last wildlife is housed in zoolike "arks," and private cars have been outlawed in favor of bicycles. A glass of pure water costs as much as the monthly rent, and jail time is ordered for anyone throwing away a soda bottle.

What are people getting around on? Mostly bicycles. "Petrol was rationed on a need-only basis," Brin writes. Mass transportation, as he saw it, would consist of "flywheel buses" and "commuter zeppelins."

Science fiction does not deliver the goods on earthbound transport. More rewarding is a look at that peculiar blend of hard reality and complete fantasy that parades in the pages of *Popular Science*. I went through a year of issues from 1960, one of our more optimistic periods. I loved what I saw. All of the fanciful inventions were real, and practically none of them had any staying power.

In just one issue, January 1960, *Popular Science* brought us such wonderful innovations as the wingless airliner that could travel at sixty-two miles a minute, the hanging TV (saves floor space), the push-button teacher, and the car that "runs on oil pumped to the wheels, without clutch, gearbox or brakes."

In Greenland, the city of the future was being modeled underground by the U.S. Army, which was proving that "the traditionally antagonistic Arctic can be tamed." (Such man-against-nature images were common at the time.) There was to be a 152-mile electric railroad, a compacted-snow landing strip for helicopters and cargo planes, snug quarters for one hundred scientists, engineers, and soldiers—and it was all to be powered by atomic energy! Luckily for the residents, it would be safe from nuclear attack, because "snow would absorb much of the shock of an atomic blast," as well as shield them from radiation and fallout.

Angeleno Al Dauphin had built an amphibious bus with retractable wheels and water jet power. He made eight knots on water, sixty miles per hour on land. Later in the year, *Popular Science* proudly tested the Amphicar, a production version of a swimming car that enjoyed a brief vogue.

Congestion problems would be dealt with by mechanized parking garages: just lift 'em and stack 'em on steel shelves. The whole process was automated. Mechanized parking was "the engineer's answer to the American motorist whom neither rain, nor snow, nor paralysis of traffic can stay from driving into the city." Traffic violators would be dealt with by helicopter-mounted cops.

Popular Science was very high on monorails in 1960. We all were. Disneyland had installed a modern German-designed system, the French were working on them, and the Japanese were trying them out, too. "Trains of tomorrow will ride on a single rail," predicted the magazine. Soon we would see "glamorous new railways in the air." The reality, unfortunately, is a wheezing system that makes a short circuit around the city of Detroit, and a trouble-plagued interterminal route at Newark International Airport. The Newark shuttle was forced to close for six months in September 2000 because cold weather had caused cracks and track corrosion. Passengers were herded onto buses. Nobody's talking about glamorous railways in the air anymore.

Today's seers aren't much better. Ray Kurzweil, the futurist who predicts that by the year 2020, a $1,000 personal computer will duplicate the processing power of the human brain, gets transportation dramatically wrong in his 1999 book *The Age of Spiritual Machines*. He thinks that by 2009 most long-distance travel will be on self-driving "intelligent roads,"[12] when in fact funding for the National Automated Highway System Consortium has been eliminated and there's virtually no chance of seeing any major automated driving in that time frame.

All this prognostication is fun, but it's serious, too. There's no reason to expect that we're any better at predicting the future today than we were in the last hundred years. The real transforming inventions, the vehicles that will totally change the way we live, are probably unimaginable to us right now.

If there's one thing that history demonstrates clearly, it's that we completely fail to recognize groundbreaking inventions when they really do appear. Wise men and women of all sorts laughed at the first automobiles, the first airplanes, even the first bicycles. But nowhere in the unique and rich saga that is transportation history is there a more illuminating tale than that of John Fitch, the man who was born too early. If eighteenth-century accounts are correct, Fitch not only conceived the first steamboat long before Robert Fulton produced the first commercial design in 1807 but he also ran it full of passengers on the Delaware River. For an encore, he designed what appears to be a railroad steam locomotive twenty years before anyone else thought of it. But, despite proving beyond any doubt that his inventions worked, Fitch became a laughingstock and eventually took his own life in the Kentucky wilderness.

Fitch came up with the idea for a steamboat in 1785 and had one plying regular routes from Philadelphia by 1790, covering more than thirteen hundred miles all told. But Fitch was an absolute failure at raising money to continue his experiments, despite meetings with such figures as General George Washington (who "received him with courtesy") and Benjamin Franklin (no mean inventor himself). Fitch crowned himself "Lord High Admiral of the Delaware" and believed he had started a transportation revolution; but, he admitted, the world and his country "[do] not thank me for it."[13]

Fitch's railroad engine, complete with flanged wheels and a track, was only a model, completed just before he took his life. He never told anyone what the model was intended to do, and many learned men of the day thought it was some kind of boat (despite the rather obvious wheels). By that time, Fitch had given up, evidently concluding that the world was determined to dwell in ignorance.

Perhaps Fitch should have waited, because all his visionary ideas were gloriously vindicated soon after he died. Steamboats crowded all of America's major waterways, and railroads knit the country together. What Fitch and the great fiction writers shared was a willingness to look beyond the conventions and limitations of their day. By imagining steamboats, airships, and space travel, they prepared the public for what was to come with remarkable prescience. They are due credit, as well, for including the downside—polluted skies and overcrowded transit routes—in their visions. Small wonder, then, that the modern science fiction writer sees the future of mankind as unfolding on other worlds, with the frequent conclusion that our home planet has been rendered nearly uninhabitable by the follies of human endeavor.

We hunger for some new invention that will transform the world like the galaxy-spanning spaceships of science fiction. Perhaps that explains the near hysteria that greeted the news in early 2001 that Dean Kamen, a brilliant and eccentric New Hampshire–based inventor, had come up with an unspecified device called "IT." And because Kamen said his invention "will be an alternative to products that are dirty, expensive, sometimes dangerous and often frustrating, especially for people in the cities,"[14] speculation quickly focused on some revolutionary form of transportation device that would soon sweep the world and replace the automobile. The enthusiasm was dampened when clues pointed to IT being some sort of gyroscopically balanced adult scooter. Without "warp drives" and other imaginary marvels, we the earthbound will have to learn to live within our means.

2

WE CAN'T GO ON LIKE THIS

WE ALL HAVE our coping mechanisms. When faced with relentless, unmoving traffic nearly every day of my working life, I read. Only a few years ago, the notion that it was possible to leaf through a newspaper or a book while driving on an interstate highway would have struck me as dangerously insane, but now I know it can be done. The necessary ingredients are a good book and an absolutely immovable traffic stream. These conditions are usually met when what is a twenty-minute commute under ideal circumstances turns into a sixty-minute bumper-to-bumper crawl. My technique involves looking up every three or four minutes to see if I need to inch forward. For some reason, other gridlocked motorists become enraged if any open space of pavement isn't immediately filled.

Joel Pellinger has coping mechanisms of his own.[1] A New Jersey–based computer systems relocation expert who commutes daily into Manhattan, Pellinger outfits his sport-utility vehicle with such familiar office comforts as his Palm Pilot, his laptop computer, his portable global positioning system receiver, and no less than three cell phones, which clock up a $1,000 monthly bill. The next car Pellinger buys will probably allow him to check his e-mail and surf the Internet as well.

My wife's cell phone is an extension of her arm while she's driving in rush-hour traffic. She participates in conference calls, leaves messages, updates consultants. A major drawback for her is the car's manual transmission, which keeps her shifting hand out of the action. I bought her a headset, but her next car will be an automatic, and she'll be able to dial in relative comfort.

We need coping mechanisms like these because commuting times are getting longer for many Americans. Tracy, California, is a former farming community about sixty miles east of San Francisco. Because housing prices in San Francisco are some of the highest in the nation, Tracy has been absorbed into the city's suburban commuter corridor. For the trade-off of a four-bedroom house for $800 a month, Tracy's commuters travel an average of fifty-eight miles one-way to work, many of them taking a 4:54 A.M. train to Silicon Valley or hitting the road at 5:00 A.M. for a two-hour drive to Menlo Park. In Tracy, housing prices are directly related to transportation distances: every mile east translates roughly into $5,000 less for a home purchase.[2]

What's wrong with this picture? Plenty. The news that all this onboard computing, dialing, and faxing is dangerous probably won't deter many harried commuters, who would be both bored out of their minds and behind at work if they didn't turn their cars into mobile offices. According to the National Highway Traffic Safety Administration, however, there's a correlation between plugged-in drivers and crash statistics. The agency says that as many as a quarter of the 6.3 million auto accidents that occur annually in the United States are related to a distracted driver. Rosalyn Millman, the agency's deputy administrator, told the *New York Times,* "We are experiencing a dramatic change in driver behavior. If we underestimate this potential risk to highway traffic safety and do not moderate drivers' use of in-vehicle systems, the price may be very steep."[3]

There are other ways of coping. My friend Jerry Nichols, a British-born musician, nurse, and beer brewer, has a long morning commute that can double if traffic is bad. His solution is unique to him: Zen-like detachment. "I simply tune it out," he said. "The traffic can be swirling around me, people can be yelling, honking their horns, and I hardly even hear it. In my mind, I've already arrived at the hospital." Jerry's other coping mechanism is a bargelike Lincoln Town Car so vast and isolating that it's hard to tell if he's even in traffic.

Nichols's methods probably won't work for the pregnant women of Atlanta, who are increasingly often having their babies in the car because of traffic jams on the way to the hospital.[4] In a city with expansive suburbs and average commutes of thirty-four miles a day, many mothers-to-be just can't get to the medical center fast enough. The state Department of Transportation's highway emergency unit says it aided six hospital-bound women in the first eight months of 2000 alone.

It can't go on like this, can it? In the new millennium, when the futurists said we'd all be wafting to work in sky cars, we're decidedly earthbound. According to Katie Alvord's book *Divorce Your Car!* a third of the average city's land is devoted to serving the car, including roads, service stations, and parking lots. In 1970, Americans drove a trillion miles per year; it's been more than two trillion since the mid-1990s. There are well over 210 million registered automobiles in the United States alone, and their numbers will soon overtake the human population. There are already more cars than there are American adults to drive them. Automotive fuel economy doubled in the 1980s, but fuel use continued to climb because of the increasing number of cars on the road.

As cities sprawl farther into distant suburbs, daily commutes also spiral upward. An hour a day in the car has become the national norm. The average family takes ten car trips a day, mostly for shopping, socializing, or recreation. For every ten travel miles, nine are taken in a car. Every year, we use up to 100 billion gallons of oil, more than half of it (56 percent) imported. If present trends continue, we'll be importing two-thirds of our oil in twenty years. As Alvord puts it, this isn't love; it's addiction.

Despite the fact that the national interstate highway system is completely built out, governments spend $200 million every day constructing, fixing, and improving roads in this country. Traffic management and parking enforcement on those roads costs $48 billion annually, and $20 billion is spent on routine maintenance. What do we get for our money? The National Transportation Board predicts that delays caused by congestion will increase by 5.6 billion hours in the period between 1995 and 2015, wasting an unnecessary 7.3 billion gallons of fuel. The General Accounting Office, a federal agency, puts the loss of national productivity resulting from traffic congestion at $100 billion a year. Currently 70 percent of all daily peak-hour travel on interstates occurs under stop-and-go conditions, and a measurable "rush hour" will soon be a thing of the past.[5]

I have a negative visceral reaction every time I see a sport-utility vehicle (SUV), and it still amazes me that the category they occupy, light-duty trucks, has overtaken cars in the national marketplace. Huge eight-passenger SUVs should not be part of the morning commute, especially with solo drivers. DaimlerChrysler was forced to retreat, red-faced, from its suggestion that the 12,000-pound Unimog could be used as a shopping vehicle. But it's no wonder that people are buying these lumbering vehicles: there's very little personal cost. Despite recent price hikes, gasoline is still cheaper than bottled water in the United States. And the cost of operating the average new car keeps going down. Dr. Paul MacCready, a pioneer of human-powered flight as well as one of the developers of General Motors' EV-1 electric car, estimates that, in 1989 dollars, driving the average new car twenty-five miles cost $4 in 1929, $3 in 1949, $2 in 1969, and $1 in 1989. Extrapolating that data to 2005 yields a net cost of zero.[6] Almost everyone I know owns a car, and I can't remember the last time anyone complained to me about the cost of keeping it on the road.

A recent *Baltimore Sun* editorial cartoon shows a shopper's eyes popping at the prospect of $1.65-per-gallon gasoline, while he's lugging such groceries as $9.87-a-gallon beer, $48-a-gallon maple syrup, and $4.52-a-gallon spring water.[7] If it were sold by the barrel, Ben & Jerry's Chunky Monkey ice cream would cost $1,105.44, according to the petroleum-researcher firm John S. Herold, Inc. At $30 a barrel, then, oil looks like a bargain. But even if it isn't, our dependence on autos is such that we swallow price hikes that might deter us from buying other expendable consumer goods.

The global mania for private automobiles, together with the means to acquire them, means a huge projected increase in the world car population in the next fifty to one hundred years. New car registrations in the United States grow at a rate of 2 percent a year. By 2100, the current 600 million cars registered worldwide (a third of them in the United States) could grow to 4.5 billion. Since cars account for a third of air pollution emissions and a quarter of global warming, this would obviously have disastrous, nearly impossible consequences for planetary health.

According to the 1995 Nationwide Personal Transportation Survey, a treasure trove of travel statistics, "On an individual household basis, vehicle ownership seems to have reached a saturation point."[8] There were 1.16 cars and trucks per household in 1969; in 1995, there were 1.78. And those cars are being driven more, too. The average family drove 22,802 miles in 1983, and 34,459 in 1995.

It's clear from all of this that we're driving more but enjoying it less. Does that mean we're actually going to change behavior that's moved relentlessly toward ever greater private car ownership since the automobile was invented more than a hundred years ago?

THE SLOW SWITCH TO TRANSIT

James Howard Kunstler, the author of *Home from Nowhere*, an impassioned plea for abandoning suburban sprawl and returning to a more authentic America, thinks change is inevitable. "Anybody who thinks we're going to be using cars 25 years from now the way we've been using them in the recent past ought to have his head examined," Kunstler writes. "That phase of our national history is over."[9] Encouraging words, if true. Kunstler thinks we're waking up from our collective automotive hangover, and one indication is the trend toward applying federal Department of Transportation money to something other than highways. He's talking about the Intermodal Surface Transportation Efficiency Act (ISTEA) of 1991 (since extended in 1998 as the Transportation Equity Act for the Twenty-first Century, or TEA-21), which at long last gave state and local governments flexibility to pay for bike trails and pedestrian walkways instead of more and more roads. The money is slowly being taken out of the pavers' pockets, though the pace of the transfer is roughly akin to that of a car stuck in Atlanta's rush hour.

The switch to alternative methods of transportation can be documented with recent statistics.[10] There are now 170,000 miles of railroad tracks in the United States, a far cry from the 300,000 that existed at the peak of railroading in the 1920s, but nonetheless a comeback. Class 1 freight traffic on those tracks increased 47 percent from 1980 to 1999. The nation's passenger-rail service, Amtrak, making a slow fiscal recovery from the dark days of the mid-1990s, now operates 250 intercity trains a day, with service to 500 communities in 44 states. Amtrak is poised for greater things with the introduction of high-speed rail service in the Northeast corridor. Another factor, though it may not qualify as "alternative transportation," is an increased market share for flying. The number of airports jumped 20 percent from 1980, to more than 18,000, and commercial air travel is now accounting for 19 percent of all household trips.

Mass transit is making modest overall gains, though it can be hard to get excited about increases that give cities bus and rail systems comparable to those they had in 1910. The nation's 556 federally assisted urban transit agencies operated 76,000 vehicles of all sorts in 1997, providing 8 billion transit trips. Buses (which still carry a majority of all transit traffic) added 60 percent more route miles between 1992 and 1997. Light-rail and trolley lines made gains of 21 percent in that same period and now cover more than 10,000 miles. Many American cities are either adding light-rail systems or extending existing ones.

I'm willing to celebrate those gains, even if they're not so dramatic. In fact, it's now possible to visit some particularly visionary American cities—Portland, Oregon, comes most readily to mind— and get near-European levels of transit choice.

THE SOLITARY COMMUTE

So we're being pushed, with no little reluctance, onto ferry docks and train platforms, and we're beginning to see the enormous costs, environmental and spiritual, of our dependence on autos. But that's not quite the same thing as really changing our habits. Only in America would commuters desperate to gain entrance to the congestion-free high-occupancy vehicle (HOV) lanes on freeways actually construct dummies to fake a traveling companion.

As Robert D. Putnam documents in his book *Bowling Alone: The Collapse and Revival of American Community*, we've become a nation of solitary travelers—a phenomenon fundamentally incompatible with mass transit. It turns out, surveys suggest, that people actually like riding in their little private auto islands. "Over the last two or three decades," Putnam writes, "driving alone has become overwhelmingly the dominant mode of travel to work for most Americans. . . . The fraction of all commuters who carpool has been cut in half since the mid-1970s, and [was] projected to reach only 7 or 8 percent by 2000. The bottom line: By the end of the 1990s, 80 to 90 percent of all Americans drove to work alone, up from 64 percent as recently as 1980."[11]

Most of the environmentalists I know drive alone to work. One acquaintance, a dedicated recycler and consumer of organic produce, told me she had twice been in carpools only to bail out of them, once because the physical distance between her and her car sharer was too great, and the other time simply because of a personality conflict. "She was emotionally distant, and it drove me nuts," my friend said. Now she drives to work by herself, trying to outsmart the traffic by taking back roads. And this in Los Angeles, where carpooling is a free pass to the HOV lanes.

I give my eighty-four-year-old uncle a lot of credit, however. Throughout his working life in Washington, D.C., this Virginia resident almost never drove to work. He was a member of a four-man car pool as far back as I can remember. The catch was that he hated driving of any kind and never took a turn at the wheel. Instead, he offered his fellow passengers their choice of financial inducement as long as he could just sit quietly in the back.

I'm no different from everyone else. Despite knowing full well the costs of cars, I drive to work alone, too. And if the traffic's not too bad, I kind of like the private time, sitting in a comfortable reclining chair, with my music playing and time to think about the events of the day.

What's my excuse? I don't really have one. None of my co-workers live in my town, but we could meet somewhere. There are certainly people I know who both live and work near me, and we could double up. And I have mass-transit options, too. I could take the commuter train, which I'm lucky enough to have available. I could take buses. I could even bike the twenty miles to work, which is something the publisher of my magazine does nearly every day in the summer. Sure, I'm very busy, and I go on assignment in the middle of the day sometimes, and I teach college courses twice a week, but everybody has reasons like these for driving.

Frankly, the main reason I drive is because—like most Americans—I prefer the convenience of choosing my own departure time, of having a car at work, of being flexible about what time I leave. I guess it's about something called freedom, which is ironic because the private automobile has done so much to enslave us into unbreakable patterns. If I rode the train, I'd know with reasonable certainty what time I'd get to work. I could read, and certainly with a lot more safety than the brief glances I get in the car. I could talk to my fellow commuters. And I could be part of the valiant effort in my county to reduce traffic on the interstate.

PAYING FOR PRIVILEGE

Frankly, if a driver like me chooses to take the highway, he or she should pay for this incredible freedom of movement. I joined with many other motorists in applauding the end of toll collection on Connecticut interstates, but in hindsight I'm not sure it was a good idea. Removing existing tolls, which is often very popular politically, "is usually a mistake, because it encourages more driving," Janine Bauer of the Tri-State Transportation Campaign in New York told me. She added that people often consider mature highways to be "paid for," when actually the public continues to spend inordinate amounts of money on maintenance and improvements.

As annoying as they are, tolls serve an important function. Through what's called "congestion pricing"—varying toll amounts by time of day—they can help reduce gridlock at peak travel times. And the revenue tolls generate can be diverted to worthy transit alternatives. That's beginning to happen in some states.

Though we think of highways and tolls as arms of the state, both started out in private hands. During the nineteenth century, as many as two thousand private companies operated toll roads. The first, operating under a state charter, connected Philadelphia and Lancaster, Pennsylvania, in 1794. In the 1840s, thousands of miles of private plank roads were constructed.[12] "No tax can operate so fair and so easy as that of paying a turnpike toll," said a happy New York user in 1796.[13]

Congestion pricing is popular with libertarian critics of light-rail transit systems. One I talked to, John Charles, environmental policy director of the Cascade Policy Institute in Oregon, believes that variable toll pricing will ease traffic conditions in ways that adding mass-transit capacity cannot. "When you pay the premium, you get a premium result," he said. "There's no need to pass judgment, but if you drive a lot, you should pay for it with a user fee. Our studies show it's only necessary to reduce traffic load a tiny amount to make it free-flowing again."

Tolls are, in fact, a pretty good way to reduce traffic buildups. But don't tell that to groups like Citizens Against Tolls and No More Tolls, both of which inveigh against accident rates and annoyance to drivers.[14] Part of the problem is with the high-tech hardware that accompanies congestion pricing, specifically the car-mounted electronic transponder that can automatically debit toll amounts from a commuter's account. It doesn't help when, a Metropolitan Transportation Authority report revealed, the E-ZPass electronic toll programs in New York double-billed transponder customers who got in the wrong lane.[15] In Florida, the SunPass toll program has been similarly plagued, though in this case the problem is uncollected tolls.[16]

In a report entitled "Curbing Gridlock: Peak-Period Fees to Relieve Traffic Congestion," the National Research Council praised congestion pricing as a potentially powerful persuader that could induce commuters to carpool, use mass transit, telecommute, alter their travel times, and combine some trips.[17] An earlier Federal Highway Administration report reached the same conclusion. There have been feasibility studies and pilot programs galore, with federal funding, in such varied locations as Boulder, Houston, Minneapolis, and Lee County, Florida. In San Francisco, where traveling in groups of three not only allows HOV travel but entitles drivers to skip the toll on the Bay Bridge, commuters—mostly strangers to one another—connect in parking lots at dawn and fill up cars for the ride into the city.

Critics, like California attorney general Bill Lockyer, say that congestion pricing on public highways is elitist, penalizing economically disadvantaged drivers. Lockyer is especially incensed that California has allowed private companies to build for-profit toll roads (known as "Lexus lanes") on public land alongside major congested highways in the state. The new highways, such as 91 Express Lanes in Orange County, near Los Angeles, allow drivers to pay for the privilege of getting to work faster. In introducing a bill to ban the use of public land for private highways, Lockyer, then a state assemblyman, said, "Toll roads are fundamentally inegalitarian. Such roads create a two-tier system, where people of ordinary means drive on roads that are falling apart, while the affluent pay tolls and drive on new or improved highways."[18] That's certainly true, especially because less-affluent people have less flexibility in their work schedules, forcing them to pay peak prices if they use the private roads.

The Lexus lanes are controversial, but so are their more popular parent, the HOV lane. "Transportation researchers find them to be of limited value in relieving congestion, and elected officials are under increasing pressure to convert these limited-access lanes into general-purpose lanes," according to a report published by the libertarian

Reason Public Policy Institute.[19] HOV lanes are a "road rage" magnet, provoking angry reactions similar to those of motorists who encounter jammed supermarket parking lots with blocks of unused handicap spaces.

Almost *any* attempt to relieve congestion by expanding highways is doomed by data that suggests that 20 to 50 percent of the new road capacity is immediately filled by opportunistic motorists who had previously been kept at home by the awful traffic. Adding an HOV lane to existing interstates, as many cities in California and other states have done, provides only temporary relief, according to information from researcher John Holtzclaw. And because HOV lanes allow traffic to move faster, they also cause the creation of 10 to 25 percent more emissions.[20] It's certainly true that HOV lanes haven't fanned American enthusiasm for car pooling. In the 1980s, carpooling declined by 19 percent; average vehicle occupancy in metropolitan areas dropped from 1.17 persons per car in 1970 to 1.09 in 1990. In the 1980s, 16 percent of commuters traveled in multiple-occupant vehicles; today, 9 percent do.[21]

TRYING PARATRANSIT

Technology has also been applied to those ubiquitous small vans with elevated and widened cabins (often with the name of a hospital, school, or rehabilitation center painted on the side) seen buzzing around many metropolitan areas. What are they up to, exactly? These "demand response" or "paratransit" vans, which are often radio- or telephone-dispatched, perform a vital function and handle a surprisingly large volume of traffic. "Paratransit is the real future of transit," Dr. Joseph Coughlin of MIT's Center for Transportation Studies told me. "It's classic demand response, having smaller vehicles go door to door when they're needed. A lot of intelligent technology can go into them to make them very efficient. Paratransit is now mainly for the elderly or handicapped, so people dismiss them as 'the old people's bus.' But there's the basis there for a suburban mobility system to address gridlock."

Dan Sperling, the author of *Future Drive* and a transportation expert at the University of California at Davis, thinks that what he calls "smart paratransit" is one of the bright spots of our transit future, along with car sharing and clean-car technology. "Smart paratransit is a modern update and major improvement over the old dial-a-ride concept and the burgeoning airport shuttle van services," Sperling says. "Up-to-the-minute service and traffic information would eliminate the need for reservations. Travelers could request rides by telephone, cellular phone, interactive television, modem-equipped computer, or public computer terminal."[22]

As Sperling puts it, "Smart paratransit would dramatically improve access for people without cars, as well as solve the dilemma of suburbs being too dense for automobiles and not dense enough for buses and rail transit. By filling the gap between large transit vehicles and cars, smart paratransit would attack metropolitan congestion head on." Sperling told me that he expects paratransit to grow dramatically in the next ten to twenty years. According to the American Public Transportation Association, demand response makes up only 1 percent of transit trips today, but the volume of travel has nearly doubled since 1985.

I decided to investigate paratransit as it plays out near my home and met up with Clarence Rogers, who drives for People to Places in Bridgeport, Connecticut. Rogers, a very tall and slender black man with a resemblance to the basketball player Michael Jordan, drives a diesel-powered Ford Econoline 350 with twenty seats and a wheelchair lift. Rogers's day with it begins at 6:30 A.M., picking up children with cerebral palsy from various Bridgeport locations and taking them to school. It continues with runs to deliver seniors to adult day care and ends with a long haul up I-95 carrying a full load of men to the state veterans' hospital. Riding with Rogers was inspiring, not only because of his great empathy with his passengers but because he was clearly fulfilling an important role and making connections for people. The fact that his work also got cars off the road seemed almost incidental.

Congestion pricing and effective paratransit can be accomplished without enormous public expenditures, and they get a modest boost from such gadgetry as the electronic transponder and the cell phone. But technology was supposed to do much more for us. Listen to this wildly inaccurate prediction from Norman Bel Geddes's *Highways and Horizons* exhibit, sponsored by General Motors, at the 1939 World's Fair in Chicago:

> Looming ahead is a 1960 Motorway intersection. . . . By means of ramped loops, cars may make right and left turns at rates of speed up to 50 miles per hour. . . . Now we are traveling high above the mountains and valleys below—a bird's eye view of a paradise for vacationers. With the fast highways of 1960, the slogan "See America First" has taken on new meaning and importance. . . .
>
> Contrast the straight, unobstructed path of the Motorway at the right with that of the twisting, winding, ordinary road to the left of the quiet and peaceful monastery. One marvels at the complete accord of this man-made highway with the breathtaking scenic beauty of its route.[23]

Imagine what's become of that "quiet and peaceful" monastery today. The liberating highway never really materialized, despite the optimism of 1960, when *urban renewal* was the watchword. The same thinking that produced Bel Geddes's utopian vision also led to the failed dream of the automated highway. On paper, all these systems work—the drawings uniformly show cars speeding unimpeded to their destinations. We have very good reasons to be wary of new highways as a solution for the bedeviling transit problems that face us today.

3

SPRAWLING OUT: HIGHWAYS TO NOWHERE

THE FAIRFIELD, CONNECTICUT, neighborhood in which I live isn't quite suburban and it isn't quite urban. If I traveled a few miles in one direction, I'd be in an inner city; a few miles in the other, and I'd be on the Gold Coast, driving past homes owned by Phil Donahue, Paul Newman, Don Imus, the late Jason Robards, and a host of other celebrities and millionaires.

My house is also only about two miles from Trumbull Shopping Park, built in 1964 as the first enclosed mall in the state of Connecticut. A large mall is an essential element of what author Joel Garreau describes as "edge cities," featureless, colorless places that have sprung up in recent years to house corporate office parks, big-box stores, and endless ribbons of highway. In his book *Edge City,* Garreau notes that "malls usually function as the village squares of these new urbs." Ever seen a sign that said MALL, NEXT FOUR EXITS? That's an edge city.

My mall began modestly. I learned to drive in its parking lot when the place was closed on Sundays, a quaint notion today. Trumbull Shopping Park has been through four major expansions since then, and it's almost always open. In keeping with the mall's limited role as a community center, it hosts personal appearances by World Wrestling Federation superstars, soap opera actors, and Elvis impersonators. Its floor space is open to the Westfield Mall Walkers and a few selected mainstream charities, but unlike a real town center, it is not open to controversy or to ad hoc activists. As a working reporter, I accompanied a group of protestors from the Act Up! AIDS group to another local mall, and our entire entourage was ejected five minutes after setting up a card table.

Within well-defined limits, mall operators love to celebrate their role as the new Main Street. The mall, noted a brief item in the *Connecticut Post,* essentially serves as Trumbull's downtown, and that's why many people feel it should have a proposed police substation. "We need to protect it," said police commission member James McNamara, who, one hopes, is equally protective of the First Amendment.

For all their apparent civic-mindedness, malls are extremely private fiefdoms exerting rigid control over shopper behavior. Researching a story, I discovered that all of the Trumbull Shopping Park's extensive security functions and even its piped-in Muzak are controlled from a single small room behind an unmarked door.

There are 166 specialty shops within the mall's walls, and four major anchors, which by themselves have a combined area of over 700,000 square feet. In place of the modest lot I knew, there are now spaces for five thousand cars.

There is also a bus stop at Trumbull Shopping Park, on the outer ring road, though its existence is not without controversy. In 1994, the mall announced plans to close its stop on weekend nights, the very time it serves as the destination of choice for carless youths from the lower-income neighborhoods of gritty, postindustrial Bridgeport. The plan drew threats of legal action from the Greater Bridgeport Transit District and cries of racism from many community groups.

But they are not without compassion at Trumbull Shopping Park. The charges may well have been heard all the way in Sydney, Australia, where the mall's image-conscious parent company, Westfield Holdings Limited, makes its home. Westfield America owns thirty-nine malls in the United States, and it's unlikely that it wanted to be a test case for transportation activists. The bus stop was restored to weekend operation, which was definitely good news for its many employees without cars.

LIVING ON THE EDGE

The Trumbull case is proof, if any were needed, of just how hard it is to serve the mass transportation needs of sprawled Edge City, U.S.A. "The suburban city embraces the automobile with exuberance and the single-minded devotion of the truly religious," note Sim Van der Ryn and Peter Calthorpe in their book *Sustainable Communities*. "The resulting pattern is a linear horizontal grid that is diffuse and uniformly low-density and undifferentiated."[1] What they're talking about are little boxes made of ticky-tacky that all look just the same.

I grew up in a classic postwar suburban development, in a split-level on a block with twenty other houses that differed only in paint color. Everyone's dad worked outside the home, and nobody's mom did. The commuter train to New York was, for most of us, our only experience of mass transportation (and we never actually rode on it ourselves).

"The United States has become a predominately suburban nation, but not a very happy one," writes Phillip Langdon in *A Better Place to Live*. "Today, more than three-quarters of the American people live in metropolitan areas, and more than two-thirds of those live in suburbs. Each year, development pushes out across more than a million acres, yet the expansion of highways, housing tracts, and other suburban construction rouses fewer cheers than at any other time in the past."[2] Suburban sprawl so enraged the shadowy Earth Liberation Front that, at the end of 2000, it torched four nearly built luxury homes on Long Island. The underground group left the message "Stop urban sprawl: If you build it, we will burn it."

The history of American suburban development is well documented and merits merely passing mention here. One can only imagine the rapture with which GIs, most of whom had been raised in cramped city apartments, returned from World War II and were met with newspaper ads like this: "Set in a spacious, carefully planned community, this ranch sensation is an architect's dream come true. Automatic kitchen, fluorescent lighting, two walls of baked enamel cabinets, radiant heat. No cash for vets, only $68 a month for every-thing."[3] I have a friend whose home retains one of those NuTone automatic kitchens, and it's like a museum of "modern convenience." The blender, for instance, is built right into the counter so as not to waste space. "The era of kitchen confusion now joins the crystal set radio and the potbellied stove as a thing of the past," said the brochure that came with NuTone's "inbuilt" kitchen.

Those vets had returned to a severe housing shortage that wasn't likely to be met by the construction of new apartment buildings in already overbuilt cities. In stepped the Federal Housing Administration (FHA), a creation of New Deal idealism and "the first federal agency to actively encourage the construction of new, single-family houses in suburban areas."[4] Another major factor was the GI Bill of Rights, which guaranteed returning soldiers a tuition-free college education and loans to purchase homes. It worked tremendously well. By 1980, census data show that the typical housing unit (57 million out of 86 million homes) consisted of a car-friendly single-family house with a yard.

The new suburbs didn't have to be as car-oriented as they turned out to be. For this, we can at least partly blame "master builders" like Robert Moses, who had an elitist attitude toward any form of trans-portation designed to move the sweating hordes. On Long Island alone, Moses built the Van Wyck, Long Island, and Seaford–Oyster Bay Expressways, the Wantagh, Bethpage, Grand Central, Northern State, Southern State, Meadowbrook, and Cross Island Parkways, and both the Whitestone and Triborough Bridges. But he fought off any attempt to incorporate mass-transit rights of way into his highway plans.

Biographer Robert Caro writes that in 1952, Moses was informed by the General Electric Urban Traffic Division that it had "costed out" installing rapid-transit lines on highway center medians and that "if provision for tracks was made in the original highway design their cost would be one-tenth of providing them later. Moses's reply? 'The cost of acquiring additional width and building for rapid transit would be prohibitive and hundreds of families would be dislocated.'"[5]

According to longtime Moses associate Frances Perkins, Moses made a distinction between the public, whom he genuinely served, and the common people, whom he loathed. As New York City parks commissioner, Moses opened Jones Beach with parking for thousands of cars, but vetoed plans for access by rapid transit and refused to allow even a Long Island Railroad link. The bridges on his new parkways were deliberately made too low to allow passage by chartered buses.[6] Moses would have heartily approved of Trumbull Shopping Park's decision to close its bus stop. With planners like these, suburban sprawl was inevitable.

Moses and colleagues like New York governor Al Smith had considerable help from the highway lobby, which made sure that their suburban landscapes were accessible by federally funded asphalt. One of the major barriers to the fledgling automobile industry at the turn of the century had been the poor state of the roads. One of the first such lobbying groups was the League of American Wheelmen, organized by the colorful electric car and bicycle magnate Colonel Albert Pope (the same man whose initial reaction to the internal-combustion engine was that you could never get people to sit on top of an explosion). "I hope to live to see the time when all over our land, our cities, towns and villages shall be connected by as good roads as can be found," he said.[7] The Wheelmen founded "good roads" associations around the country and, in 1891, began lobbying state legislatures.

Many of the early roads and parkways built in America were private, funded by tolls. As in the modern science of "congestion pricing," the tariff varied by time of day, load carried, and other factors, but the motivation was profit, not easing the traffic burden. One such early road was the forty-five-mile Long Island Motor Parkway, entirely financed by the racing enthusiast William K. Vanderbilt Jr., who was angry after receiving some speeding tickets. Vanderbilt's toll-collection plan fell short of expectations, and in 1938 he was forced to give up his road to three county governments in lieu of back taxes. Only short sections remain on western Long Island, including stretches still called Vanderbilt Parkway.

By 1916, Congress was funding federal road projects with $75 million over five years. By 1930, the annual budget was $750 million. It was the $25 billion Interstate Highway System, created by act of Congress in 1956, that really set the course for the future development of America, making it possible to commute to work into the city from distant suburban towns. In 1956, when the legislation was signed, 72 percent of American families owned a car; by 1970, when the national road network comprised 30,000 miles, 82 percent owned cars, and 28 percent had two or more.[8] Ironically, one major motivator for building the new roads was to achieve fast and efficient urban evacuation in the event of a nuclear attack. Such concerns are ingrained in the minds of every suburban kid who had to go through "duck and cover" exercises, or whose parents built a nuclear shelter in the backyard.

Imagine the combined lobbying efforts of such current and former groups as the American Association of Highway Builders of the North Atlantic States, the American Association of State Highway Officials, the American Concrete Paving Association, the American Road Builders Association, and the American Automobile Association—and those are just the groups with "American" in the title. The American Automobile Association—which most people think of as an apolitical group that aids stranded travelers and provides good maps—is a fierce lobbyist for highways and against clean air legislation. In 1970, Americans spent $131 billion on highways and $75 billion for education. There are now 170,000 miles of roads in the United States receiving federal aid.

The highway lobby is very much still with us today, in the form of the American Association of State Highway and Transportation Officials, which represents all fifty state highway departments and has a $14 million annual budget. Another link in the chain is the Washington-based American Highway Users Alliance, which has a staff of twelve and a $2 million annual budget. Formerly the Highway Users Federation, it was created in 1932 by General Motors, "on the not unreasonable assumption that healthy GM auto sales required plenty of roads."[9] Funding comes from member organizations like the American Trucking Association (itself a $35 million lobbying group), the Alliance of Automobile Manufacturers, and the American Petroleum Institute.

It's not surprising, then, that the American Highway Users Alliance sees the solution to America's congestion problem as building more roads, especially interstate interchanges. "Our overstressed road system needs additional capacity at key points," the alliance opines in a report entitled "Unclogging America's Arteries: Prescriptions for Healthier Highways." Removing strategic bottlenecks, the report maintains, "will reduce the amount of time commuters have to spend on the road, save hundreds of lives, prevent thousands of injuries and help us safeguard the environment." If we pour money into highways, says the Alliance, "emissions of smog-causing volatile organic compounds would drop by 44 percent, while carbon monoxide would be reduced by 45 percent."[10] In other words, not only can we build out of congestion, but we can build out of pollution, too.

FIGHTING BACK AGAINST SPRAWL

The highway lobby's legacy to the United States is urban sprawl, one of today's most hotly debated topics. We live in a country with 60,000 square miles of paving, covering 2 percent of the country's surface area and as much as 10 percent of its arable land.[11]

Minnesota legislator Myron Orfield, a national antisprawl leader who directs the Metropolitan Area Research Program, told me in an interview that, like some incredibly tenacious disease, sprawl can actually occur in cities that are *losing* population. "Metropolitan Detroit lost 8 percent of its population and grew 35 percent in land area in the last twenty years," he told me. "Cleveland lost 11 percent of its population and grew 38 percent in land area. There you have shrinkage and sprawl. A lot of us in the environmental movement say that we're not against growth—we just don't want it to waste resources or land unnecessarily, or cause excessive traffic congestion."

But despite the huge challenges posed by the relentless pace of sprawl, not all the news is bad. Especially encouraging is a phenomenon known as "smart growth," which amounts to a municipal plan for controlled, environmentally sensitive development. Although the term wasn't used until 1995, smart-growth initiatives have been adopted in more than thirty states.[12]

As an example, Loudoun County, Virginia, the third fastest growing county in the country, could easily become the outermost link in the Washington, D.C., "edge city" corridor. The commute to the nation's capital is only an hour and a half, land is cheap, and five-thousand-square-foot homes are invading the landscape with all the force of a flock of locusts. Over the next five years, forty thousand new houses are slated for development on county open space and farmland. A recent Mason-Dixon poll of northern Virginia residents found that 84 percent agreed with the statement "The current pace of development and resulting traffic congestion has resulted in my family spending more time in traffic and less time with each other."[13]

But in 1999, in an extraordinary move, Loudoun County activists decided that it was time to call a halt to the congestion, pollution, and destruction of green space threatening their way of life. A slate of eight antisprawl candidates challenged the incumbents on the County Board of Supervisors—and won.

"It was an astounding victory," says Joe Maio, director of Voters to Stop Sprawl, a political action committee that endorsed all eight of the newly elected supervisors. "It was a complete repudiation of the way business is done around here."[14] Such changing attitudes are mirrored around the country. A national survey conducted in 2000 by Smart Growth America found that 60 percent of Americans favored spending more on mass transit, even if it meant spending less on highways, and 76 percent said their states should do more to manage growth.[15] In 1999, voters passed more than 70 percent of 240 local ballot initiatives around the country governing preservation of open space, creating more than $7.5 billion in funding for land conservation. A record 1,000 state land-use reform bills were introduced in legislatures that year, and more than 200 of them were enacted into law.

In Maryland, Governor Parris N. Glendening deserves credit for launching a revolution in urban-suburban thinking. In 1997, Glendening and his charismatic lieutenant governor, Kathleen Kennedy Townsend, pushed through the state legislature a three-point smart-growth package designed to save the state's most valuable natural resources before development ate them up; support existing communities and neighborhoods; and save money for taxpayers by limiting sprawl and the costly municipal infrastructure required to support it.

The legislature approved Glendening's plan because of some inexorable demographics. Maryland is expecting a million new citizens by 2025, and if they push sprawl out into now rural counties it could consume more state open space than disappeared in the last 250 years. On the other hand, Baltimore lost 350,000 residents between 1950 and 2000, and it and other Maryland cities could accommodate the new wave of settlement without a heavy environmental price. Serving urban populations with effective transit is infinitely easier than accommodating the same people in new suburban developments. The challenge is to revitalize the cities and make them attractive destination points.[16]

The smart-growth legislation limits state economic-development funding to twenty-three "priority funding areas" in each county. The funding areas are like circles drawn around existing population centers. If the counties build outside these growth boundaries, they get little state assistance. Businesses that choose to locate in these zones are provided with tax credits, and additional tax advantages are available for job creation. Rural areas are protected through such programs as conservation easements, which provide financial benefits to landowners who agree to keep the developers at bay.

Maryland's smart-growth initiatives also include a pilot Live Near Your Work (LNYW) program that can drastically reduce commute times for its participants. If home buyers working for participating employers agree to locate in approved LNYW neighborhoods near their offices, the program provides a minimum of $3,000 in housing assistance. The buyers must also agree to live in the house for at least three years.

By limiting developer liability and coordinating a voluntary cleanup program, Maryland is also encouraging redevelopment of the abandoned and contaminated urban industrial sites ("brownfields") that mar many cities and make repopulation difficult. According to the federal Department of Housing and Urban Development, the United States has 450,000 brownfields, which exhibit a wide range of serious environmental problems.

Once the center of American steelmaking, Pittsburgh was so contaminated by heavy metal and coal fires in the first half of the last century that streetlights burned during the day and residents called the city "hell with the lid off." Since then, Pittsburgh has moved aggressively to rejuvenate dozens of sites around the city and return them to productive use. "Effective reuse of brownfields can actually prevent urban sprawl," says Deborah Lange, executive director of the Brownfields Center, a joint project of Carnegie Mellon University and the University of Pittsburgh.

The cleaned-up brownfield sites are bringing new residents and jobs back into Pittsburgh. A case in point is Washington's Landing, an island that was once the site of an extensive meatpacking and rendering industry. The smell, according to one resident, was "foul enough to make a fellow just about swear off breathing." Electric transformers on the island leached polychlorinated biphenyls (PCBs) into the soil.

Today, after a $26 million restoration and environmental cleanup, a spruced-up Washington's Landing plays host to a mix of residential town houses, commercial office buildings, restaurants, and such recreational uses as a three-hundred-boat marina. The city projects are helped along by a two-tier tax system that encourages the redevelopment of vacant downtown land.

New Jersey is another smart growth leader, and voters there approved a bond issue to preserve a million acres of open space—half of all the undeveloped land in the state. Former governor Christine Todd Whitman, who resigned in her second term to head the Environmental Protection Agency, drew criticism from some green groups in New Jersey for defunding environmental regulation, and praise for supporting smart growth. One initiative of hers was designed to simplify building codes to make it easier to renovate urban buildings than to erect new rural ones.

Georgia is another state with urgent reasons to develop smart-growth initiatives. When metropolitan Atlanta nearly doubled in size between 1990 and 1996, with resulting sharp increases in gridlock and smog readings, the city was hit with an EPA moratorium forbidding it to spend federal transportation funds on road building. The federal order delayed forty-four highway projects, but it was lifted in 2000 after the state agreed to spend more on mass transit and emissions testing. Although environmentalists in Georgia mistrust the state's intentions, in 1999 Georgia enacted legislation creating a new watchdog agency with veto power over sprawl-inducing land use and transportation plans in the Atlanta region.

Not everyone likes smart growth. According to the *Washington Business Journal,* in Maryland Governor Glendening's initiatives "have placed him in some hot water with business interests, who want to see new roads and highways."[17] The *Pittsburgh Tribune-Review* editorialized that sprawl should be regarded positively as "growth fueled by man's age-old desire to migrate out of population centers." Pittsburgh commuters, stalled in traffic as they head out to the suburbs, may be less sanguine about this manifest destiny.

THE NEW URBANISM

In concert with open-space preservation and smart growth, a new science of sustainable community has sprung up. At the heart of it is "New Urbanism," the neighborhood-based reclaiming of America's depressed central cities. One of the leaders of this movement is Peter Calthorpe, an urban designer based in Berkeley, California. "I think we are just on the cusp of major changes," Calthorpe notes. "The first and most profound sign of it is the antigrowth movement in which people are saying, 'I don't want any more development.'" The private automobile is Calthorpe's public enemy number one. "I've focused in the last ten to fifteen years on just how destructive the automobile is—socially, aesthetically, and environmentally. Given that we are actually tripling the number of vehicle miles traveled per household per year, this upward spiral of auto use grabs my attention the most."

Calthorpe defines a smart urban design as, in a word, walkable. "A well-designed city is a place where you enjoy walking, where your destinations are close enough to walk to, where you feel safe enough to walk," he said. "It's a place that is interesting enough socially to make you feel that walking is perhaps something more than just getting from A to B—perhaps seeing your neighborhood, smelling the blossoms on the trees, or watching some kids play."[18]

Walkable communities are of necessity high density. Author Bill Bryson, upon returning to the States after two decades in England, was struck by the near impossibility of walking from place to place in strip America, which is built solely to accommodate cars. Density is a prerequisite for mass transit, too. According to Robert Cervero's *The Transit Metropolis,* "[E]very 10 percent increase in population and employment densities yields anywhere between a five and eight percent increase in transit ridership."[19]

The challenge, as Dr. Joseph Coughlin of MIT's Center for Transportation Studies points out, is to "develop an alternative vision that is more attractive than living in a single-family detached home in the suburbs. Despite the problem that sprawl presents for the environment . . . we have been unable to develop a lifestyle that has been as successful in capturing the hearts and imaginations of so many people."[20]

What are some prime models of New Urbanism? I saw some wonderful examples on my visit to Portland, Oregon, which has done much to forestall unwanted growth by erecting an urban-growth boundary. Many planners point to Curitiba, the capital of Paraná state in southern Brazil. Upon taking office in 1971, Mayor Jaime Lerner made converting downtown streets to pedestrian walkways his first priority. Some forty-nine of Curitiba's downtown blocks are now car-free. Robert Moses would have been appalled by Lerner's integration of highways and mass transit. The city has dedicated busways that keep transit out of the main traffic stream. High-rise, high-density apartment buildings line the transit corridors, with retail shopping on the ground floor.

Curitiba does not have light rail, but it has one of the most efficient—and profitable—bus systems in the world. There are twenty intermodal stations and five busway corridors, giving Curitibans a one-fare ride to nearly anywhere in the metropolitan region. Per capita ridership figures approach those of New York City, the most transit-dependent city in the United States. The city's Volvo-built buses can carry 270 passengers each, a density achieved by having more than three-quarters of them stand up. Curitiba's buses carry nearly twice the percentage of all city commuters as do the buses in car-dependent São Paulo.[21]

In the United States, model cities take different forms, many of them built with self-conscious nostalgia for the picket-fence neighborliness of an earlier America. Phillip Langdon, in his book *A Better Place to Live: Reshaping the American Suburb,* uses the example of Seaside, a Florida panhandle hamlet whose slogan is "The new town, the old ways." There are indeed white picket fences in eighty-acre Seaside (fences that *must* by law differ from those of their neighbors) and also spacious front porches. Streets are narrow, slowing traffic down, and sandy footpaths welcome pedestrians. Gazebos stand at intersections. One gets the feeling that if we could all live in Seaside, America would be back on track.

Unfortunately, places like Seaside, though on the upswing in America, are overwhelmed by the population-heavy edge cities that Joel Garreau talks about. Eighty percent of these character-free cities have sprung up in the last twenty years, he reports, and they hold two-thirds of all American office space (which, of course, makes them prime destinations for commuters). Just as the Boston-Washington corridor has fused into one long strip of continuous development, so it is possible to imagine new waves of population growth turning the last American open space into the last pieces of the sprawl mosaic.

POPULATION MATTERS

The danger, of course, is that all the smart planning and urban reinvestment can get overwhelmed by the sheer number of new
Americans. Some environmentalists talk about urban sprawl and the
loss of natural space as if they were completely self-contained phe-
nomena. In fact, although sprawl does occur in cities that have
stopped growing, it is largely, relentlessly, a product of American
population growth. And that growth threatens to swamp the modest
gains we're making in automotive fuel efficiency, transit use, species
and land protection, and development of pedestrian-friendly suburbs.

Our finite planet welcomed its six billionth citizen in 1999.
Population activism, a small but growing movement around the
world, tends to focus—laudably—on global growth. After all, no
country can "solve" population problems on its own. But nation-
states have no business lecturing the world if they haven't made
progress on the home front, and the United States is a prime offender.
According to the U.S. Census Bureau, the United States should get
ready for a dramatic doubling of its population by 2100.

From 281 million Americans in the 2000 census, we can expect to
grow to 571 million in the next hundred years, says the U.S Census
Bureau. That's actually a fairly conservative projection. One of the
bureau's projections actually predicts that there could be 1 *billion*
Americans in 2100.

The effects of all those new Americans has an immediate and
measurable effect on all forms of transit, because the United States is
so car-dependent. The automotive population grows even faster than
the human one in the United States, and Americans love to drive. If
an immigrant arrives here from, say, France, he can expect his time
spent in an automobile to double. In 1990, Americans used their cars
for 82 percent of all trips, compared to just 48 percent for Germans
and 45 percent for the British.[22]

In 1996, the President's Council on Sustainable Development
listed ten goals, the eighth of which was moving toward stabilizing
U.S. population. The report noted that U.S. population was growing

at a rate double that of Europe, putting in peril both economic objectives and the quality of the environment.

An environmental assessment that cataloged the problems America faces today (from loss of species and farmland to polluted air and water) could well conclude that the current 281 million is a violation of the continent's carrying capacity. Imagine, then, those problems magnified by a doubling of the population. The Associated Press reported in January 2000, "The new population projections . . . conjure images of twice as many cars jostling for position on the highways and twice as many shoppers crowding the aisles at Wal-Mart."

The prospect of a billion Americans, however remote, is certainly alarming enough to take seriously. Carl Haub, a demographer with the Population Reference Bureau, says that to imagine an America with a billion inhabitants, just look at India. "They've got more people than that, and even less space," he says. "But if we went that way, we'd be a different country. The American dream would have to be changed. Half-acre-lot suburbanization couldn't continue. We'd have to look at models like Hong Kong, where all the new development is straight up."

Take just one arena, energy demand. Even ignoring Americans' status as the world's worst energy gluttons, U.S. dependence on foreign oil could be ended through population stabilization. According to energy specialist John Holdren, if the United States still had 135 million people, its population during World War II, it could meet current energy demands without either importing oil or using coal at all. We would, in other words, achieve energy independence and end the massive damage caused by burning coal, all in one stroke.

A halving of the American population isn't likely, but other developing factors *are* likely to reduce fossil-fuel use. The nature of work is changing, and with it the daily commute.

THE ELECTRONIC COMMUTE

Population growth has *huge* impacts on traffic congestion and urban sprawl. That's obvious when you look at Los Angeles, where the nation's fastest rate of human growth—the equivalent of two Chicagos over the next twenty years—fuels a 3 percent annual growth in the number of cars on the road. But there are ways of altering the equation, and Los Angeles is one of the places where that's happening through the vastly promising field of flexible work.

If you work for the City of Los Angeles, for instance, you have the option of letting go of a nine-to-five schedule and switching to a staggered flextime schedule known as a "compressed work week." Work nine hours a day for eight days and you're on track to get an extra day off every two weeks, according to the city personnel department. If you can stand working four ten-hour days, you'll end up with a four-day workweek. (Some insomniacs even work three twelve-hour days for their full week.) Flextime, says author Joel Kugelmass, "works well for those who must (or feel they must) bring themselves to work by automobile." He adds that it reduces emissions by as much as 40 percent to put drivers on the road at times when they can move faster. Flextime, Kugelmass notes, "is at once the flexible work program most easily implemented on a large scale and the least difficult to manage."[23] At the U.S. Environmental Protection Agency office in Research Triangle Park, North Carolina, seventy-four workers are on flextime, and a "flexiplace" option allows them to spend up to two days a week at an alternative work location.

The next step is getting out of the office altogether through telecommuting, which is also encouraged for Los Angeles employees (though it's a "management option, not an employee entitlement"). Telecommuting is exploding across America, and it's beginning to affect travel patterns. In 1999, 19.6 million Americans took advantage of the new digital workplace and got to work that way at least part of the week, up from just 4 million in 1990.[24] In 2000, the "Telework America 2000" report said that telecommuting was growing at a rate of more than 20 percent a year.[25] In a survey, *Modern Office Technology* magazine found that 95 percent of its readers did at least some overtime work at home, and 40 percent of all home computers are purchased to meet that need.

Jack Nilles, the author of *Managing Telework,* runs a management-consulting company from his home in California. "The annual growth rate of telecommuting is something like 20 percent," he told me. "I'd expect to see 40 million people telecommuting by 2030, and after that I give up forecasting."

Nilles may be a bit optimistic on those telecommuting numbers, but there's no doubt that the effect of even modest increases is great. He projects that southern California could reduce daily trip generation by 5 to 10 percent by 2020 if the region embarks on a massive campaign of commuter education and marketing. An Arthur D. Little study concluded that if only 12 percent of the U.S. workforce telecommuted a single day a week, it would result in 1.6 million fewer car accidents annually and 1,100 fewer traffic-related deaths.[26]

According to a federal Department of Transportation projection, vehicle miles saved through telecommuting could triple between 1997 and 2002, from 10 billion to 35 billion. At the upper end, that means 1.6 billion gallons of gasoline (worth nearly $3 billion to consumers) that will never leave the pumps. Seen in terms of time savings, it means 110 hours for the average telecommuter over the course of a year, or a total of 1.6 billion hours.[27]

Most telecommuters do own cars, says Nilles, but "not as many as would otherwise." Nilles, who's personally cut down on business travel through the medium of teleconferencing, says it's a myth that working from home interferes with promotability and can lead to social isolation. "When you're out of the office, you become more proactive in keeping in touch with what's going on than if you were there," he said.

Companies are not only beginning to encourage telecommuting but have come up with novel ways of promoting it. At the insurance company Aetna, where 2 percent of the workforce stay home, telecommuters are assigned "office buddies" so they can stay in touch with home base. Ten percent of Sun Microsystems' 40,000 employees are permanently "unassigned" and are allowed to work anywhere there's space, including at home. In a survey, 80 percent of Sun's employees said they worked at home at least part of the time. Cisco Systems, another telecommuting leader (66 percent of the workforce)

offers both ergonomic furniture and twenty-four-hour technical support for stay-at-homes. Merrill Lynch employees, 5 percent of whom
telecommute, can test out the lifestyle in a two-week simulation.[28]
The telecommuting stars are mainly large companies, because corporations with more than one hundred employees are feeling pressured
by state law to reduce their commuter populations.

An array of state statutes, prompted by the federal Clean Air Act,
encourages trip reduction (Arizona, Illinois, New Jersey, and
Washington) or telecommuting for state employees (Arizona,
Connecticut, Florida, Minnesota, and Oregon). In Arizona, for
instance, state employees can get 100 percent reimbursement for taking public transit or van pools and can also get paid back for what's
known as "telecommuting connectivity," or setting up a home office.

Connecticut grants six-month telecommuting trial periods to state
workers, with supervisor approval, but extensions are possible. Since
1994, state agencies in Florida have posted listings of job classifica-
tions and positions that they consider appropriate for telework.
Missouri provides benefits for telecommuting recipients of Aid to
Families with Dependent Children. North Carolina has the goal of
using telecommuting incentives to reduce state employee vehicle
miles traveled by 20 percent, and offers periodic reports on progress
that began in 2000.[29]

The whole business of work is changing, with vast implications
for the rush-hour commute. Remember the old Who song "Goin'
Mobile"? That seems to be what is happening to our jobs in the
American edge city, reports Neil Strother of ZDNet. In an on-line
column, he reported that large U.S. firms with more than 1,000
employees support almost 5 million telecommuters, with 9 million
projected by 2004. These same firms host nearly 1 million remote
offices around the world. The average company supports 96 such
offices, a number that will jump to 153 by 2004.[30]

Today's mobile office can be nothing more than a briefcase containing everything a "road warrior" needs to do work away from a
desk. According to major telecommuting supporter AT&T, mobile
offices increase the amount of time salespeople spend with customers

by 15 to 20 percent. Andre'a Chetam, manager of IBM's national mobility project office, says that in 1994 its marketing and service sales force increased productivity 10 percent after moving out into the field.[31]

IBM is just one of a number of companies taking advantage of telework centers, which offer rental space in large, basically anonymous facilities. Mobile employees commute into them to use a temporary desk, telephone, and other necessities. These satellite offices let workers share technology and computer equipment, and they also offer the advantage of proximity to workers' homes. Some telework space is simply paid for on an as-needed basis. Kinko's, for instance, offers office space, computer and fax rentals, and even conference facilities without the encumbrance of a lease or other details.[32] A variation, "hoteling," lets floating employees check in once or twice a week at any one of a company's offices to use vacant space. Such work patterns take millions of people out of the regular rush-hour grind.

These developments don't quite add up to wholesale abandonment of the central office tower in favor of the "electronic cottages" that futurist Alvin Toffler imagined. But work is definitely changing. And so is shopping. On-line shopping through companies like Amazon. com and eBay takes a huge number of cars off the road, though the environmental impact depends on several factors. Some of what would have been trips to and from malls is offset by new mileage for diesel delivery trucks working overtime to make deliveries. The big shopping services also create a new and significant waste stream of cardboard boxes and styrofoam packing peanuts.

Joseph Romm, in a study prepared for the Center for Energy and Climate Solutions, sees great significance in the fact that energy consumption remained constant in 1997 and 1998, despite 8 percent growth in the gross domestic product. The explanation, he says, is that the Internet is making e-commerce more efficient and reducing transportation-related fuel expenditures. Romm thinks that telecommuting growth will eliminate the need for 3 billion square feet of office space by 2007. And his report also attempts to quantify energy savings from Internet-based shopping. To buy two five-pound items at a mall ten miles distant from the shopper's home burns a gallon of gas. To have the same items air-freighted burns 0.6 gallons, and to have it delivered by truck, just 0.1 gallons.[33]

Information technology, the vast field that barely existed two decades ago but now accounts for a significant percentage of American employees, is helping shape a new and less predictable workforce. Given the rapid pace of technological change, any predictions made today about the future of the great American commute could turn out to be dead wrong tomorrow. But it's certainly true that when increasingly sophisticated home-computer technology meets gridlocked highways, the solution is often workers in their bathrobes and slippers.

Dealing with the challenges ahead requires planning, and there are some pretty good role models for that in the urban landscape. But viewed historically, planning has also been part of the problem, as in Robert Moses's auto-centric vision or the massive urban-renewal programs of the 1960s. Not all the transportation examples I studied are good ones: some cities are innovating with smart growth, others getting stuck in a tangle of highways. There are lessons to be learned from both types.

4

TRANSIT CITIES

WHAT MAKES A CITY LIVABLE? Is it the parks, symphony orchestras, and corporate headquarters proclaimed in promotional handouts? Or a certain hard-to-define quality of life? To make the peppery stew of a lively city, a diversity of ingredients is necessary. Leave out any one of them—like effective public transit—and the recipe can easily go awry. I've seen that firsthand.

Just up the road from where I live is the city of Stamford, Connecticut, once a blue-collar manufacturing city (the birthplace, among other things, of Phillips' Milk of Magnesia, the Page automobile, the Eagle bicycle, and the electric dry-shaver industry) but now America's third-ranked "corporate headquarters community." Soaring glass towers are emblazoned with the logos of GTE, Xerox, Pitney Bowes, Clairol, GE Capital, Champion International, and a recently acquired crown jewel, Swiss Bank. Even the World Wrestling Federation is headquartered in Stamford.

"Stamford: The City That Works!" proclaims the mayor's office. And by a lot of standard measures, that's true. Stamford, which went into stark decline in the 1950s as the manufacturing sector fled south and abroad, now has a huge tax base, good schools (many of them racially integrated), abundant housing stock, twenty-five-mile proximity to New York City, and, at least on paper, great transportation. Stamford is served by the Connecticut Turnpike (I-95) and the historic Merritt Parkway, as well as the Metro North commuter railroad.

That's on paper. In reality, Stamford is an absolute transportation nightmare. Zooming real estate prices have meant that many commuters are forced to live thirty or more miles from Stamford itself. Ghastly stop-and-go commutes of an hour or more are frequently cited in corporate exit interviews and feature in business-relocation decisions.

Like many other cities of similar size and population, corporate Stamford is struggling to find solutions for getting people to work on time. Clairol, for instance, has 60 of its 850 employees riding in four company-supplied fourteen-passenger vans. According to Bill Andersen, Clairol's manager of security and employee operations, riders pay $28 a month to take the vans in a program that is heavily subsidized by the company.

Clairol also offers a shuttle bus (decorated to resemble an Herbal Essences shampoo bottle) that makes four trips each morning and four each afternoon from the train station to its headquarters near Stamford's downtown. At GE Capital, more than 100 commuters get up to $60 a month off their train tickets through a company-supported voucher system run through the transit district. GE Capital also runs four twenty-one-passenger commuter vans to the Stamford station.

These programs are laudable, but they're also very small. Most Stamford commuters drive, and they spend a fifth of that highway time stuck in bumper-to-bumper gridlock. It's rather ironic that Stamford can't get moving today, because the city was built on effective transportation. A canal, completed in 1833, allowed schooners and sloops to dock right in the heart of what was then a small town. Only fifteen years later, the railroad arrived, "accompanied by much drama and excitement," as the Stamford Historical Society describes it. The trains, complemented by local trolleys, gave manufacturers a way to get their goods to market and also provided an access point for the immigrant labor pool the city desperately needed.

By the 1960s, when I first saw it, Stamford's downtown was still graced with two- and three-story Civil War– and Victorian-era buildings, and it was both walkable and manageable. And though the trolleys were long gone, the tracks were still visible. I once leafed through a picture book of old Stamford and was startled to see what a livable city it had once been, with expansive homes and inviting storefronts.

Today, as a mini-Manhattan without New York's transit infrastructure, downtown Stamford is hazardous duty for work-bound pedestrians and bicyclists, who must face a gauntlet of whizzing traffic in a grid of streets where sidewalks are an afterthought. The people-centered city of years past, with parks and tree-shaded promenades, has been replaced with densely packed office towers, each a separate fiefdom.

Most commuters head straight for the subsidized parking garages attached to every office tower. At night, they head right out again, which is one reason that most retail businesses close at five P.M. and the arts have to be heavily subsidized by the city's corporate giants.

Stamford is a role model, certainly, but of what? As an example of urban revitalization, it has succeeded wildly, earning the envy of many other cities. Economic growth has soared, and Stamford's reputation as a financial center makes it an investment mecca. But Stamford "works" only on balance sheets. Too much thoughtless expansion and a complete lack of municipal planning have strained its quality of life. If the city's corporate growth had been accompanied by affordable housing construction and development of a regional light-rail system with links to satellite commuter towns, it could be well positioned as a livable city today. Other cities have taken that route, and it has worked.

In researching this chapter, I visited five American cities: Los Angeles and Arcata in California, Boston, New York City, and Portland, Oregon, each with a different lesson to teach about our transportation future.

The automobile built Los Angeles, birthplace of American drive-in culture, and the sprawled city is paying the price for its devotion with the nation's worst smog and—despite endless cloverleafs—immobile traffic. Los Angeles's belated attempts to build a mass-transit infrastructure are admirable, and desperately difficult.

By contrast, New York City embraced transit from the beginning and remains—by a wide margin—the least car-dependent city in America. But there are troubling trends in New York that threaten its livability, as well as a sense that the city doesn't fully appreciate its unique legacy.

As a city that, like New York, was laid out before the automobile, Boston benefits from an abundance of healthy, walkable neighborhoods and an enduring appreciation for transit. But Boston has committed itself to a massive highway-reconstruction project that is eating up every transportation dollar in the state, and its other transit problems languish from lack of attention.

Arcata, California, fully embraces transit—it just doesn't really have any. One of America's greenest small cities, Arcata would love to free itself from the tyranny of the automobile, but the only thing it's got now is a fleet of smelly diesel buses.

Of these cities, only Portland seems to be merging its vision with its accomplishments. Portland has big transit dreams, and the determination to make them real. It's a living laboratory of innovation in the complicated science of getting people from home to work and back again.

BOSTON: BLEEDING ARTERIES

It is popularly believed that Boston, America's oldest city, is full of bad drivers. But perhaps they simply have bad roads to drive on. I've frequently been lost in the Boston area, particularly in Cambridge, which is a warren of zigzag streets. I attempted to find the heralded Museum of Transportation while researching this book but gave up after repeated fruitless searches on the border between Brookline and Roxbury.

Boston's founder, John Winthrop, had wanted to make "a City on a Hill," but instead, in 1630, he built one on a peninsula. There are hills, though, on the western side, and a beautiful natural harbor that became the new colony's most important shipping route in the seventeenth and eighteenth centuries. Ferries crossed to what would become Chelsea and East Boston as early as 1638.

It was the new settlers (and their cows, as Ralph Waldo Emerson famously added) who laid out the winding streets, in the English pattern. Boston was actually a pioneer in the municipal management of highways—Roxbury had a street commission in 1652. The first Charlestown street surveying occurred in 1670, followed by, in 1760, a lottery to pay for the paving of Main Street.

As Boston swelled with textile and shipbuilding wealth, the tradition of managed growth continued. The roads and bridges of the nineteenth century were built as private toll-producing enterprises. (When the Charles River Bridge was opened in 1786, Harvard College was compensated for the loss of ferry revenues.)

Public transit, in the form of horse-drawn carriages on set schedules, was established in the 1820s. Horses also pulled the first commuter railcars, which plied routes beginning in the 1840s. Heavy rail, in the form of steam locomotives, also made its appearance. Boston was transforming itself into a modern city, complete with poverty and blight. Urban renewal was already under way in the 1860s, and the first of what would soon be an endless torrent of city planning studies, *The Most Beautiful City in America: Essay and Plan for the Improvement of the City of Boston,* was issued in 1872.

By 1900, Bostonians could move about easily on a municipal electrified streetcar system that was the largest in the world, making it possible to work in the city and live in the suburbs. At the same time, beginning in 1897 with the Tremont Street line, an enterprising city built the country's first subway, designed to ease downtown congestion.[1] The *Boston Daily Globe* (as it was then known) wrote breathlessly on opening day, "Over 100 persons were aboard the car when it rolled down the incline leading to the Boylston Street maw, and they yelled themselves to the verge of apoplexy."[2]

Boston, like many other American cities, hosted a patchwork of private transit systems until 1947, when they were finally consolidated under public ownership. That led, in the 1960s, to the creation of the Massachusetts Bay Transportation Authority (MBTA) to oversee rail, bus, and boat operations.

"T" FOR TRANSIT

The historic subway, known as the "T," consists of four color-coded rapid-transit lines. All the lines run aboveground for at least part of their route, and there are more than seventy-five stations. The MBTA bus network, with 160 routes, complements rather than duplicates subway service. Most buses connect commuters to T stops, instead of bringing them directly downtown. Others run directly between the four color-coded subway lines, which are notorious for defying easy transfers. MBTA also operates a commuter-rail train service that extends to such tourist destinations as Rockport, Gloucester, and Salem.

There are commuter boats, too, like the service between the elegant and historic town of Hingham and downtown Boston, which carries forty-five hundred riders every weekday. The ferry service was specifically conceived in 1973 as an alternative to new highway construction.

The admirable transit system built in Boston has many admirers, but they'd be the first to point out its seemingly intractable flaws. As early as 1909 the need was recognized for a link between North Station, where Maine and North Shore passengers disembark, and South Station, the end of the line for New York, Rhode Island, and the South Shore. But, then and now, political will and available capital have never coexisted.

Boston is one of the most determinedly walkable cities in the United States, with its pedestrians organized into an aggressive constituent group called WalkBoston. Jane Holtz Kay wrote in *Asphalt Nation* that "Boston's pedestrians are notable—or notorious—for their assertive stance against the automobile. Indeed, the word 'jaywalker' was invented [t]here."[3] Despite a growing automotive invasion, WalkBoston persuaded the city to try out such traffic-calming measure as retimed traffic lights that result in longer green lights for pedestrians. The group also fought hard to build pedestrian-friendly roads into the redesign of the city's Central Artery. Katie Alvord's *Divorce Your Car!* proclaims Boston as one of the best American car-free cities because of its "auto-free streets and corridors" and "excellent advocacy support for walking."[4]

Boston also has a car-sharing program, Zipcar, launched in 2000 by two women (one a German geochemist and the other an MIT management-school graduate). Zipcar estimates that each car-share vehicle replaces four to eight privately owned cars.

Bike riders are well organized, too. Because of political pressure from groups like MassBike, cyclists can take their two-wheelers on any MBTA rapid-transit or rail line without a fee or a special pass. Crosstown buses have bike racks that any passenger can access. MassBike is also behind an ambitious plan to restore what's known as the Emerald Necklace. Stretching from the Charles River to Franklin Park, the Emerald Necklace was a continuous linear greenway designed in the nineteenth century by Frederick Law Olmsted, but since bisected by highways.

The Depression stopped the expansion of Boston's rail lines, leaving many expansion plans on the drawing boards, and widespread private auto ownership began to slowly strangle the streetcars. Downtown traffic continued to swell, however, and the Central Artery, a six-lane elevated highway designed to slash through the congested city streets (and, unfortunately, cut Bostonians off from their waterfront), was first proposed in 1930, but was not actually built until the 1950s.

The Central Artery is formally known as the John F. Kennedy Expressway, but Kennedy would be none too proud if he could see what was wrought in his name. When it forced its way through downtown, wrote Lawrence W. Kennedy in *Planning the City on the Hill*, it "quickly earned a reputation as an outdated eyesore. Scarcely a decade after its opening, planners began to dream of tearing it down."[5]

THE BIG DIG

When it opened in 1959, the Central Artery carried 75,000 cars a day, but by the 1990s that number had swollen to 190,000. Traffic backed up eight to ten hours a day, and the accident rate was four times the national average for urban interstates.[6]

With city traffic at a breaking point, the state is finally tearing down the Central Artery as part of a spectacular plan known as the Big Dig. Burying the Central Artery underground is what the History Channel describes as "the most complex and expensive highway project ever undertaken in the United States." The project, which finally broke ground in 1990, was originally proposed in 1969 by Fred Salvucci, then Boston's transportation commissioner. Salvucci, who became state secretary of transportation in the 1970s under Governor Michael Dukakis, has since come full circle on the Big Dig and is now one of its fiercest critics.

The project as it is now unfolding under the direction of the Massachusetts Turnpike Authority (MTA) has two major components: a ten-lane underground highway to replace the Central Artery (part of I-93) and an extension of the Massachusetts Turnpike (I-90) through the Ted Williams Tunnel to Logan International Airport, one of the few big-city airports in America not reachable by an interstate. Five new highway interchanges and two new bridges over the Charles River are also part of the plan, and the city will gain thirty acres of parkland above the underground road. The Big Dig, originally projected to cost $2.5 billion, had ballooned by 2001 to $14.1 billion. Deriding the Big Dig's mushrooming costs and savage impact on commuters, who must negotiate around the frequently shifting construction sites, is a popular sport in Boston.

According to its contractors, who love statistics like these, the Big Dig will span 7.5 miles of highway and 161 lane miles, and excavate 13 million cubic yards of soil. Building the highway will consume 3.8 million cubic yards of concrete. Completion, already pushed back several times, is now slated for 2005.

The Boston press has been merciless about the Big Dig, daily bannering headlines about new corruption investigations, lawsuits, construction delays, and cost overruns. The project's Web site got included in the *Boston Phoenix*'s 1999 "Best of Boston" issue—as "Best Waste of Taxpayer Money." The Big Dig was also awarded the "Porker Award" by Wisconsin Congressman Tom Petri, a Republican antitax crusader, in 1997.[7]

The state's own attorney general, Scott Harshbarger, teamed up with Boston's Conservation Law Foundation (CLF) and sued every agency involved in the Big Dig for their failure to keep their promises about improving the city's bus and transit lines. Seth Kaplan, a CLF attorney, says that the suit, now settled, demanded that the MTA live up to its commitments with upgrades to subway service, cleaner buses, improved ferry service, and better park-and-ride facilities.

A nine-year review of Big Dig management problems by state Inspector General Robert A. Cerasoli concluded in the spring of 2000 that the project's contractors had essentially been allowed to police themselves, an arrangement that was "an invitation to fraud, waste and abuse."[8] The MTA chairman and project director who presided over the cost overruns, James Kerasiotes, was forced out just before the review was concluded.

The Big Dig's size makes it ripe for corruption. According to Ron Killian, the MTA's manager of environmental permits and procedures, just to get the Big Dig approved, the contractors had to make more than two thousand individual commitments and navigate the bureaucratic hurdles of one thousand different permit actions. Congressman Petri describes one such commitment: "The Boston Fire Department wanted a fire boat. So project administrators had a contractor go out and buy a glorified dinghy at a cost of $230,000. . . .And after the purchase was made, the boat had to be redesigned because firefighters with their equipment on couldn't get into the cabin."[9]

I decided I had to see the Big Dig for myself, and joined a tour led by Sean O'Neill, MTA's spokesman. The first thing I saw, after being hassled by a security guard who was fiercely protecting the MTA's parking lot, was a thirty-foot-long glass-covered model of the completed project. Dotted with green space and punctuated with tiny strolling pedestrians, it looked like a utopian cityscape of the kind Edward Bellamy had imagined for Boston in the nineteenth century.

The tour group was already milling around, and it was soon joined by the very energetic O'Neill, who displayed a thick Boston accent to go along with his job as what he called a "professional spear catcher for the biggest show on earth." He started right in disarming the critics. "There's a hullabaloo around this project because it's not happening in a field in Kansas," he said, "but instead, right in the heart of an historic city." O'Neill assured his visitors that simply fixing the Central Artery as it was would have cost $6.5 billion.

We took the elevator to the top of MTA's skyscraper and saw the construction project spread out in a panoramic 360-degree view, seeming to take up half of downtown. We donned hard hats and safety vests and walked along narrow pathways strewn with building debris and old coffee cups. Huge steel girders were being dropped into place by ten-story cranes, and hundreds of cables were being readied for the seemingly impossible feat of lining up 45,000-ton concrete tunnel sections to within a sixteenth of an inch. Men clung to metal gridwork on the tunnel walls like flies caught in spiderwebs. PROUD TO BE UNION TUNNEL WORKERS read a truck bumper sticker. O'Neill looked around admiringly. "If we didn't do this project, we might as well shut down Boston," he said, ignoring the fact that the city was practically shut down anyway.

We descended 120 feet of steps into what will be the tunnel for I-93 north. It was rather spooky, standing in the middle of an empty highway. "The next time you're in here, you'll be moving at sixty miles an hour," O'Neill said. And maybe he's right.

Complaining about the Big Dig has become almost as much a ritual in Boston as eating baked beans. Among the most vocal are residents of western Massachusetts, who have seen their transit projects wither as $8.5 billion of state money was committed to the Boston boondoggle. City transit gets shafted too, critics say. According to Dick Bauer, a Greater Boston Legal Services attorney and bike enthusiast, "There's now no money in the whole state of Massachusetts for any other transportation project."

Fred Salvucci, who now lectures at the Massachusetts Institute of Technology, is blunt about the ways in which his project went astray. "The connector roads, in a part of East Boston which has high ratios of Hispanic and Asian immigrants, were supposed to be at or below grade," he said angrily. "There was also to be major park expansion in the area to mitigate the effects of these connectors on the surrounding communities. The plans also called for a good shuttle-bus and subway system in the area, the new Blue Line extension." Instead, Salvucci said, the East Boston connectors are not on or below the ground; they're a series of fifty-three-foot-high ramps. The park expansion didn't happen, and the Blue Line extension was canceled. "These are violations of environmental justice," Salvucci said.

Salvucci is also upset about the failure to include the transit link between North and South Stations as part of Big Dig planning. Such a link, which would considerably simplify Amtrak passage through the city, was championed as part of the Boston Transportation Planning Review process in the 1960s. As the *Boston Globe* described it when the link was actively moving forward in 1994, the link "would buy Boston and New England a world-class transit system that would be a major engine for the region's economic growth. The $1 to $2 billion Rail Link would serve as a crucial connector for all the different modes—rail, highway, and air—and would create a seamless commuter transportation system within and among the region's suburban and urban centers."[10]

There's only one significant mass-transit component of the Big Dig as it exists today, the Silver Line. I naively thought during my tour that this new route between the World Trade Center and South Station was a rail system. Instead, it's a dedicated bus tunnel that is supposed to start ferrying passengers in 2003. And it might not end up doing much good. Massachusetts Environmental Affairs Secretary Robert Durand told the *Boston Globe* in the summer of 2000 that projections for the Silver Line to carry 62 percent of waterfront commuters are "hopelessly optimistic."[11]

The woes Boston is experiencing in attempting to build out of congestion are hardly unique. Don Chen, executive director of Smart Growth America in Washington, D.C., points out that America's capital city is itself undergoing similar headaches with its improvements to the notorious Springfield Interchange, a.k.a "the Mixing Bowl." Originally projected to cost $300 million, in the early stages the project quickly ballooned to $450 million. "Cost overruns are a matter of course with highway projects," Chen says. "To get the Big Dig built, a lot of commitments and promises were made early on that were not upheld. This is becoming politics as usual for these highway projects."

I hadn't seen Boston's historical South Station in some years, so I paid it a visit while I was in the city. At the time of my visit in 2000, the station had just undergone a $170 million renovation and was formally named the South Station Intermodal Transportation Center. I'd say it was struggling to achieve intermodality, with a bus terminal for Peter Pan and Greyhound lines being built next door. Amtrak and the T's Red Line stop give some flexibility to travelers. The terminal serves 45,000 rail passengers and 15,000 bus riders daily.

Boston's subway is, overall, a very good one, but there are some challenges for the traveler at South Station. Without the Rail Link, connecting to North Station for northbound Amtrak trains is difficult, and two changes, from Red to Orange to Blue, are necessary to get to Logan Airport. I was amazed by the station itself, which has been so thoroughly swallowed up by glitzy commercial renovation that you can hardly see the train announcement boards. It's a fine place to go if you want to try the bread at Au Bon Pain or the Asian specialties at the China Café.

This kind of thing is inevitable. I was to see similar station makeovers on my travels to Los Angeles, Washington, and New York. At Grand Central Terminal in Manhattan, the entire lower level has been transformed into a gigantic food court, but at least the main floor still feels like a railroad station.

I left Boston with mixed feelings. There's little doubt that the aging Central Artery had to go. If thirty acres of park land does get built in the city's downtown, everyone will benefit. And Bostonians will be able to rediscover their waterfront. But replacing one highway with another, even if it is going to be underground, is unlikely to lead to long-term and lasting benefits. Twenty years from now, new highway studies will land on municipal desks, proposing yet another way to build out of congestion.

PORTLAND, OREGON: SUSTAINABLE CITY

After taking off my hard hat in Boston, I was eager to visit a city that has firmly rejected highway-based solutions to transit problems. Portland's reputation preceded it, but I'd never visited there. I had the impression that Portland enjoyed a spectacular setting in a fertile valley, which is true enough, but there are also six months of cold, misty weather. It's state-of-the-art public transportation that makes Portland so notably livable. Portland was lauded in 2000 as one of America's ten most environmentally friendly cities by the Environmental News Network, which cited it as "the only U.S. city to come close to balancing investments between roads and public transit."

Make no mistake, though: compared to most European cities, Portland remains heavily auto-dependent. By offering light-rail links to just about everywhere, the city is only hoping to lessen that dependency a little bit, from 92 percent of all area trips now to 88 percent by 2040—and that's under one of the more optimistic scenarios. Like most American cities, Portland is ringed by interstates that carry the bulk of its commuters. And like many of those American cities, projected population increases threaten to nearly double the cars on the road by 2050. The difference is that Portland said yes to transit and no to more roads, with a 1997 decision not to build an urban beltway and to limit highway construction to less than forty miles over the next forty years. The result is that from 1990 to 1996, transit ridership grew 20 percent faster in the metropolitan region than did vehicle miles traveled.

There's no better way to be introduced to transit-friendly Portland than by taking the No. 12 bus from the airport to downtown. This is a city whose transit agency, Tri-Met, provides its citizens with 80 million transit rides a year, three-quarters of them on the bus.

Portland's Tri-Met bus drivers are courteous and say, "Have a nice day now" as their passengers get off. A few stops down, we braked for a helmeted cyclist, who flung his bike onto a rack on the bus's nose.

Bicycles always ride free on Tri-Met, even during rush hours. Cyclist Earl Weston, whose handlebar mustache gave him a passing resemblance to the rock star David Crosby, told me that the racks, which come in two different styles, have made life much easier for him. "To get a rack pass, they make you watch a six-minute video that shows how the mechanism works," Weston said. "Now I use them every day and they save me forty-five minutes of riding in morning rush-hour traffic."

The bus dropped me off in downtown Portland, a thriving commercial center. It wasn't so popular thirty years ago. In 1970, according to a Tri-Met study called "Beyond the Field of Dreams," a depressed downtown provided only 50,000 jobs and suffered air-quality violations on one of every three days; by 1997, it provided 105,000 jobs and hadn't had an air violation in ten years.[12] Buses and gaily painted light-rail cars buzzed past, and private cars, too, but not so many that traffic slowed to a crawl.

SHARING CARS

I was on time for my meeting with Portland's ambitious car-sharing program, which is doing its best to get cars off the city's streets. CarSharing Portland, while a private enterprise, is located in the city's decommissioned courthouse, a grand tribute to Depression-era architecture. My visit coincided with that of Warren, a tall, thin computer-software consultant with the sensitive features and long hair of a poet. Warren was the latest of approximately three hundred city residents who'd decided to leave full-time auto ownership behind. His orientation was run by Maren Souders, the crisply efficient young woman who is CarSharing's one full-time employee.

It's hardly surprising that Warren does computer work. Intel has more than eleven thousand employees in Portland, and there are many high-tech start-ups in the increasingly affluent city. Warren works out of his house and had sold his car recently. But he also has a wife and two kids, who frequently use the one vehicle the family still owns.

Souders explained the rather complicated drill. CarSharing Portland, which was founded in 1998, is part of a new wave of such programs in major urban centers, including Seattle, Boston, Chicago, and San Francisco. European systems, which are much older and much bigger, are the models. Mobility CarSharing in Lucerne, Switzerland, for instance, has thirteen hundred cars at eight hundred locations and uses advanced electronic-chip cards to simplify access.

CarSharing Portland's complicated reservation system is handled entirely over the telephone, by a computer program. The software schedules nineteen vehicles, mostly compact Dodge Neons and Saturns, but the fleet also includes a pickup truck and an ultramodern Honda Insight gas-electric hybrid car.

A gigantic map of Portland decorated with pushpins shows not only the cars' locations but those of the members. Most people borrow cars parked within walking or bicycling distance of their homes. They gain access to them through lockboxes not unlike those displayed on houses for sale. Car sharers pay $1.50 an hour, plus 40 cents a mile for gas. "The last time it was this cheap to drive a car, it belonged to your parents," reads a CarSharing slogan.

Souders ran down the rules, which are many. "We bill in hourly increments, depending on the time you reserved the car—even if you don't use it," she explained. "If you bring a car back late, there's a twenty-dollar fine, plus you're liable for up to one hundred dollars of other charges related to the driver you stranded. The lockbox contains the ignition key and a gas card. You're the only person who can drive the car. No racing or testing, no smoking in the cars, no use outside the United States, no animals unless they're in an approved carrier." It was all a bit overwhelming, Warren said.

President David Brook, who based the Portland program on the Mobility plan in Switzerland, says that Europe—which has 150,000 people in 450 cities involved in car-sharing programs—is much further along. "They haven't had the effects of sixty years of widespread private-car use over there," he says. Brook points out, however, that Americans who drive less than 7,500 miles a year will definitely save money by sharing rather than owning a car. Most drivers, he adds, factor in only gasoline when computing their automobile expenses, but there are also regular bills for insurance, repairs, parking, and maintenance.

Brook thinks that car sharing is a low-cost, low-overhead approach to easing congestion. "I look at plans for the automated highway, for instance, and I don't see the point," he says. "Why spend all that money on technology just so we can squeeze a few more cars on the existing highways?"

Some car-sharing programs are used primarily by commuters, but Portland's is aimed at the casual weekend and errand user. The San Francisco Bay Area's ambitious CarLink program, by contrast, puts its cars onto a complicated schedule that includes use by both inbound and outbound commuters making connections at rail stops, as well as short in-town missions. "I think that's expecting the system to do too many things," says Brook.

If one hundred more new members come in the door, CarSharing Portland will break even. Maybe then David Brook can start paying himself a salary and Maren Souders won't be so overworked. Until then, they might consider adding discounts from bicycle retailers to the mix, as AutoShare in Toronto does. Portland is the most bicycle-friendly city I've ever seen. Another approach, used by Switzerland's Mobility, is to make use between 11:00 P.M. and 7:00 A.M. free of hourly rates. That's a smart form of congestion pricing.

BIKES RULE!

On a Tri-Met bus I met a young man named Ed Chang, who offered me his business card, which identified him as a consultant and also revealed that he was an MIT graduate. "You should contact a group called the Bicycle Transportation Alliance," he said. "They do a lot of good work in Portland." Chang added that he doesn't own a car and plans never to own one. I later learned that the Bicycle Transportation Alliance (BTA) lobbied hard for the on-bus bike racks, and also sponsors such whimsical innovations as Bicycle Commute Challenge, which provides prizes for employees who pedal to work, and the annual Providence Bike Pedal, which closes Willamette River bridges to all but human-powered traffic.

Bicycles have the right of way in Portland, and BTA is one of the main reasons why. Since 1990, the group has agitated for bikers' rights statewide, and its very active Portland chapter is usually on hand to make sure that bikes are considered in any new transit scheme. During repairs to the Hawthorne Bridge in 1998, for instance, BTA convinced the city that better bike access should be part of the work. When city agencies balk at adhering to Oregon's very bike-friendly Bicycle Bill, BTA takes them to court, as it did successfully in 1995 to force inclusion of legally required bike lanes around the then-new Trailblazers arena. BTA also administers a bike-locker rental program at transit stations and has developed a comprehensive bike-safety education program.

Portland is one of the few American cities with a Bicycle Master Plan, adopted in 1996. In its first two years, the plan resulted in sixty miles of new bikeways, two thousand new parking spaces for bikes, and sharply elevated bike use citywide. An informal count of central-city riders in 1997 clocked more than two thousand passing by between 4:00 to 6:00 P.M. When two slots opened up on the city's Bicycle Advisory Committee in 1998, twenty-six people competed fiercely for them.

A 1998 update on the Bicycle Master Plan estimated that downtown bike riders save the city up to 5.5 million vehicle miles every year, resulting in a 1,700- to 2,800-ton reduction in carbon dioxide emissions. Portland will only get more bike-friendly. A law that went into effect in 1997 requires all new buildings and all buildings undergoing major renovation to install bike parking. Through a program called Bike Central, there is even bike parking at several city athletic clubs, which also provide showers and changing facilities for commuters at a small monthly fee. Bicycles are part of intermodal Portland: they're on bus racks and riding along on the city's Tri-Met light-rail system.

PORTLAND BY RAIL AND BUS

Light rail is well established in Portland and is at the heart of the city's sense of itself. Portland's transit hub is Pioneer Courthouse

Square, a former parking lot in the city's center that is now laid out like a Roman coliseum, with descending circles of steps. On a recent sunny Friday during my visit, kids ran around laughing, office workers caught some rays, and strollers grabbed some lunch from pushcart vendors. Traversed by buses and Portland's ultraspiffy Tri-Met MAX light-rail system, and with hardly a parking space in sight, this is transit-based development in spades. In fact, if you ride the rail or bus within the downtown core, known as Fareless Square, it's absolutely free. If Mayor Vera Katz has her way, fares will be suspended permanently on the whole system.

Portland's MAX is truly remarkable, a single thirty-three-mile line of efficient light rail running east and west to connect the city with the communities of Gresham, Beaverton, Orenco Station, and Hillsboro. A newly built five-mile extension connects the city with Portland International Airport. Tri-Met is fond of pointing out that Portland is the only region in the country where transit ridership is growing faster than vehicle miles traveled. MAX, first opened in 1986, now makes 62,000 passenger trips a day and enjoys a 90 percent approval rating from its riders (most of whom also own cars).

I met Lynn Ann Peterson from Tri-Met, the city's transit agency, in Pioneer Courthouse Square. Peterson, who's white-blond, wears John Lennon glasses, and is extremely impassioned about smart-growth issues, is hardly a typical transit bureaucrat. She is, in fact, a very recent transfer from One Thousand Friends of Oregon, which is perhaps the state's most prominent advocate for open-space preservation and planned development. Peterson chants a mantra that often includes the phrases *high density, mixed use,* and *pedestrian friendly.*

With Peterson and Tri-Met's Phil Colombo, I took the MAX light rail along the system's Westside line eight miles to Orenco Station, a mixed-use development with two thousand housing units on two hundred acres that is winning national attention. Critics claim that the MAX system suffers from low ridership, but it didn't seem that way as we rode standing-room-only through Washington and Forest Parks, a cluster of kid-friendly natural escapes that together constitute the largest urban green zone in America.

Light rail drives smart development in Portland, and that's evident even at MAX's next stop, Beaverton, which borders the city across the Willamette River. Peterson pointed out with a shudder that Beaverton is dominated by "strip malls and big-box stores." But Beaverton also has mixed-use development going up right along the light-rail tracks.

The Westside line passes through farmland, a sticking point for federal funders. According to Peterson, "They didn't want to give us money because we couldn't show that we'd have the ridership. But we wanted to build the line and have the development grow around it. They did finally agree to funding, and we didn't have to give the money back because we did get the ridership." Tri-Met estimates that if 7,000 new housing units move in around the transit line, at least a quarter of the twelve thousand new residents will ride light rail.

Orenco Station, when we did arrive there, was picture-postcard pretty, looking almost like a housing development on a movie set. In fact, it resembles the Disney-built exercise in instant nostalgia known as Celebration, Florida, though its residents would hate the comparison. What we saw is a result of an extensive market study, fitting smart development into a city convinced it doesn't want any other kind.

We disembarked from MAX, then strode down an access road that, Peterson exclaimed, featured nearly every textbook traffic-calming device and pedestrian-friendly feature. "Look," she said. "Those are curb extensions that make the road appear to be narrower, slowing the traffic down. There's a stamped-concrete crossing. There are street trees, benches, trash cans . . ."

Then–vice president Al Gore opened Orenco Station, which was draped with a BUILDING LIVABLE COMMUNITIES banner for the occasion, in 1998. Now its town houses and cottages, which range from $192,000 to $250,000, are filling up fast and prices are rising. All the houses feature front porches, broad sidewalks, and extensive gardens, and are within walking distance of the town's manicured center, which sports a Starbucks and an Indian restaurant. Some of the town houses even have urban-style stoops, so that neighbors can get to know one another. Intel is a short distance away, and a shuttle bus serves its campus. No one in Orenco Station needs to own a car, even though most of the homes have (tastefully hidden) two-car garages.

"It's all very yuppie," Peterson admits, looking at the plastic lobsters on display in a model home. "Right now it's attracting retirees and double-income high-tech workers looking for their first home." We bought some iced coffee at Starbucks, then toured a 514-square-foot mother-in-law apartment, proof that Orenco Station values the extended family.

MAX delivers Orenco residents downtown in half an hour, for $1.50. From there, bus lines, light rail, and an in-town trolley service can whisk smart-growth true believers to every corner of the city and connect them to the airport and Amtrak, too. Is there anything wrong with the picture of better living at Orenco Station?

Gentrification and inadequate shopping, to name two. In a *New York Times* op-ed piece, Alan Ehrenhalt of *Governing* magazine wrote of his own visit to Orenco Station. Ehrenhalt noted the possibility of car-free living and the presence of Starbucks, but he also noticed something missing: a drugstore and a grocery. "[T]he biggest problem for previous New Urbanist projects hasn't been home sales," he wrote. "[I]t's been an inability to attract the commercial infrastructure of everyday life: grocery stores, pharmacies, bakeries, barber shops, bookstores. It takes a whole streetful of merchants to make a village; without them, it is hard to see how Orenco or any development like it could change the face of suburban America in the way its promoters promise."[13] Orenco offers merchants a built-in base of well-heeled consumers, but what it doesn't offer is very much retail space. Orenco may be "the future of the country," as developer Rudy Kadlub put it at the opening,[14] but it has to figure out a way to incorporate a real, thriving Main Street, or those two-car garages will get a lot of use.

Gentrification is a charge leveled at many of Portland's high-density developments, including Orenco Station. Phil Colombo pointed to the rising home prices in Orenco as proof that transit-oriented development works, but this same phenomenon has also driven poor and working-class families out of many neighborhoods within Portland. Only 14 percent of Tri-Met's riders take transit because they have no car available, which doesn't tend to put the problems of the urban poor front and center.

Portland's bus system seemed remarkably healthy to me, with relatively new buses riding nearly full on 102 routes. The buses, which carry three-fourths of Portland's transit passengers, are fully intermodal, with 88 bus lines connecting to MAX at light-rail stations. Seniors can ride for only 60 cents, less than half the regular fare. But critics like Jonathan Richmond, the author of a Harvard University transit study, claim the buses are being shortchanged by light rail in terms of both new equipment and the designation of new routes. Richmond also points out that only a third of Tri-Met's new rail passengers gave up cars; the rest were former bus riders. Portland transit activist G. B. Arrington, a former Tri-Met strategic planner now with the consulting firm Parsons Brinckerhoff, counters that Richmond is "twisting numbers" and ignoring light rail's role in shaping new development patterns.[15]

I spoke with Robert Liberty, executive director of One Thousand Friends of Oregon, and he admitted that transit-oriented development can and does cause both gentrification and accessibility problems. "It's a concern that our coalition shares," he said. "In Los Angeles, they've gutted the bus lines to support high-speed rail to the suburbs, and I don't think that's fair. It's also not fair to remove access to transit for people without cars. We have to be sure that transit is always available for Portland's low-income neighborhoods."

Transit defender Arrington describes the city as "a tangled web of strategies and policies, with all kinds of effects." And he poses a provocative question: "Who said gentrification is a bad thing? The real question is what other policies are being pursued to deal with the consequences of it. The next big challenge the region faces is to address affordability in a comprehensive region-wide manner." That view is widespread in the city, so Portland may well avoid some of gentrification's pitfalls.

GENDER GAPS AND TRANSIT BURDENS

In visiting Portland, I was fortunate to know Linda Baker, a journalist who contributes excellent work to the journal I edit, *E: The Environmental Magazine.* Linda is a fine researcher who, just prior to my visit, had written a long piece for *E* on urban sprawl and its solutions. And some of the best of those solutions were coming out of Portland. Our piece featured a photograph of the Belmont Dairy, a high-density condo complex of thirty-three units that happens to be located near her home in a revitalizing southeast Portland neighborhood.

Baker, who has two young children, recently wrote an op-ed column in the *Oregonian,* Portland's daily newspaper, contending that women, and in particular women with kids, get the short end of the stick when it comes to transportation options. "I hate to drive," Baker wrote.[16] "Only recently have I realized how inextricably connected driving and motherhood really are. And in the process, something personal—chauffeuring my kids around town—has become something political: understanding the harmful effects of an automobile-centered society on women, children and the institutions that sustain them."

Baker's story continued:

According to a study released last year by the Washington, D.C.–based Surface Transportation Policy Project, spread-out development caused mothers with school-aged children to spend more than an hour a day driving. Whether they work outside the home or not, women with kids now make as many as five car trips a day, 20 percent more than the average for all women and 21 percent more than the average man. Even in a mass transit, neighborhood-friendly city such as Portland, figures like these come as no surprise. "Women drive more because they do the bulk of household production tasks such as shopping for groceries and dropping kids off at day care—what we call 'trip chaining,'" says Catherine Lawson, a researcher at Portland State University.

Women's fender benders are different, too, according to a 1998 study by the Federal Office of Road Safety, which found that accidents involving women typically occur at intersections and in lower-speed zones during the day—in other words, in school zones and shopping districts. "This is due to an increase in the number of women obtaining drivers' licenses and an increase in the amount of travel they are undertaking," the report said.[17] More than half of all new mothers bought a car within the year before their delivery date, according to data on female driving habits from Ford.[18]

As we waited on line at the Cup and Saucer restaurant, situated on a Sunnyside neighborhood street that ten years before had housed mainly transients and methadone clinic habitués, Baker explained her thesis. "Land-use and development patterns really shaft women, low-income women especially," she said.

"And there's definitely a class element to this," Baker continued. "Because of welfare reform, poor women are forced to take jobs, and since they don't often have cars, that means taking the bus. And because of urban disinvestment, many of the jobs are now in the suburbs, which are poorly served by the bus lines. So they can't get to the jobs that do exist. Yes, Portland has light rail, but only one line that runs to the western suburbs.

"In Portland," Baker explained as our breakfast arrived, "the old paradigm is sprawl. The new paradigm is urban reinvestment in city neighborhoods. Of course, that means gentrification, and some of the older residents are displaced."

Kids are also players in another Portland drama, Baker says. She's concerned that much of the new development—including the showplace $265,000 Belmont Dairy condos, which entirely lack yards—isn't kid-friendly but is targeted at the kind of double-income, no-kids-yet young professionals seen walking the streets in droves.

"I think attracting families to these neighborhoods is key," Baker said. "But all the new recreational centers around here are big boxes surrounded by busy arterial highways. They have very good programs for kids, but there's no way to get there without a car."

The first phase of redevelopment, Baker says, was rebuilding abandoned neighborhoods as attractive places to live, attracting home buyers and businesses. The second phase, she adds, "is to really think about the kind of people you're attracting. Families may not sit in chichi restaurants as much as couples without kids, they may not go out as much, but they're essential anyway. Without them, for instance, the public schools deteriorate, and that usually means the neighborhood does, too."

Baker volunteered to give me a tour of Portland, and we walked through the Pearl District, once a decaying neighborhood of abandoned warehouses but now a thriving home to artists and upscale, mixed-use condominiums. An innovative group called Eco Trust was rebuilding a warehouse on the edge of the district as the Natural Capital Center, a virtual temple to sustainability, housing many progressive businesses. Its anchor is upscale outdoor-clothing retailer Patagonia. New restaurants and, in particular, coffee bars, were everywhere.

We drove through Laurelhurst, an older neighborhood of fine Tudor and Craftsman homes surrounding the jewel-like Laurelhurst Park. Here was proof that city real estate can retain value, since these immaculate homes command prices of $500,000 and up, much more than comparable homes in the Portland suburbs. We also took a ride up Skyline Boulevard, where newly built mansions in the mammoth Forest Heights subdivision command sweeping views of the city. These five-bathroom abodes for dot-com millionaires seemed the antithesis of smart growth, but the developers point to the wilderness corridors on the property that were maintained as part of construction. They also note that Skyline Boulevard is well within Portland's famous urban growth boundary (UBG), which restricts sprawl.

All urban areas in Oregon have been required to have a UGB since 1973, when influential Governor Tom McCall lashed out in a speech to the state legislature against the "ravenous rampage of suburbia in the Willamette Valley." In Portland, the UGB is overseen by Metro, Portland's regional government, which has modified it dozens of times, releasing about five thousand acres to developers between 1980 and 2000. Environmentalists say that UGBs have allowed Oregon to retain far more farmland and open space than states with comparable population growth; critics charge that the UGB in Portland has precipitated a housing shortage, and that by funneling high-density development into the urban core it is destroying the delicate balance of the city's neighborhoods. But the neighborhoods I saw looked revitalized, not destroyed. And Portland's careful transit planning is key to the process.

I rejoined Baker and her family for a picnic in Laurelhurst Park later that evening. In preparation, Baker rounded up her children and we walked to Zupan's, a snazzy neighborhood supermarket that—this is unthinkable in most of the country—has no adjoining parking lot. Baker and the kids walk to Zupan's nearly every night.

I left Portland the next day, just as the Providence Bike Pedal was getting under way. The streets were thronged with cyclists making their way over the Hawthorne and Morrison Bridges. The shuttle-bus driver swung onto I-5, and I could see the sun glinting off the helmets of hundreds of riders as they crossed the bridge. It was a stunning sight, and very symbolic of Portland's human-sized approach to transforming transportation.

NEW YORK CITY: GRIDLOCK IN THE TRANSIT UTOPIA

Though you won't hear the fact touted in the tourist brochures, New York City is the least car-dependent city in the United States. It's a situation that derives more from population density and land-use patterns than any inherent love of transit. In a city of just 321 square miles (or 205,000 acres), there are more than 8 million people, 750,000 buildings, and 3 million housing units. More than two-thirds of those housing units are in multifamily buildings.[19]

On a slightly larger scale, the New York metropolitan area, incorporating the commuter parts of New York State, Connecticut, and New Jersey, is the largest urban region in North America, with 20 million people in 12,000 square miles and a 1,250-mile rail system that carries 40 percent of the total transit ridership in the U.S.

How car-free is New York? John Kaehny, executive director of the bicycle-promoting nonprofit group Transportation Alternatives, told me that 55 percent of the households in the city have no car at all. Some 18 percent of all trips in New York are taken by pedestrians. Of the commuter traffic arriving in midtown Manhattan during the morning rush, 90 percent comes in on subways, buses, or suburban rail. New York's only Achilles' heel is freight: goods are moved in and out of the city mainly by truck. A proposed rail tunnel between Brooklyn and either New Jersey or Staten Island would eliminate 130,000 truck miles a year but would be very expensive. "The transit system helps to make New York City unique and interesting," said Kaehny. "The density creates an overall ferment that is of a different order than anywhere else."

New York City and Portland are, in fact, engaged in an amiable competition about which city is friendlier to transit. Kaehny derides Portland as "not even close," because car ownership is much higher and only 10 to 15 percent of the population takes mass transit. But I also spoke to Portland's bicycle-riding Democratic congressman, Earl Blumenauer, who repeats the mantra that his city is "the only metropolitan area in the U.S. where transit ridership is growing faster than vehicle miles traveled." He cautions that the New York numbers are deceiving, because of urban sprawl outside the city's boundaries. The sprawl, he said, is growing faster than the population increase. "Don't just talk to me about what's going on in the New York City core," he said. "Let's look at what's happening in Connecticut and northern New Jersey."

Let's. From 1970 to 1990, vehicle miles traveled grew by 60 percent in the metropolitan area. "Growing use of automobiles, trucks and buses is also the key reason why the region is second only to Los Angeles in number of days that air quality fails to meet federal standards," wrote Robert D. Yaro and Thomas K. Wright in *Cities in Our Future*.[20]

But New Yorkers do *everything* in a big way. Yes, a million cars a day drive into midtown Manhattan. But those metro New Yorkers also take some 2.5 *billion* transit rides a year, on buses, subways, and suburban-rail networks. In 1998, regional rail transit, bus and ferry ridership, and subway trips all increased dramatically, according to the New York Metropolitan Transportation Council.[21] According to a poll in late 2000 by the Straphangers Campaign, a riders' group, passengers' biggest complaint about the subways is the fact that they're overcrowded. According to Farouk Abdallah, the survey's field organizer, many of the problems are due to a 17 percent ridership increase since 1997.[22]

A TRANSIT TOWN

I've lived in the shadow of New York City all my life, and I'll always think of it as primarily a transit town, where walking is a given. When I visit the city, I walk more than I do anywhere else, and I even adopt that hurried stride that is so characteristic of New Yorkers. I become part of the city's vast sidewalk sea, congregating on curbs and waiting for the light to change. Probably 90 percent of my subway experience is in New York, though I've been lucky enough to ride the competition in London, Los Angeles, Tokyo, and Paris. (The others are cleaner; New York's are both more dangerous and more exciting.) I love New York's distinct and walkable neighborhoods, like SoHo and Park Slope, Brooklyn. The beautiful brownstone apartment buildings feature neighbor-friendly stoops that I saw echoed in Orenco Station outside Portland.

You'd never live in New York if you hated people, because they surround you every day. For all its size, New York has a human scale, and that's why *Money* magazine, in its 2000 "Best Places to Live" survey, praised the city's "unmatched vitality."

I'm ashamed to admit, though, that when I'm in a hurry or headed somewhere far downtown, I drive into the city just like the 2.7 million other people who cross the rivers on bridges or in tunnels every day (up from 1.4 million in 1980). Driving in can be both quicker and cheaper, since parking is often free in neighborhoods south of midtown. I almost invariably take the car when flying from one of the metropolitan area's three airports, since public transit links are poor at best. I have high hopes, however, for the new Airtrain light rail system, which will link JFK Airport to the city's subway by 2003.

In recent years, the city seems to have gone out of its way to favor me and my kind over the car-free majority of pedestrians and transit takers. In the late 1990s, Mayor Rudolph Giuliani made his views abundantly clear by cracking down on jaywalking and erecting crosswalk barriers on five avenues to aid motorists. In the city, pedestrians race for the safety of curbs through a gauntlet of wildly swerving yellow cabs, lead-footed commuters, and speeding trucks. The fact that the traffic is in gridlock most of the time inflames motorists to heights of advantage-grabbing derring-do.

Bike and transit groups say they consider themselves under siege from an invading horde of cars and trucks. Transportation Alternatives, in a letter to the New York City transportation commissioner, urged the department to emphasize traffic reduction and focus new investment on alternatives to driving. "Business leaders, environmentalists, civic organizations and neighborhood groups agree [that] the problem is too many cars," the letter said.[23] As an alternative, the group proposes an end to relentless taxi cruising in the midtown area, additional bike paths in Manhattan and on the East River bridges, traffic-calming programs, and car-free trials for Central and Prospect Parks.

There have been a variety of setbacks to transit forces in New York. In a parallel to Florida's infamous "butterfly ballot," voters in New York State narrowly defeated the $1.6 billion Transportation Infrastructure Bond Act of 2000 (which would have funded a host of subway, bus, and train improvements), possibly because of extremely confusing ballot positioning and labeling.[24] A proposal for a bike lane in Brooklyn's Borough Park neighborhood linking existing paths at Shoreline and Ocean Parkways foundered when Orthodox Jewish residents objected to "scantily clad cyclists."[25]

On the brighter side, New York's legendary vitality extends to its bike and transit advocates. Transportation Alternatives is a vigorous campaigner for the 105,000 bicyclists who brave some of the world's fiercest rush-hour traffic on a daily basis. And if the group's within-the-system lobbying is too tame for you, there are more militant organizations. One of those is Right of Way, a streetwise grassroots group dedicated to ending "car violence." Right of Way was founded by Charles Komanoff, a former antiwar and antinuclear organizer who ran Transportation Alternatives for a time in the 1980s before concluding that the group was too policy-oriented for his activist tastes. "I consider myself a kind of low-level David Brower," he said, referring to the late pioneering environmentalist whose penchant for founding—and then quitting—activist groups was legendary. Komanoff actually grew up in one of Long Island's more pedestrian-friendly suburbs and didn't even learn how to ride a bicycle until he was an adult living in New York. Now you can't get him off his bike.

"The great advantage of New York, something it shares with the older parts of Boston and Philadelphia, is that most of its streetscape predates the car," Komanoff said. "The density more or less forces people out of cars and into alternatives. The crime of New York City transportation policy is that, like nearly every other city in the country, it bends over backward to privilege drivers at the expense of people."

There's not much doubt as to where Right of Way stands on the issues. "Cars suck!" it proclaims. One of the group's principal activities is illegally stenciling lifesize outlines of pedestrians killed on city streets. Since 1996, the group has stenciled more than 250 death sites. "Every year, more than two hundred New York pedestrians and at least twenty bicyclists are killed by automobiles," said Komanoff. "That's twice as many as in Tokyo, London, or Paris. The city has become a killing zone." According to the group's statistics, in 1996 only 20 percent of drivers found to be at least partly at fault for striking pedestrians received summonses.

One of the dead, the subject of a Right of Way vigil in 1997, was Dr. Rachel Fruchter, a women's health researcher who contributed to the landmark book *Our Bodies, Ourselves*. She was struck by a van while riding her bike in Prospect Park and dragged fifty feet. Judging by the skid marks, police estimated that the van was traveling at least forty miles per hour, far over the legal limit in the park. Rachel Fruchter was dead, Right of Way said at the time, "because the police investigate only a fraction of the several hundred pedestrian and bicycle fatalities every year, and refer only a mere handful of these to the district attorneys for prosecution."[26]

Right of Way is just one of the city groups that have been participating in regular Reclaim the Streets events since 1998. Echoing a similar campaign in Europe, Reclaim the Streets bills itself as a "free-form dance performance protest street party," and its events feature live performers, traffic blocking, and even pirate radio broadcasts. The first event, on Broadway in Manhattan in October 1998, drew a thousand people into the street. As in San Francisco, Chicago, Austin, and other cities, Critical Mass rides are held once a month in New York, impressing—and irritating—motorists with their sheer numbers. "We're not blocking traffic, we *are* traffic!" the riders proclaim.

The creative environmental group Time's Up! has done much to promote bike travel in New York City with themed mass rides, including a Christmas event in Brooklyn to see the "miracle mile" of Christmas lights in Dyker Heights, a New Year's ride in full costume to Union Square Park in Manhattan, and even a "Mystery, History, Murder and Money Tour" that included legendary crime lairs in lower Manhattan.

Transportation Alternatives is leading the campaign to limit cars in the city's enormous Central Park, which was built with crosstown traffic arteries. In 1999, it collected one thousand signatures to have the idea tried out on a three-month trial basis. The group even enlisted the biographer of the park's legendary designer, Frederick Law Olmsted, in a campaign to prove that the park was never intended to host motorized traffic. Transportation Alternatives has also campaigned to keep New York's bridges open to bikes and is trying to start a "rack and roll" program so bikes can ride on transit buses.

Transportation Alternatives' Kaehny says that the number of bicycles in New York City is growing rapidly. In 1990, there were 70,000 bicycles in daily use in the city; in 2000, there were 105,000.

"Bicycling is up in the city, despite car traffic that grew by 20 percent in the last five years," Kaehny told me, adding sardonically, "The problem is that the city correlates car trips with the health of the economy. Some of the river bridges are free, and that's an inducement to drive into the city. Parking in the central district is incredibly cheap, given the scarcity of space."

New York is in many ways looking up for cyclists: there are new bicycle paths on the Queensboro, Williamsburg, Manhattan, and Brooklyn Bridges. Still, the vast potential is unrealized when only one-half of one percent of all the trips taken in the city are made on bicycles.

THE WEST SIDE HIGHWAY: THE AUTOMOBILE TRIUMPHANT

The venerable West Side Highway (State Route 9A), which in its glory days ran from the Henry Hudson Parkway at the top of Manhattan to the Brooklyn-Battery Tunnel at the bottom, is worth looking at in some detail, because it provides a microcosm of New York's transportation priorities. The elevated highway along the Hudson River, constructed between 1927 and 1931, was part of the huge grid of limited-access highways designed by "master planner" Robert Moses. Typical of Moses's plans, it cut off public access to the waterfront and exalted the private automobile over other forms of transit. "Moses was an absolute monster," says Right of Way's Michael Smith. "He did more damage to New York than the black plague did to medieval Europe. He considered transit a poor people's thing."

By 1957, 140,000 cars a day were taking Route 9A and the road was visibly deteriorating, sparking the first of what has turned out to be an endless series of studies on the highway's future. The 1957 study, and a later one in 1965, advocated widening the road and adding lanes, reflecting the thinking in vogue at the time that you could build out of congestion.

The studies went nowhere. It took a disaster to finally spur redevelopment of the highway. "On December 16, 1973, in the most ironic of circumstances, a cement truck that was traveling to make repairs [on the highway] caused a 60-foot section of the northbound roadway to collapse at Gansevoort Street," according to a detailed history of the West Side Highway. "Immediately, the entire highway from the Battery to 46th Street was closed."[27]

A "temporary" replacement to part of the highway was constructed and stayed in place for more than twenty-five years as a primary north-south traffic conduit. Meanwhile, the abandoned and rotting hulk of the elevated road became a popular running and biking path, as well as a staging area for concerts and a home for the homeless. The elevated highway was finally torn down completely in 1989.

Even before the road collapsed, planners had envisioned replacing it with a new interstate expressway, to be called Westway, that included provisions for a new subway line or a dedicated bus lane. There would have been 85,000 apartments and a 150-acre park built alongside the riverside highway. But opposition began building as early as 1974, led by then-congressmen Hugh Carey (a future governor) and Ed Koch (a future mayor). Westway's opponents claimed it would generate even more traffic into the city and would amount to a giveaway to developers, who'd get to build those apartments. Throughout the 1970s, Westway was a favorite target of reform politicians and muckraking journals like the *Village Voice*.

The highway proposal went through some remarkable twists and turns. By 1978, Westway had won the support of both Mayor Koch and Governor Carey, formerly its bitterest foes. President Ronald Reagan, newly elected in 1981, supported Westway too. But did the highway get built? No, thanks to an environmental assessment that concluded that Westway would devastate the Hudson's striped bass population and to some obstinate judges who refused to issue construction permits. Westway was finally abandoned for good in 1985, and to the joy of public transportation advocates, $1.7 billion of its construction cost was deeded over to mass transit.

It wasn't until 1993 that city and state officials cobbled together the Joe DiMaggio Highway, with just three lanes in each direction, as a replacement expressway for the West Side of Manhattan. To enlist the support of environmentalists, the plan includes both a bicycle path and a walkway, as well as what are described as "ample pedestrian refuge areas." The Hudson River Greenway will make it possible to bike from the southern tip of Manhattan to 155th Street when the highway is finally completed in 2005. "There will be five thousand bicycles an hour on the Greenway, making it the busiest bike path in the United States," says Kaehny. And New York pedestrians, bikers, and in-line skaters will finally get back their access to the Hudson River, denied them by the tunnel vision of Robert Moses more than seventy years earlier.

PUTTING CARS ON THE DEFENSIVE

New Yorkers should be proud of their unique and pioneering transit history. There was public transit in the city as early as 1827, when Abraham Brower began operating a twelve-seat stagecoach along Broadway from the Battery to Bleecker Street. By 1904, there were 147 ferryboats registered in New York City, all privately owned. That changed dramatically a year later, when the city-owned *Manhattan* made its maiden voyage from Whitehall Street to Saint George, Staten Island. The event was marked by a gala ceremony attended by newspaper tycoon William Randolph Hearst, whose Municipal Ownership League promoted municipal transportation ownership. The *Manhattan*'s run is the same one made by the Staten Island Ferry today, with the added inducement that passage is now free.[28] Ferry service could grow substantially in New York if plans for a twenty-five-stop ferry around New York Bay, announced in early 2001, are realized.

Manhattan's legendary elevated railway began running in 1870, and its clatter serenaded generations of immigrants. (It was shut down for good in 1955.) The subway, one of the world's first, was opened in 1904 with twenty-eight stations. Both gasoline-powered buses and electric taxis operated in New York before 1910.

In many ways, despite the loss of the transportation bond issue, New York City's transit system is still in good shape, though the long-term financial picture is cloudy. The subway, operated by New

York City Transit, serves 4.3 million customers on an average week-day, 1.3 billion a year. Unlike public transportation in other cities, the trains run twenty-four hours a day. Stronger-than-expected revenues from record passenger traffic have allowed the longest fare freeze since the 1960s. The state legislature adopted a five-year, $17.1 billion transit program in late 2000 that calls for more than two thousand new subway cars and buses. And some of those buses will be fueled by natural gas.[29] Things have definitely improved since 1966, when the mayor's Task Force on Urban Design described the city subway system as "the most squalid public environment in the United States."[30]

Commuters were stunned when, in the summer of 2000, the No. 6 train pulling into the Thirty-third Street station was, instead of the usual graffiti-covered wreck, a gleaming and brand-new stainless steel car with wide doors, indirect lighting, ergonomically correct bench seats, electronic signs, and working air-conditioning. "I feel under-dressed," said commuter Maureen Leroy, a paralegal. "I wish I had worn something more appropriate, a ball gown maybe."[31] More than one thousand of the $1.4 million cars, made by Bombardier and Kawasaki, will eventually replace the battered Redbird trains, built in the 1950s.

But there are other signs of stasis. Plans for dedicated bus lanes have not been realized, though some express bus service is being added. The city's aging municipal infrastructure, especially its maze of increasingly derelict and outmoded underground tunnels, remains an issue. Although the incredibly busy Pennsylvania Station, which serves both Amtrak and subway passengers, is being massively remade on a grand scale, some city officials wonder about fire evacuation and other safety conditions in the ninety-year-old tunnels beneath the $800 million project.

Subway overcrowding has become a serious problem. In 1951, city voters approved bonds to pay for a Second Avenue subway line. Aside from a brief flurry of work on a tunnel in the 1970s, nothing has been done since to build the vitally needed line. The defeat of the state transportation initiative means straphangers may end up waiting interminably, even as crowding increases because of the new connection between the Long Island Railroad and Grand Central Terminal. If work did begin on the subway line, it would take decades to complete. The *New York Times* columnist John Tierney, a free-enterprise advocate, recently championed an alternative plan—the Second Avenue Free Way—in which anyone with a motor vehicle could pick up passengers for a mutually agreed upon price.

Charles Komanoff probably wouldn't go for that idea. He wants to strengthen the city's public transit, not weaken it. Komanoff recently cannibalized an AUTO-FREE NEW YORK sticker for his bike so that it reads AUTO FEE NEW YORK. He wants drivers to pay dearly for using the city's streets and support transit in the process. "I'd like to see the city using the automobile as a cash cow to fund mass transit," he says. Under his system, cars entering any part of New York City would have to be equipped with an electronic transponder, which would effectively meter them like a taxi for the time they spend in the five boroughs. The fees would be arranged on a sliding scale based on each area's average traffic density. In a program similar to variable congestion pricing at tollbooths and bridges, cars that had the highest impact on gridlock would pay the highest rates.

It may be some time before every car entering New York has a transponder, but congestion pricing—with higher tolls at peak travel times—is beginning to take hold in the city. The Metropolitan Transit Authority (MTA) has debated such a fee structure for the city's bridges and tunnels, and then-mayor Rudolph Giuliani championed the idea in 1997 and again in 1999 as a way of getting trucks off the roads during peak periods.

A variable toll *was* adopted by New York's Port Authority, which operates such Hudson River crossings as the Holland and Lincoln Tunnels, the George Washington Bridge, and the Staten Island bridges. Cars using the electronic E-ZPass system on the George Washington Bridge to New Jersey, for instance, pay $4.00 in off-peak hours and $5.50 during peaks. Trucks get a significant fare reduction if they make deliveries between midnight and 6:00 A.M.

The New Jersey Turnpike has also introduced an E-ZPass-based congestion-pricing scheme, which has proven so popular that, ironically, the extra expenses involved in administering the program are expected to generate a $65 million deficit by 2008. Officials had planned on 35 percent driver participation; instead, more than 50 percent of motorists taking the turnpike are using the E-ZPass. "The bottom line is that the more that people use E-ZPass the less congestion and the greater the benefits to the traveling public," said James Weinstein, New Jersey's transportation commissioner.[32]

Whether through congestion pricing or simply congestion, auto travel will get increasingly difficult in New York City. Janine Bauer, executive director of the region's hardworking Tri-State Transportation Campaign, is enthusiastic about the possibilities that opens up. She sees the greatest transportation growth potential in biking and walking. "I'm optimistic," she says. "The automobile has seen its heyday, and the transportation investment tide is turning. Through biking and pedestrian pathways, people in New York are rediscovering quality of life. The ideal today is to walk to work, or work where you live."

New York City has not been a leader in developing bikeways and bike parking. According to Tri-State, the city has "lagged behind the pace and scale of improvements seen in far-smaller cities like Philadelphia" and needs "less planning and talk and more construction."[33] If the city did want to make New York more bike-friendly, groups like Transportation Alternatives could provide them with a wealth of information. According to the group's *Bicycle Blueprint,* New York's transit would be considerably more accommodating if it offered more bicycle parking at rail stations, greater access for bicycles on peak-hour trains, and "rack and roll" bicycle racks on buses, like the ones I'd seen in Portland.

In another report, "The Wrong Foot Forward—2000," Transportation Alternatives notes that the city gives short shrift to pedestrians and cyclists in safety spending. Looking ahead through the 2004 budget, the group says that "despite representing 48 percent of all traffic deaths, walkers and cyclists will receive only 5 percent of available safety funds" during that period.

John Pucher, a transportation specialist who teaches in the department of urban planning at Rutgers University, says New York's legions of walkers and cyclists need to band together and lobby the way the competition does. "For some strange reason," he told me, "cyclists and pedestrians are among the worst-organized groups, while motorists and the auto, highway, and oil industries are *very* well organized. Walking and cycling are so efficient and resource-conserving that they don't generate the profit levels of the motorized modes, hence the lack of deep-pocketed lobbyists to promote them."

Things are considerably different in Europe. In *Transportation Quarterly,* Pucher and co-author Lewis Dijkstra point out that pedestrian fatalities in the Netherlands and Germany are less than a tenth of what they are in the United States, and bicylist fatalities are only a quarter as high. "Over the past two decades," the authors write, "these countries have undertaken a wide range of measures to improve safety: better facilities for walking and bicycling; urban design sensitive to the needs of non-motorists; traffic calming of residential neighborhoods; restrictions on motor vehicle use in cities; rigorous traffic education of both motorists and non-motorists; and strict enforcement of traffic regulations protecting pedestrians and bicyclists."[34]

Pucher and Dijkstra note that Dutch and German bikeways "serve practical destinations for everyday travel, not just recreational attractions, as most bike paths in the U.S. do." In the Netherlands, from 1980 to 2000 the network of bike paths and lanes doubled in length; in Germany, it almost quadrupled.[35]

New York City could learn a lot from Europe. But maybe things are starting to improve, if only very gradually. When, in late 2000, the New York Jets proposed a massive domed stadium with seating for 75,000 on the West Side of Manhattan next to the Javits Center, Mayor Giuliani did not instantly applaud. Instead, that very pro-car civil servant pointed out the stadium's location between Eleventh and Twelfth Avenues, far from any subway stop. Sounding like a newly minted member of Transportation Alternatives, he said that the expansion of public transit to the site would be a "critical element" of the plan.[36] The mayor proposed extending the No. 7 subway to the Javits Center, no doubt a costly option but one New York's small but growing transit lobby could support.

LOS ANGELES: REVERSING AUTO DEPENDENCE

According to the *Los Angeles Almanac,* the first known automobile in Los Angeles was built in 1897 by a man named S. D. Sturgis. By 1904, it had 1,599 other cars for company and the city's die was cast. There are now 10 million people in Los Angeles County, and more than 5 million cars. The city is literally choking on its auto dependence.

Traffic congestion grows 3 percent a year in Los Angeles, a pace that can only accelerate as southern California adds a projected 7 million residents between 2000 and 2020. Los Angeles County has 5 million licensed drivers, a quarter of the total for the entire state, and the four busiest highways. By 2010, the Southern California Association of Governments predicts, the average urban rush-hour traffic speed will drop from thirty-five miles per hour to just fifteen. The combination of Los Angeles, Orange, and Ventura Counties rates as the nation's most congested area, claims the Texas Transportation Institute, with traffic delays costing area residents some $10.8 billion annually in lost productivity.[37]

Ninety-seven percent of all travel in Los Angeles is by car, leaving a small but growing public transit system (including a new subway, extensive bus routes, and commuter rail) to transport the rest. Los Angeles's longstanding love affair with the automobile has cost it heavily. The city vies with Houston for the dubious distinction of worst urban air in the nation. According to "Out of Breath," a 1996 Natural Resources Defense Council report, "The South Coast is the only region in the United States classified by the EPA as an 'extreme' ozone problem area. Peak concentrations for ozone [a formative agent for smog] can reach three times the allowable EPA maximum, and violations are known to occur in some areas on more than 150 days a year. In addition, the Air Basin routinely violates the federal standards for carbon monoxide, particulate matter, and nitrogen dioxide."

Chillingly, the report adds that 2.5 million preadolescent children in southern California breathe highly polluted air.

These numbers have improved since Los Angeles began the painful process of taking cars off the street and cleaning up the exhaust, though much remains to be done. In 2000, there were no first-stage ozone alerts anywhere in Los Angeles, Orange, San Bernardino, or Riverside Counties. Since 1987, ozone concentrations have declined by two-thirds, though the gains could be wiped out by the region's relentless population growth. Cracks are developing in the pavement of the region's automotive monolith, and little flowers of resistance are blooming there. I decided I wanted to see how they were growing.

ON THE HOV HIGHWAY

My cousin Charlie picked me up at LAX in a white Honda. We both remarked on the natural gas–powered shuttle buses buzzing around. A graphic artist and industrial designer, Charlie has lived in Los Angeles for six years. He grew up in Virginia, lived in Boston for many years, and then moved to L.A. because his wife got a job at the J. Paul Getty Museum. The place still doesn't feel like home, he says.

I told Charlie that I'd like to get a feel for the freeways and to see if we could find 91 Express Lanes, the private-pay highway in Orange County that combines the new science of congestion pricing with private enterprise. The ten-mile private road is in the median of State Route 91, which crosses Los Angeles from east to west.

A toll road like 91 Express would be possible only on a seriously congested highway. The idea is that motorists, fed up with crawling along from Orange County to Los Angeles and back again, will pay a premium—which increases sharply during rush hours—for an exclusive "Lexus lane." This profit-making enterprise, with the state's cooperation, offers the privileges of a high-occupancy vehicle (HOV) lane without the extra passengers.

The creation of 91 Express was made possible by 1989 state legislation that invited entrepreneurs to build roads on state property in exchange for potentially lucrative operating contracts. California

Private Transportation Company was the first business to get involved, spending some $135 million to build the highway and receive a thirty-five-year franchise. The road opened in 1995. The scheme is high-tech in that drivers are required to have special battery-powered transponders mounted on their windshields that can be used to bill them for the ride. One-way fares range from 75 cents between midnight and 6:00 A.M. to $3.75 on Fridays between 3:00 and 7:00 P.M. There are even 91 Express Lane gift certificates.

Neither Charlie nor I knew precisely where 91 Express was, so we traveled the length of the regular Route 91, which grows from a four-lane city street into a major ten-lane highway. Even in the late morning, long after the rush hour, it was still crowded. Since there were two of us, we traveled regally in the HOV lane, which has very few access points. I noted the ever present smog layer, which had improved slightly since my last visit several years ago, and the signage, which was attempting to enlist the public in a grand traffic-reduction scheme: METRO RAIL STATION—PARK AND RIDE read one. Another offered an 800 number for car-sharing information.

"We've been thinking of moving out of the city, and the traffic is a major impetus," Charlie told me. "They're talking about the metro area adding millions of new residents in the next ten years, and that scares me. They keep allowing development, pushing the edges of the city out, without making any plans to accommodate the traffic." I got the sense that getting stuck in traffic is a major topic among Angelenos.

Suddenly, 91 Express loomed. 91FASTRAK, NO CASH, the sign on the entrance ramp said, as a flashing signal announced the tariff as $1.50. We were warned to stay off if we were in a single-occupant car without a FasTrak transponder. (Car-pool drivers get a free ride.) The private highway does indeed move quickly. We sped along with traffic that was moving at seventy miles per hour or more. Per the instructions on a sign, we tuned to 1620 AM and listened to FasTrak radio: "What would you do with an extra twenty minutes?" an announcer asked. "In a year [of FasTrak driving], you'll gain seven days!" An amazed motorist was heard to exclaim, "I could see my kids before they go to bed!"

We made fast work of the express lane and were soon back in regular traffic. Though 91 Express is a private road, the California Highway Patrol enforces violations of the transponder law, which range from a $100 fine for a first offense to $250 for the second time.

Making money by building highways may prove elusive. In 1999, California Private Transportation was involved in a bruising debate involving a possible sale of the highway franchise to another private company. Because of vocal protests from municipal officials in Orange and Riverside Counties who thought the company was profiteering with state investments, that plan was dropped. Currently, 91 Express is complemented by a similar experiment on I-15 in San Diego, making California a national leader in the congestion-pricing experiment. But other congested states are trying it out as well. In late 2000, New Jersey inaugurated an E-ZPass system on twenty-seven toll plazas that charged commuters 8 percent more for using the highways during rush hour. Some planners in New York State think that a congestion-pricing scheme for the Tappan Zee Bridge over the Hudson River could reduce peak-hour travel enough to avoid a very expensive widening of the bridge.

THE L.A. EXPRESS: TRAINS IN AN AUTO-CENTRIC CITY

Since 91 Express is one ten-mile stretch of highway, it may be helping a few Orange County residents get home earlier in the evenings, but it isn't doing much for the bulk of the metro area's commuters. For that, the city needs mass transit. And after many years of just talking about it, the city has finally made a modest start at it.

It may be some time before the fact that their city even *has* a subway penetrates the consciousness of most Angelenos. And you're not likely to find members of the city's environmentally conscious film community hanging on to the next strap. I talked with Alexandra Paul, a former *Baywatch* and *Melrose Place* actress. Paul is in almost all ways an exemplary environmental citizen. She drives a General Motors EV-1 electric car and produces documentaries for young people on such subjects as overpopulation and excessive consumption. A member of the Alliance for a Paving Moratorium, she says,

"Highways cause a tremendous amount of damage and ruin it forever for wildlife and nature." But Paul, who lives in Malibu, admits to having never taken the subway. She last rode the bus when she arrived in town in the early 1980s. "I'm guilty as charged when it comes to public transit," she said, and many other environmental activists would probably say the same thing.

Using L.A.'s subways requires a complete mind-set change, and the system offers only a limited numbers of stops in an excessively sprawled metropolitan area. My cousin Charlie had never ridden the subway, either, when he and I met Richard Silver at the so-called Kiss 'n' Ride. That's the parking lot where harried North Hollywood commuters get dropped off for the Metro Rail run into Los Angeles. Silver, an energetic fellow in his late fifties with salt-and-pepper hair to match his name, has an encyclopedic knowledge of the Los Angeles transit system. And not just L.A., either. As head at that time of both the Train Riders Association of California (TRAC) and the similar Rail Passengers Association of California (RPAC), groups that were later to merge, Silver was constantly on the move around the state. A justice of the peace who performs weddings as a sideline, he does not own a car.

TRAC was the driving force behind Proposition 116, a $2 billion citizens' rail-bond initiative approved by voters in 1990. It funded a wide variety of mass-transit initiatives in California, including the preservation of several Amtrak trains, the CalTrain from San Jose to San Francisco, and the Coaster from Oceanside to San Diego.

Both TRAC and RPAC have been major supporters of Los Angeles's 17.4-mile subway system. The $4.7 billion system needs a lot of defending because it was built through the heart of a congested city and cost the exorbitant amount of more than $250 million per mile. But critics should perhaps be required to come up with another alternative for a city being slowly throttled by smog and traffic.

In 1980, Los Angeles voters approved a sales-tax increase for mass transit that provided $200 million annually to various projects, including the Metro Blue Line from downtown to Long Beach, which opened for public use in 1990. It was followed in 1993 by the Red

Line, which now reaches North Hollywood, and the Green Line, to Redondo Beach, in 1995.

The North Hollywood station, which was only a few months old at the time of my visit, is surrounded by a slightly seedy San Fernando Valley neighborhood that Metropolitan Transportation Authority (MTA) officials have hopefully dubbed the "NoHo Arts District." Whether that upscale appellation will take or not is still anyone's guess, but if the jam-packed six-hundred-space parking lot was any indication, rents should soar in the down-at-the-heels apartment buildings that surround the station. As the *Los Angeles Times* put it, "Lately, commuters at the North Hollywood subway station have been circling like sharks. Their prey: the elusive parking space."[38]

We descended into the station, which represents the last approved extension of the subway's Red Line. Though the line just barely makes it into the Valley, cost overruns and community opposition (including a citywide referendum that cut off future funding) means it's unlikely to go any farther. That hasn't stopped Angelenos from hoping they'll one day have a subway stop near their homes. When an anonymous group of L.A. artists surreptitiously erected eight very realistic billboards announcing the forthcoming debut of the subway's eleven-stop Aqua Line ("Connecting Downtown to the Westside") in the summer of 2000, excited crowds gathered.

For Charlie, taking the Red Line to work is out of the question because getting to this stop would mean a half-hour—or longer, depending on traffic—drive along the horrific San Diego Freeway. "They're dying every day on that highway," said Charlie, and he had a point: that same morning, a three-car accident on the 405 put seven people in the hospital. Traffic accidents killed 1,666 people in Los Angeles County, including 215 pedestrians, in 1998.[39]

The station itself was clean and decorated with colorful tile murals. The Los Angeles subway works on an honor system similar to those in Europe. Commuters buy tickets from automated machines ($1.35 for one-way rides; $2.70 for all-day round trips) but only occasionally have to produce them for conductors' spot checks.

The cars, new and clean of graffiti, are color-coded to match the name of their line. We sat on bright red seats as a conductor intoned, "Good morning, ladies and gentlemen, and welcome aboard." Critics have derided the subway system as a cappuccino express for the rich, but more than half the passengers we encountered during a long day on Los Angeles mass transit were black and Hispanic. It's undeniably true that the city's minority residents ride buses (which carry 1.2 million passengers a day) more than they do subway trains (about 155,000 a day), but none of the cars I rode in were filled with gray-suited businessmen sipping lattes.

The train ran through stops at Universal City, Hollywood and Highland, and Vermont and Santa Monica. By the time we reached the hub of Union Station in downtown L.A., it was more than half full.

On a good day, 1.5 million of Los Angeles County's 7.5 million people ride some form of transit to work, according to the MTA. The figure contrasts rather neatly with San Francisco, which, according to Silver, gets 750,000 people on transit every day—a population larger than that of the city of San Francisco itself. "There's still a long way to go for transit here," said Silver. "Maybe they could have done it better and faster. But it's a start." Los Angeles's system, built at an exorbitant cost, recovers perhaps 20 percent of its operating expenses from the fare box, versus 68 percent (the highest rate in the state) on the San Francisco BART line. Nobody expects trains to make money, and construction costs are effectively written off. Defenders point out, however, that phenomenal highway construction costs and frequent repairs are always glossed over by asphalt advocates.

The Spanish-style Union Station, a triumphant reconstruction of a venerable city institution, offers travelers upscale restaurants and a choice of subway lines, Metrolink heavy rail, or Amtrak trains. We paused at Union Bagel and contemplated our next move. The trip down from North Hollywood, on a dedicated rail line that never suffers from traffic jams, had taken forty minutes. On a good day, said Charlie, it would take only twenty minutes to drive. On a bad day, he added, it could take an hour and a half.

We decided to take a quick trip on the Blue Line, which runs mainly aboveground and serves low-income neighborhoods. At this point, were we riding a subway or light rail? "Who cares?" says Silver. "If it has steel wheels on a steel track, it's a train." On the way across the platform, we encountered a horde of yellow-shirted schoolkids, visiting from Ribet Academy. "We're on a field trip to see the subway," Robert "Mr. Fitz" Fitzgerald explained. "We've seen the Children's Museum and now we're hopping on the train to go to Hollywood." Even at 1:10 P.M., the Blue Line train was crowded, with standing-room-only passengers. It was clear that, even if the subway is not serving anything like a majority of Los Angeles's commuters, it is at least making a difference in highway congestion.

We returned to Union Station with a few minutes to spare before climbing aboard a "heavy rail" Metrolink train to Santa Clarita, a fast-growing suburb now chockablock with new housing developments. The trains, pushed and pulled by diesel locomotives, are beautiful double-decker affairs made by Canada's Bombardier. Passengers sit in four-seat cubicles with tables. Ridership was light during the middle of the day, but that is likely to change. NOW SELLING! OAK RIDGE SINGLE-FAMILY HOMES! reads a sign for a cluster of housing units only a few yards from the tracks.

ON AND OFF THE BUS

I had planned to get a more complete look at Los Angeles's transit picture by riding the municipal buses with someone from the Bus Riders Union, an arm of the activist Labor/Community Strategy Center. Unfortunately, the group rebuffed my repeated attempts to set up such a ride. I was also unable to talk with Eric Mann, the union's principal strategist, who has a reputation for dodging the media.

Despite getting the cold shoulder, I have considerable respect for what the Bus Riders Union is doing. It's undeniably true that buses carry far more commuters than light-rail trains do. The public transportation fleet in the United States consists of 129,000 vehicles, 58 percent of them buses and only 1 percent light-rail cars. Sixty-one percent of all public-transportation employees work for bus services. Of the 8.7 billion unlinked trips taken by American travelers in

1998, 61.6 percent were taken in buses (and only 11 percent in the "all other modes" category that includes light rail). Since 1984, however, light-rail trips have doubled while bus trips have stagnated, proof that transit agencies—and passengers, too—have become entranced with this modern way of getting around.[40] But light-rail growth may have come with social costs attached.

The Bus Riders Union thinks that bus passengers get short shrift in Los Angeles, and that there's a racial component to it. The union was formed in 1992 and quickly began a Billions for Buses campaign to defeat what it calls "the transit racism reflected in the policies of the Metropolitan Transportation Authority of Los Angeles."

The group has a big job ahead of it, because there's ignorance about transit at the highest levels of government. During a Los Angeles stop in the early days of the 2000 presidential campaign, then–Republican candidate George W. Bush showed his "sensitivity" to the city's bus passengers. At a Univision Town Hall meeting designed to help the candidate reach out to Hispanic voters, Bush listened to the complaints of a man who rides two buses to work every day. The man wanted to know how Los Angeles's public transportation system could be improved. "My hope is that you will be able to find good enough work, so you'll be able to afford a car," replied Bush.[41] This "silver spoon" remark went largely unnoticed in the press.

In 1994, the union filed a civil-rights lawsuit charging the MTA with running a separate but unequal system that punishes 94 percent of its passengers, the 350,000 bus riders, and rewards the "primarily suburban and business district" rail system. The union contended in the suit that the MTA spends 70 percent of its operating budget on the 6 percent of its ridership who are rail passengers. The bus riders, it said, are 81 percent black, Latin, and Asian; 60 percent female; and 60 percent poor, with incomes below $15,000 a year. In the last decade, the union said, the MTA had reduced its peak-hour bus fleet from 2,200 to 1,750. It also subsidized subway riders eighteen times more than it did bus riders, according to the suit.

In what was undoubtedly a surprise to transit officials, *Labor/Community Strategy Center et al. v. Los Angeles County Metropolitan*

Transportation Authority was a successful suit. In 1996, a federal district court ruled that such inequities do exist. In a court-ordered consent decree, the MTA agreed to invest more than $1 billion in bus-system improvements in the ten years until 2006. It was the first successful attempt to use Title VI of the 1964 Civil Rights Act against a transit agency and the largest settlement in civil-rights history. As Martin Luther King Jr. pointed out, "Urban transit systems in most American cities are a genuine civil rights issue."[42]

Instead of spending money on light rail, the union supports a $1.6 billion plan to create a six-hundred-mile network of bus-only express lanes, similar to those in Curitiba, Brazil, on Los Angeles's freeways and major surface roads. Such a system, it estimates, could carry 2 to 3 million people a day more than the present 1.2-million-passenger bus system. The buses would do away with polluting diesel engines, of particular concern in Los Angeles, and would have natural gas power.

The union is willing to play hardball to achieve its goals. It seeks a total moratorium on construction of any new rail lines in the Los Angeles area and has in particular tried to stop an extension of the MTA's $1 billion light-rail Blue Line to Pasadena. The union also launched "Don't Play Ball with a Racist City," a campaign that attempts to thwart funding for a new football coliseum in Los Angeles until the MTA agrees to buy an additional 481 buses.

The fight over light rail in Los Angeles is not a clear-cut black-white issue. Three of the more prominent black and Hispanic MTA board members support Pasadena light rail. The union's attempt to label the rails as for suburban and business use oversimplifies what is plainly a complicated ridership pattern.

Critics like Richard Silver claim that the Bus Riders Union represents no real constituency in Los Angeles. But the group plainly has a point: light rail is very expensive to build, and each mile of new construction has the potential to cause a cost reduction in other parts of the system. The L.A. transit system, under the best circumstances, has a difficult time coping with a metropolitan region that was wholly built up around the needs of automobiles. Mass transit provides a major safety valve for the overloaded highway system, as was made clear during the city's agonizing transit strike in the fall of 2000. Without buses or light rail, a new fleet of entrepreneurial "bandit operators" took to the streets in cars and vans, many of them gouging the 3 percent of Los Angeles's commuters who are otherwise wholly dependent on public transportation to get to work.

GETTING AROUND: THEN AND NOW

I wanted to visit the opulent Petersen Automotive Museum on Wilshire Boulevard to cap my L.A. visit because I was curious to see how it would celebrate the city's car culture. Also, I just like car museums.

As befitting its home in the city where the drive-in was invented, the Petersen has a certain worshipful quality to it. Cars are shown in their element: there are full-scale hot-rod shops, suburban bungalows, even a complete Chrysler dealership, circa 1935. As luck would have it, the exhibit that was current during my visit celebrated the car in the city of Los Angeles. The displays offered a graphic picture of how the automobile ruined a sun-dappled paradise of orange groves and graceful Spanish architecture, though that's not what the curators intended.

Los Angeles had only 11,183 residents in 1880. What transformed the city, as Mike Davis reports in his book *City of Quartz,* was the completion of the Southern Pacific's Sunset Route to the city in 1883, followed by the arrival of the Santa Fe line in 1886. The railroads "transformed the geographic and economic setting of Southern California," Davis notes. "With immense investments tied up in their new transcontinental lines, and as the region's largest landowners, the railroads acquired a huge stake in the rapid development of Los Angeles and adjoining counties."[43]

The resulting population boom of 1886 to 1889 rivaled the 1849 Gold Rush for populating California. Eager to show off the western paradise, Southern Pacific offered the writer Oscar Wilde a special train with private cars if he would consent to visit Los Angeles. The railroad, along with the Santa Fe line, maintained what author Kevin Starr describes as an "elaborate publicity operation to promote travel to the

Southland."[44] At its height from 1870 to 1900, Southern Pacific (known universally as "S.P.") virtually controlled the California legislature.

The old photos in the Petersen exhibit, combined with a full-scale 1920s Los Angeles Yellow Car (which provided local trolley service, complementing the long-distance travel of the Red Cars, also city-run), provided a picture of a long-gone city where world-class transit was taken for granted. The city very nearly had a rapid-transit system in 1907, when S.P. bought up the Los Angeles Pacific Company trolley system and proposed to turn it into an ultramodern grid with tunnels through Hollywood and the Wilshire District. Unfortunately, a financial panic stopped construction shortly after it began. By 1921, the Red Car interurban service was one of the best in the world, with a thousand miles of track and 250,000 passengers a day. That's almost twice as many passengers as the MTA's system today. And that level of ridership represented nearly a quarter of the city's population in 1921. The debonair rail passenger of that era could easily travel by rail to Pasadena, San Bernardino, Venice Beach, Long Beach, Redondo Beach, and many other places.

"As car ownership increased during the 1920s," the Petersen exhibit placards said, "cars and trolleys competed for space on the streets and congestion grew worse." Meanwhile, car ownership meant freedom to live away from the trolley lines, and "new homes went up with dizzying speed. L.A.'s population almost tripled in the 1920s, to 1.2 million." Everyone wanted the California dream, and that meant a bungalow—94 percent of the city's population lived in single-family homes by that time.

The oil boom in Los Angeles began in the late nineteenth century when a sand dealer named E. L. Doheny found a greasy black substance in some of his wagon loads. "By the 1890s, the oil developments were ruining whole sections of Los Angeles County. . . . Nearly 1,500 derricks rose where Los Angeles's lawns and flowers had once been."[45] And what kind of oil city travels on streetcars? The same public relations machine that had encouraged immigration to Los Angeles, now, in the pay of the oil industry, persuaded its citizens to give up mass transit and try their luck with a private car.[46] It worked spectacularly well. The drive-ins that proliferated in the 1930s were just an extension of a city and a state that had gone car crazy.

Attempts to extend rail service in Los Angeles since its heyday in the 1920s have taken on a surreal aura. In 1949, downtown power brokers, concerned about losing their hegemony in a rapidly sprawling city, proposed a rail rapid-transit system, with downtown as its hub. A suburban united front deemed the plan "socialistic" and defeated it in the city council. The MTA proposed a forty-five-mile, $165 million monorail from Panorama City through Hollywood and downtown Los Angeles in 1954. "Doubts as to economic feasibility, unresolved engineering questions and, very likely, aesthetic considerations helped put the monorail plan on the shelf with Los Angeles' growing pile of discarded rapid transit proposals," writes Robert P. Sechler.[47]

In 1987, the original route of the Los Angeles light-rail system to the San Fernando Valley became hotly controversial because it moved along Chandler Boulevard, through an Orthodox Jewish neighborhood whose Saturday worship would have been disturbed. Metro Rail went underground, at much greater cost.[48]

Sympathy must be extended to a transit system struggling to adapt itself to a city wholly built around the car. In the video for the hit "I Love L.A.," songwriter Randy Newman is seen racing down what looks like the Pacific Coast Highway in a convertible, enjoying the sun, just as the Beach Boys had twenty years earlier. But in L.A. today, the cars are no longer racing toward a golden future, and the ardor seems to have cooled.

ARCATA: GREEN REFLECTIONS IN NORTHERN CALIFORNIA

It is with some chagrin that the current residents of Arcata, California, one of the greenest, most environmentally conscious communities in the United States, admit that their town was founded on the lust for resource extraction.

Tribes of Hupa and Yurok Indians made their homes on Humboldt Bay for many centuries, living simply on the plentiful salmon, shellfish, and waterfowl. The Spanish were the first Westerners to set eyes on the northern California coast, in the sixteenth century. The rocky inlets were treacherous to their wooden boats, so they looked elsewhere for gold. Sir Francis Drake, who called California "New Albion," may have visited the mountainous Humboldt coastline on board the *Golden Hinde* in 1579, but the historical record is unclear on that point. The Russians were next, in the eighteenth century, exploiting the lucrative trade in sea otter pelts, but they visited only briefly and made no permanent settlements.[49]

The first American gold miners arrived in 1849 and named the place Union; they changed it to Arcata in 1860. Transportation was on their minds, particularly a route from their Trinity Mountain mining camps to the Pacific Ocean. A party of exploration led by physician Josiah Gregg got lost in Humboldt County's legendary redwood trees and nearly starved to death before stumbling on the Pacific, Humboldt Bay, and a navigable waterway, which, in their raving state, they named the Mad River. To celebrate, they killed and consumed a bald eagle.[50]

Miners poured into the newly discovered bay to exploit the region's mineral wealth, and they were soon joined by settlers whose primary occupation was cutting down the incredibly dense stands of giant redwoods. One acre could yield a million board feet of lumber. By 1878, steamers plied the route from San Francisco, and a thousand ships a year were entering Humboldt Bay.[51]

Land transportation inevitably followed. Until 1914, the only route south was by stagecoach, but that year engineers completed the arduous task of connecting the region to San Francisco, 280 miles to the south, by railroad. Only a few years later, Highway 101 was built through difficult terrain that included unruly rivers, unstable soil, and sheer slopes. The first airport was built in 1942. Fog-shrouded Humboldt County, a place of great natural beauty preserved through physical isolation, was slowly revealing its treasures to the outside world.[52]

But the logging and fishing industries that had sustained Arcata's economic life began to decline in the postwar years, and with them went the effective mass transportation that had helped make the region's growth possible. The federal highway bill championed by President Dwight Eisenhower passed in 1956, and the next year utilitarian passenger-rail service on the North Coast was defunded, "primarily because federal subsidies shifted from rail to highway."[53]

Natural disaster also played a role. The state-owned line between the Bay Area and the Humboldt County seat of Eureka (six miles south of Arcata) has been unusable since 1998, when landslides took out sections of track in the Eel River Canyon. Service to Arcata itself, a line known affectionately as the Annie and Mary Railroad (apparently named after two secretaries) hasn't been available for several years. The tracks sit empty, and some of them have been ripped out in an ill-considered redevelopment scheme.[54]

Sustained by Humboldt State University and a population of 15,000, half of them college students, Arcata has turned its back on exploiting natural resources. Instead of salmon and redwoods, the town exports compost and potting mix. At Humboldt's Campus Center for Alternative Technology, students build solar showers, pedal-powered washing machines, and sustainably designed permaculture gardens. Roving bicyclists take over the city's downtown once a week as part of a Critical Mass "street-reclaiming" effort. There's even a commuter bus fueled by vegetable oil, as well as a pioneering biological wastewater facility (also known as the Arcata Marsh and Wildlife Sanctuary).

In a proclamation signed by Mayor Connie Stewart, in 2000 Arcata became a charter partner in the Cities for Climate Protection Campaign. Twenty percent of Arcata's voters have Green Party registration, and they get stirred up by environmental causes, including a contentious plan by the state transportation agency, Caltrans, to widen Highway 101 to four lanes. The *Utne Reader*, which named Arcata one of America's "ten most enlightened towns" in 1997, called the successful fight to stop the superhighway a "heroic tussle."

Nobody likes cars much in Arcata, even if they are the main mode of transportation. When the local Nissan dealer brought some sport-utility vehicles to show off at a semipro baseball game between the

Humboldt Crabs and the Aloha Knights, they were hounded off the field. "Three gallons to the mile!" screamed one spectator. "Looks like it's time for a wild practice pitch!" yelled another. "Ride a bike!" hollered a third.[55]

Riding bikes is indeed very popular in compact Arcata, a walkable city that is only a couple of miles across. There is a very vigorous community bicycle program in town, and new bike lanes have been springing up since 1990. That's good news for people like Minerva Williams, who hasn't let the fact that she's sixty-five years old keep her off her bicycle. "Arcata is very bicycle-friendly," says this Los Angeles native. "You can go just about anywhere by bike, and there are marked bike paths."

Williams, who fled Los Angeles twenty years ago after developing chemical sensitivity, has one big complaint: she doesn't like having to circumnavigate the new roundabouts, put in place by a city council that was trying to "calm" downtown traffic. The roundabouts, which have measurably reduced auto accidents, are a symbol of the new green Arcata, and not all the older residents approve of the moves against the car.

"Transportation is always in a state of change here," says Kevin Hoover, editor of the folksy *Arcata Eye.* "There are a lot of visionaries who want to depave everything, and a lot who want alternative transportation, human powered if possible."

Indeed, Arcata is home to the Alliance for a Paving Moratorium, led by a visionary, Jan Lundberg, who did indeed depave his own driveway. "Transportation in Arcata is a pretty mixed bag," says Lundberg, who campaigns locally against new highway projects when he's not trying to depave America in his magazine *Auto-Free Times.* "It's nothing to shout about."

Doby Class would probably agree with that, but he's working overtime to make things better. Arcata's deputy public works director, Class was responsible for installing those three roundabouts, as well as a host of other traffic-calming measures, including wider sidewalks and narrower roads. He may be one of the few public works officials in America to exhibit a strong bias *against* big road projects.

Class can say things like "We're working to create a more walkable community" and actually mean it. Arcata has plans to spend up to $3 million in federal and state funds on transportation-enhancement projects in the next few years. "Typically, the projects take away from cars and give to bicyclists and pedestrians," he said. "But people want us to fix the potholes, too."

Ramps have gone in alongside stairways downtown to make it easier for parents pushing baby carriages. A prominent road, Samoa Boulevard, has been reduced by a lane and is now a city street instead of a state highway. Some intersections now have circular planters in the middle, creating an all-way yield that forces drivers to slow down.

Rodney Brunlinger, a volunteer member of the Transportation Safety Committee, which advises the city council, is another progressive thinker. Humboldt Bank's genial credit analyst once even entertained a proposal to make the downtown Arcata Plaza, the home base for panhandling ex-Deadheads, car-free, but the idea was quickly hooted down by local merchants. "It turned into a political stink bomb," says Brunlinger gloomily.

The plain fact of it is that public transportation in Arcata is limited to three or four old diesel-powered buses that traverse the city only in hourly intervals.

Brunlinger has gone beyond just talking about the lack of mass transit in Arcata. In 1993, he took matters into his own hands—or, in this case, feet. Brunlinger opened a one-man pedal-cab business in Arcata. "It was a state-of-the-art $3,000 rickshaw, kind of like a bicycle with a big butt end on it," he said. "There was room for two passengers. The rickshaw was very well received, but the insurance was frightfully expensive." Reluctantly, he sold the high-tech pedicab to an entrepreneur in San Francisco and moved on to other things.

"Arcata should lend itself to public transit, because it's a very compact small town," Brunlinger says. "Instead, we have buses that operate only ten hours a day. You can wait an hour for them, when a car can take you anywhere in town in one or two minutes. Students can take the buses for practically nothing, but not that many ride because it's so inconvenient." On the other hand, as Class points out, not many cities of Arcata's size even *have* bus service.

You might expect Brunlinger to get excited about the talk around town of reviving the old rail line, but instead he's ambivalent. "I don't want to see a railroad coming in here to haul away natural resources, which is what it was used for in the past," he said. "Trains could be an aid to logging and carrying off our river gravel."

The resource extractors are indeed very much in favor of reviving the Eureka–San Francisco line. Daniel Wood, director of production for Pacific Lumber, said at a recent public hearing that the train is "an important part of the transportation infrastructure on the North Coast," adding that some large trucks can't navigate sections of Highway 101.[56] According to State Senator Wesley Chesbro, a working rail line would take 30,000 to 60,000 trucks a year off the north-south road.

In 1989, the California legislature created the North Coast Railroad Authority (NCRA) to maintain a rail corridor. It has been a rocky ride, marred by numerous line closings. Ongoing financial dis-organization has held up state funding. The NCRA's own five-year plan admits, "During its short history, for every step forward, the NCRA has taken a half step back." The plan even questions whether NCRA should continue to exist (before concluding that it should).

Jim Shields, the editor of the *Mendocino County Observer,* is one voice wishing the NCRA out of existence. "Folks are no longer sur-prised when NCRA transgressions are brought to light," he opined in a recent column. "The NCRA has set new standards for lowered expectations."[57]

Meanwhile, Arcata's train advocates dream of a limited rail revival of their own. They envision a closed-circuit passenger train that would act much as a light-rail line does in larger cities. Rail advocate Daniel Pierce imagines something like a "bus on tracks," a trolley linking north and south Arcata, with Humboldt State in the middle. "It would be easy," he says, "because there is no through traffic. A simple turnaround at each end of the city limits is all that would really be needed for the City of Arcata to have its own little trolley system, with the very real possibility of collecting money from the state to pay for it."[58]

Every proposal that reaches the city council in Arcata is viewed with deep suspicion by at least half the city's residents, so don't expect to see trolleys anytime soon. But that's just fine with another group of citizens; they're trying to turn the old six-mile Annie and Mary Railroad route along the Mad River into a hiking, biking, and equestrian trail. "Our goal is to create an alternative transportation and recreation network so you can get around the county without having to be strapped to a car," says Jennifer Rice, a Friends of Annie and Mary Rail-Trail supporter who also heads the Redwood Community Action Agency.[59] The railroad corridor is owned by the state, and the Friends would like to see it handed over to California's state park system.

A number of obstacles stand in the way of a rail-trail, including a lack of funding and the fact that the tracks pass through some abandoned industrial properties and cross rickety railroad bridges. But the plan is moving forward, a few dollars at a time. If you buy a pound of Annie and Mary Brew at the Muddy Waters Coffee Company, fifty cents goes to the rail-trail.

On a faster track is a plan to switch Arcata Transit's diesel buses to cleaner-burning liquefied natural gas (LNG) within a few years. Christine Parra, an enthusiastic research engineer at Humboldt State's Shatz Energy Lab, is backing efforts to bring in an LNG pipeline to fuel the buses. But she knows the city could have even cleaner transit. In one of Arcata's many ironies, the Shatz Energy Lab is pursuing cutting-edge research on hydrogen-powered vehicles, helping to build twenty-first-century transportation in a town that still gets around the old-fashioned way.

Shatz's work has hardly any effect on Arcata at all. The lab has built four operational zero-emission fuel-cell vehicles, but the small car and three golf carts are in daily use eight hundred miles south in Thousand Palms, California, near Palm Springs.

I asked Parra why the lab doesn't simply test its vehicles in Arcata, where such highly visible demonstration projects would be very welcome. She replied that California's South Coast Air Quality Management District provided $300,000 to fund the pilot project in Thousand Palms, where the existing SunLine transit agency has converted its entire bus fleet to natural gas. Working with SunLine, Shatz has built the country's first solar-powered hydrogen generator, which produces enough fuel to keep the golf carts and a two-passenger El-Jet car on the road.

Parra, who bicycles to work herself, would certainly like to see hydrogen-powered buses plying the streets of Arcata, but she admits that such a reality is still a long way off. Her own calculations show that hydrogen-generated electricity is still at least twice as expensive as photovoltaic solar energy, which itself has trouble being cost-competitive.

The chances are that if you take a tour of Arcata—visit the solar dorms, admire the waterfowl in the bioremediation marsh, stop in at Green Party headquarters, say hello to Shatz's fuel cells, buzz the roundabouts, and get panhandled at the plaza—you'll make your trip in a dirty, polluting, old-technology internal-combustion vehicle. As Arcata's aging buses make their way around town, the scent of diesel smoke still hangs in the air. Try as hard as it might, Arcata is still an American city, with a painful legacy of near-total auto dependence. It hasn't yet found its way out of the modern transportation quagmire.

Arcata is hardly alone in trying to retrofit itself for transit; that's happening in cities all over America. Reclaiming territory from the automobile is an ongoing battle in our urban centers. Unfortunately, we have very few good models in America, though Portland comes closest. The best examples of modern people-friendly transit development are in Europe, where the car is being held at bay through determined municipal planning.

5

EUROPE AND AMERICA: DIFFERENT ROADS TAKEN

ON A RECENT TRIP to Germany and Switzerland with my family, I did what most Americans in Europe do: I rented a car. I assumed I'd need one, as I would on any tour of U.S. cities. One of my first stops was Zurich, where I quickly learned a lesson in transit-friendly planning. Ignoring the posted signs, I blundered into a lane that was reserved exclusively for light rail. Zurich's citizenry takes this kind of infraction seriously, and people waving their arms and pointing to the tracks soon surrounded me.

I wouldn't make that same mistake again, because I've learned a great deal about transportation preferences in Europe. Perhaps more than anywhere else in the world, Europe is putting the car in its place, refusing to let it dominate the development process and overshadow other forms of transit. The results are dramatic.

While cities like Portland are trying to follow the European model, they are still far more car-dependent than Zurich or many other urban centers. Only 6 percent of Portland's commuters use mass transit. In Stockholm, Sweden, by contrast, 70 percent of peak-hour trips are on public transit, and in Berlin, Germany, it's 40 percent (though the long-term goal is 80 percent). Helsinki, Finland, can boast that 55 percent of all trips are made by "environmentally friendly" means, including transit (30 percent), walking (16 percent), and biking (9 percent). Copenhagen, Denmark, actually has 34 percent of its commuters riding bicycles.[1]

What's striking about European transit development is that it has evolved from a rigorous planning process, precisely what is lacking in most American development models. European cities ask themselves, Where are we going? How do we want to get there? What can we do to make it happen?

In the United States, the auto industry and its close friend, the highway lobby, are in the driver's seat. American cities were built around the car, and its priorities still dominate. It's not surprising, then, that many of the solutions offered as a way out of gridlock are based on improving the car, not on eliminating it in favor of other forms of transit. With government partners, the auto industry has experimented with automated highways to speed car-based travelers along, toyed with high-tech traffic regulation, and offered megabytes' worth of in-car computer power to help the driver stay informed and avoid accidents.

Both Europe and the United States are working to reduce serious traffic and pollution problems, but their approaches could not be more different.

TRANSIT IN EUROPE: PUTTING THE CAR IN ITS PLACE

Zurich, with a city population of a third of a million in a metropolitan area of 1.2 million, is a good place to start. Even though it's one of the wealthiest cities in Europe, with a high rate of car ownership, the average resident makes 560 transit trips per year. That's one of the biggest transit commitments in the world, and it comes about by municipal design.

In recent years, Zurich has experienced modest population decline because of a flight to the suburbs that's all too familiar in the United States. At the same time, it has become a business center, with a doubling of office space since 1970. If most of Zurich's office workers were commuting in from the suburbs by car, the highways would be a disaster. To prevent that from happening, Zurich both built a world-class transit system and took a variety of measures to discourage drivers. A "transit-first" philosophy was set as early as 1973 in a citywide referendum.

Opened in 1990 by Zurich's regional government, the underground S-Train carries commuters into the city; along with other inbound transit modes, it carries about 30 percent of the suburban load.
In town, an excellent light-rail system handles 40 percent of all
travel. People who both live and work in the city have the highest use
of work-bound transit, 76.1 percent.[2]

How did Zurich attain these impressive numbers? It made transit
cheap and convenient, and driving expensive and difficult. It also
helps that gasoline costs five dollars a gallon. A policy in place since
1979 aims to speed up "green" travel. The dedicated light-rail lane I
encountered exists for buses, too, getting nearly all the transit out of
the traffic stream. A special traffic-control system gives bus and light-
rail drivers schedule information and a string of green lights at intersections, speeding them to more on-time arrivals. Transit tickets are
intermodal, good for buses, light rail, and the regional train service.
Trains and buses run every six to eight minutes, making it unnecessary to memorize a complicated schedule. Stations are ubiquitous
throughout the metropolitan area.

As Robert Cervero describes it in *The Transit Metropolis,* Zurich
realized that "promoting 'ecological transport,' in and of itself, was
not enough. The odds still would be stacked in favor of car travel;
trams and buses, for example, could never match the door-to-door
service qualities of the private automobile."[3] The city instituted a policy of no net increase in highway volume: when a new road and tunnel were built in the 1980s, the carrying capacity of other highways
was correspondingly reduced by eliminating lanes. Traffic lights and
reduced speed limits are also used to slow cars down as they make
their way through the city. Like Portland, which mandates bike racks
at new or renovated buildings, Zurich is using parking as a political
tool. It halved the number of required spaces for new buildings or
major reconstructions, and it allows no new spaces in the older, historical part of town. Parking fees downtown have risen sharply, a policy decision backed by a 1994 public referendum.

U.S.-based light-rail critics focus on high per-mile construction
costs and limited cost recovery from the fare box. Cities like Zurich,

which see light-rail systems as a public good, don't expect them to make a profit. But Zurich's work to both increase transit ridership and reduce auto traffic has paid off with 66 percent fare box recovery, a very high rate. Los Angeles's light-rail system recovers only 20 percent of its operating expenses.

Zurich's priorities are mirrored across Europe. Freiburg, Germany, for instance, has banished free parking in its downtown, eliminated some car lanes on major highways (replacing them, in some instances, with bus-only lanes), and reduced the price of transit tickets. All of this boosts use of Freiburg's excellent light-rail system, which is fully intermodal with the bus lines. Airports in Europe are intermodal, too. Even if they arrive at three A.M., airline passengers at Amsterdam's Schiphol Airport can walk through the terminal, descend an escalator, and buy a high-speed train ticket for Paris or Berlin.[4]

A very effective tool in reducing Europe's congestion problems is the strategy of "traffic calming," which includes such tactics as narrowing roadways, landscaping medians and planting trees, installing speed bumps, widening sidewalks, and tightening turns at intersections. The Dutch are world leaders in developing what they call the "living street," a people-friendly place that includes speed bumps and physical barriers to slow traffic down, sidewalk extensions for pedestrians, and the use of extensive greenery alongside streets and in parking lots. As in Arcata, California, roundabouts are also used as a traffic-calming measure.

According to Timothy Beatley's *Green Urbanism,* "One town in the Netherlands even uses sheep as a way of slowing traffic."[5] Although Beatley doesn't detail exactly how that works, I've certainly been "calmed" myself on rural roads in Wales when herds of sheep crossed to the other side.

Odense, Denmark, severely limits auto access at certain intersections and protects pedestrians and children from traffic with vertical wooden posts. At one such intersection in the town, limiting cars has made it possible to create a large children's play area, flanked by large trees and benches.[6] In Heidelberg, Germany, the Weststadt district designed curves and bends into narrowed streets to create a more livable neighborhood. Heidelberg witnessed a 31 percent drop in accidents and a 44 decrease in casualties after making those changes. A study of traffic-calming techniques in German neighborhoods found that they had reduced idle times by 15 percent, gear changing by 12 percent, braking by 14 percent, and fuel use by 12 percent.[7]

In Freiburg, Germany, "reducing motor car traffic" is the first point in the city's traffic plan, transit is emphasized, and 90 percent of the population lives in zones with speeds limited to twenty miles per hour. The results are measurable. Public transit ridership in Freiburg has more than doubled since 1984.

Copenhagen, Denmark, abandoned road building as a priority in the early 1970s, and instead built bus priority lanes and a huge network of bike paths. The result, as noted above, is a huge number of bike commuters—an 80 percent increase in the use of bicycles since 1980, and a 10 percent drop in car traffic. Together, public transportation and bicycles account for two-thirds of all commuter travel.[8]

Despite all these positive developments, however, Europe has hardly escaped auto dependence. In England, for instance, miles traveled by bus, train, and bicycle since 1952 have remained relatively constant, but car use has increased by a factor of ten.[9] But where European cities have resisted the auto's onslaught, the results have been impressive.

THE AMERICAN ANSWER:
AN INTELLIGENT TRANSIT MODULE

Though traffic calming and transit-centered development have been introduced to the lexicon of many urban planners in the United States, they are priorities today in only a few progressive pockets, like Portland and Arcata. It's impossible to consider a design for the American sustainable city without factoring in some role for the automobile. Today's New Urbanist architect may, in a moment of optimism, sketch out a housing complex without garages, but the chances are that there will be a parking lot somewhere, even if it's discreetly hidden behind a fringe of trees.

The automobile has an astounding centrality in American life; it's as much a part of our day-to-day culture as television. Weaning us from its extremely seductive clutches and its implied freedoms requires a cataclysm.

But isn't daily traffic gridlock, forcing us to spend longer and longer periods trapped in our cars, precisely that kind of cataclysm? It certainly seems to have the potential to create a nation of spurned lovers, even if it means accepting something as inherently novel to Americans as mass transit.

There is no evidence yet to suggest that drivers are abandoning their cars, but the auto industry is certainly mindful that the romance could wane. It's working hard to improve not so much the car as the in-car experience. The short-term goal is a living room on wheels, with much of the work of driving handled by electronics and all the comforts of home available at a touch of a button. New cars will be extensions of our homes. A harbinger of the times is Ford's Windstar Solutions minivan, a show vehicle that boasts not only the latest electronic aids but a washer, dryer, microwave, and refrigerator, too.

Watts Wacker, a futurist who heads the Connecticut-based consulting firm FirstMatter, notes that half of all fast food sold today is retailed through the drive-through window, and that technology to enable even more auto-based multitasking is on the horizon. "Children today are avid multitaskers," he told me, "and when they start driving they'll expect to have that capability." Wacker envisions electronic gauges that will offer not only oil pressure and fuel level but stock prices, a list of phone messages and e-mails, the whereabouts of family members, and other personal information. Wacker imagines that if the driving function itself could be automated, full-scale business meetings might take place in the car, with the other participants represented by holographic images.

In Wacker's view, the three traditional domains of American life—personal, professional, and societal—have been enlarged with the addition of a fourth domain: mobility. "And anything people do in those other areas, they'll expect to do when mobile," he concludes.

In its ultimate form, the newly disengaged driver would waft to work on an automated highway, paying as much attention to the road as today's train passenger does. The prospect raises the intriguing possibility of the automobile, in fact, *becoming* a form of mass transit. Instead of the wild and woolly beast that occupies our driveways and garages now, we'd be climbing into what amounts to a personality-free intelligent transit module for our trips to work. Try to picture orderly rows of commuters reading the *Wall Street Journal* as they move down an automated highway at one hundred miles per hour, their bumpers only a few inches apart. Sounds like a train, doesn't it? It's also a prescription for an end to the romance between the driver and the automobile he or she controls.

A new generation of sophisticated electronics makes that startling vision possible, promising breakthroughs in automotive intelligence and centralized highway management. The realization of such a dramatic vision in the near term, however, remains clouded at best, though electronics are already doing much to improve safety conditions on our highways.

I remain very skeptical, however, that electronics will provide any kind of real answer to the present dilemma on our highways. By eliminating such factors as driver error and "rubbernecking" at accident scenes, they'll move traffic along more smoothly, but the gains will be marginal and soon overwhelmed by population increases. For obvious reasons, however, the auto industry prefers technical solutions that will "fix" the car to alternatives that would eliminate it, like national mass-transit networks.

THE CAR IN CHARGE

Knowing just how much the automakers have invested in electronic Band-Aids, I went in search of the car of the future, stopping first in Kokomo, Indiana. Delphi Automotive Systems is a $29 billion company that makes electronic components for automobiles. Its huge campus, with 17,000 employees dedicated to making everything from microchips to car stereo systems, appears to be taking over Kokomo. As recently as the 1970s, the only electronic components in your car were the radio and the voltage regulator. Today, more than

20 percent of the automobile's content is electronic, involving everything from engine-control modules to point-free ignition and trip
computers.

Automotive electronics, called "telematics" by an industry eager
to capitalize on it, is projected to be a $7.2 billion business by
2005.[10] "Visualize a car equipped with a wireless voice and data communications system that combines features such as automatic airbag
deployment notification, vehicle tracking, real-time traffic data, emergency aid, and entertainment in a central service center," says the marketing company Frost & Sullivan. "Automotive telematics have made
this scenario a reality, and if manufacturers can convince the end user
of its usefulness, huge profits are expected to follow."

In Kokomo, I drove a supercharged Jaguar XKR convertible that
represented the first beachhead for Delphi's adaptive cruise control, a
radar-based system that not only keeps cars from hitting each other
but also takes over management of the gas pedal. You say you've
already got cruise control, as do 80 percent of the other cars on the
road? Forget about it. That's dumb technology. The new generation
thinks.

Adaptive cruise control first gained acceptance in Europe and
Japan, in the former because they drive very fast and treasure the ability to make quick avoidance maneuvers and in the latter because they
love new technology and experience a lot of stop-and-go traffic. The
systems work by imaging moving objects, via either front-mounted
laser guns or radar. All the driver does is steer, as the car assumes a
mind of its own. Pull out from behind the slowpoke, and the car
speeds back up to 55. Override the system with the gas pedal, and
you'll risk a warning chime for following too closely.

I took the adaptive Jaguar out on a fast run from Kokomo to
Indianapolis on U.S. 31, accompanied by Delphi's Dennis Aldridge, a
collision-warning-systems manager. I zoomed past fields of corn and
beans and got in line behind a green panel van. A small icon lit up
on the dash, indicating that the radar had spotted the vehicle, and
it soon seemed as if the van was towing us on an invisible rope.
Moments after I saw brake lights, my car decelerated, slowing to a

crawl. The van then sped up and we took off, too. We swung onto I-465, Indianapolis's version of the Beltway, and I tempted fate by swerving behind a passing Lincoln Continental. The system lit up like a Christmas tree, sounding a tone and gently applying the brakes.

In later versions of adaptive cruise control, according to Delphi safety executive Tonya Goodier, short-range sensors may get proactive in accident situations, pretensioning seat belts or deploying a roll bar. After the collision, they may automatically detect airbag deployment and make an ambulance call on the built-in cell phone. Other versions detect objects or people behind the car, sounding a warning if, for instance, you're about to hit a child on a tricycle.

Adaptive cruise control is just one way that high-end electronics are invading the automobile. Another product that's becoming almost commonplace is the global positioning system (GPS) receiver, which takes the place of the dog-eared and coffee-stained Rand McNally atlas that's been a fixture in seat pockets for thirty years. Combining satellite data to get a fix on your location with comprehensive maps stored on CD-ROMs, GPS can guide drivers quickly and accurately to their destinations. Most systems combine a touch-sensitive screen with synthesized voice directions, so drivers can keep their eyes on the road.

All this interactivity can be distracting. The owner's manual for a Lexus GPS system I tested warned in boldface type: "Do not use any feature of this system to the extent it distracts you from safe driving." Carried out to its full lawyer-inspired meaning, that would probably result in disconnecting the system. I was dismayed to encounter Beverly Hills Motoring's customized version of the Ford Expedition, which features not only two high-resolution TV monitors in the back of the front-seat headrests but a third monitor in the dashboard, facing the driver. And if that SUV isn't plugged in enough, there's always the colorfully named "Cigarette OnShore," a $165,000 Chevrolet Suburban with two video screens connected to a DVD player, games, and wireless Internet. But those vehicles are expensive toys.

While at Delphi, I found myself sitting in the deep leather seats of a Cadillac Seville, with the next generation of mobile electronics star-ing me in the face. Nestled in the Caddy's dash, where the radio would be, was Auto PC, a full-service unit that goes way, way beyond the radio-CD-cassette unit seen in cars today. If you think cell phones are a distraction for the driver, just think of the attention this inte-grated system will demand.

The Auto PC at least makes an effort to reduce driver distraction. It will receive e-mail through a built-in modem and read it back with a synthesized voice. It has a hands-free phone. It will record and play three-minute reminder memos from the driver. It has full GPS equip-ment, with maps of the entire United States. It can interact with an on-line service to deliver news and sports scores on demand, and it will also read them aloud.

Even if nobody will actually look at a screen while driving, these telematic features—including those designed, ironically enough, for added safety—can be dangerous. "The thing is, there is a limit to how much you can pay attention to, and people already are multitasking beyond the level of their abilities," says Stephanie Faul, communica-tions director for the AAA Foundation for Traffic Safety. "Once you pile on the distractions, who knows what kind of effect you will have?"[11]

Carmakers chant a mantra that goes something like "Both eyes on the road, both hands on the wheel," but people conditioned by a life-long addiction to television have a tendency to look at a display screen when it's covered with moving images. In 1997 Dr. Donald Redelmeier, a professor of medicine at the University of Toronto, con-ducted a study on the effects of cell-phone usage on driving. "Our data show that cell phone conversations decrease the ability to pay attention and drive safely, and those detrimental effects far outweigh the benefits," he said.[12] The study showed that a driver using a cell phone is four times as likely to get into a crash as a driver not using one.

The best uses for intelligent transportation systems may be *off* the car. There are several efforts under way in Europe to re-duce traffic congestion and accident rates with electronics, including the Program for European Traffic with Highest Efficiency and

Unprecedented Safety (PROMETHEUS). Rather than distracting the driver with onboard gadgetry, these systems provide a kind of electronically aided roadside assistance exemplified, in its simpler form, by the signs that flash messages such as EXPECT SLOWDOWNS AT EXIT 27, which are now appearing on many American interstates. The Japanese government's network, which is well established, involves radio transmittal of congestion information, route guidance systems, and a research program that looks at traffic problems twenty years ahead.

In the United States, the impact of 6 million crashes a year—with 41,000 fatalities—can be reduced through intelligent transportation systems. Commuters nationwide can dial 511 on their cell phones to access real-time traffic information for specific highways, says the Federal Communications Commission, which approved the Department of Transportation's plan in July 2000.

The 511 announcement was made at the first National Intelligent Vehicle Initiative Meeting in Washington, D.C. The Department of Transportation, which has coordinated a national 511 number for accessing real-time traffic information for specific highways, also announced a national goal of incorporating intelligent vehicle safety systems in 10 percent of light-duty vehicles and 25 percent of commercial vehicles by 2010. What's more, twenty-five metropolitan areas are to have deployed an intersection collision-warning system by then.

Many states have already moved ahead. In Colorado, a federally funded Mayday system helps locate vehicles in distress and provides special weather broadcasts on an AM band subcarrier. Special sensors on I-70 measure trucks' speed and weight, then flash them a recommended safe speed through a variable message sign.

San Antonio, Texas, has a central traffic-control system that makes use of advanced electronic systems, and Massachusetts has a SmarTraveler dial-up phone service for traffic and transit conditions.[13] In California, FasTrak transponders in commuters' cars help them speed through toll plazas. Boston's Big Dig project, described in chapter 4, is installing a sophisticated network of quick-response and

driver-communication devices to limit accidents on its new underground highways.

THE AUTOMATED HIGHWAY: A ROAD TO NOWHERE

At least in theory, today's telematics could be a pit stop on the road to
a complete surrender of driver control. Any highway planner will tell
you that 90 percent of accidents and a good deal of congestion are
caused by human error. One in twenty-five accidents, for instance, is
caused by bad judgment or poor visibility during lane changes or
merges. And who can doubt that rubbernecking, that tendency we
have to slow down and look at accidents or police activity, causes a lot
of backups? The advocacy group ITS America estimates that a fully
functioning driverless highway could double or triple the amount of
traffic it processes.

The automated highway would be possible only on limited-access
interstates. Drivers would proceed to an entrance ramp under their
own power. Sensors in their car would then react to magnetic strips or
other devices in the road surface, and a computer would seize control.
The driver would relax until he reached his exit.

It's not a new idea. A working model of an automated highway
was a huge hit with the public at General Motors's 1939 World's Fair
exhibit. The company went on to experiment with "hands-free" driving in the 1950s, trying out systems for automatic vehicle guidance,
speed control, and obstacle detection. Using ideas similar to those
now actually being implemented for road-maintenance work, General
Motors showed how robot trucks could carry loads in open-pit mines.
In the 1960s and 1970s, Ohio State University researcher Robert E.
Fenton was able to demonstrate wire-guided cars moving in circles
around a test track.[14] There has been some limited deployment of
automated vehicles, including a driverless maintenance truck in the
English Channel Tunnel and guideway-based, wire-controlled buses
made by Daimler-Benz and used on the O-Bahn in Essen, Germany.[15]

By the 1980s, microprocessors and wireless communications had
come so far that the idea of automated highways was reborn. In 1991,
Congress approved funding for a prototype system that would be

demonstrated in 1997. The National Automated Highway System Consortium demonstration occurred right on time, in the summer of 1997, on a blocked-off 7.5-mile stretch of I-15 in San Diego, California. A single file of eight driverless Buick LeSabres equipped with magnets, radar, and video cameras in the rearview mirrors followed visual cues along the road. The Buicks performed flawlessly, following serpentine tracks at speeds no hands-on driver could duplicate.

Researchers from Ohio State equipped four miles of the interstate with radar-reflective tape and performed passing maneuvers with two automated cars outfitted with special radar systems and video cameras. Carnegie Mellon University demonstrated collision-warning equipment in a bus and a car. (The bus had apparently traveled part of the way to San Diego under its own control.) Toyota showed off its version of adaptive cruise control. It all worked.

And then the federal government shut the program down. It was rather a reversal of the usual "Star Wars" demonstration, which proceeds disastrously but then gets increased funding. What went wrong? In the case of automated highways, it was those same human factors that cause accidents. Back in 1992, the Federal Highway Administration contracted with Honeywell to study how humans might interact with an automated interstate. Experiments were conducted on a high-fidelity, full-motion base-driving simulator at the University of Iowa. While the results were in some ways encouraging—drivers were perfectly comfortable traveling at speeds of up to ninety-five miles per hour on the simulated road—they were terrifying in other respects. Apparently, 50 percent of drivers experienced dramatic fear of a collision when another car moved into the automated traffic stream ahead of them.

And *leaving* the automated highway and retaking control was a huge problem, researchers found. "Drivers who were . . . given an advisory to leave the automated lane exhibited a large number of collisions and lane incursions," the report says in the dry language of such documents. Worse, after they got off, they turned into speed demons. Exiting the ninety-five-miles-per-hour automated lane and assuming control, "drivers exhibited speeds significantly higher than the posted speeds."[16] Even if these difficulties were sorted out, there are others. What happens when a disengaged driver has fallen asleep and needs to take control again?

Soon after the San Diego demonstration, the federal Transportation Research Board delivered a quietly devastating report on automated highways, recommending that funding for the program be discontinued.[17] "[D]aunting technical, social and institutional issues must be addressed and resolved," it said. Insurance liability was a major issue: who would be responsible for the accidents caused by an equipment failure?

NASA scientist Dennis Bushnell, who heads the Langley Research Center in Virginia, was blunt about federal disenchantment with the program. "The automated highway is the world's worst alternative," he said, "because the maximum benefit is twice the amount of traffic throughput, which would be chewed up in about a year and a half of building congestion—at incredible cost."

The research money that had gone into automated highways was redirected to safety systems like adaptive cruise control and collision warnings. Some diehard supporters think their dream will eventually be realized, but for all practical purposes the experiment is over.

Jonathan Gifford, an associate professor of public management and policy at George Mason University, says that the vast infrastructure needed remains an insurmountable barrier. "You need a separate right-of-way for automated vehicles," he said. "It's expensive in a lot of ways, including from both environmental and land-use points of view. There's a chicken-and-egg question: you can't deploy it, because it doesn't have any users yet. And there won't be any users unless it is built."

Another intelligent vehicle researcher, Srinivas Peeta, a civil engineering professor at Purdue University, admits that "there are very real obstacles to actually putting a system into use. You'd have to have some kind of driver override, because, psychologically, people would want the ability to take control back if the system fails. But what happens if a driver takes back control and then panics? Who's responsible?" Such questions are unlikely to ever be answered satisfactorily. And that means people, not computers, piloting America's auto fleet for the foreseeable future.

The automated highway was probably doomed by, among other things, its imperfect fit with human nature. The control aspect is, unfortunately, what Americans *like* about their cars, and they're willing to put up with quite a lot to stay in place at the wheel. America's car-dependent drivers in some ways resemble the frog that will sit in a pot of water as it slowly heats up and boils him to death. Since the traffic buildup is incremental, many of us adjust to it.

There is a great deal we can learn from Europe, if we will pay attention to its hard-won victories against the automobile. Transit is a critical element in most European efforts to build a livable city. Unfortunately, it's highly unlikely that the United States, with its sprawl development, will achieve European levels of transit use. Political will is largely lacking, too.

So if we are determined to remain in our cars, it's critical for our environment that they get not only "smarter" but cleaner, too. That process is already under way.

6

RETHINKING THE CAR:
A FUTURE FOR FUEL CELLS

THE AUTOMOBILE is unquestionably evolving, but its basic function as the backbone of American transportation infrastructure is unlikely to change. Given that, by 2050, we will still mainly be driving to work and play, can we take comfort from thinking that the car of tomorrow will be considerably smaller, smarter, and much cleaner?

I'm confident that we will see dramatically cleaner cars, as significant a transportation development as the invention of the automobile one hundred years ago. My previous book, *Forward Drive,* traced the emerging development of hydrogen-fuel-cell cars and discussed how they might help relieve the pollution associated with a society that is more or less totally automobile-dependent. Since I wrote it, considerable progress has been made in turning the dream into reality.

Arguments for the fuel cell, which produces electricity from hydrogen and oxygen in a chemical reaction, can be met with counterarguments. After all, a car with a nearly zero-pollution fuel cell is still a car, taking up space on the highway and pushing auto-centric development. The electric-car pioneer Dr. Paul MacCready told me that when he gives talks on the future of transportation, he says "that a Ferrari sport-utility vehicle running on cold fusion or hydrogen might have many benefits, but it won't do much about traffic and parking problems."

That's true. Environmentalists have valid reasons for questioning the idea of "clean cars" as a panacea for our transportation problems. But if hydrogen can be harnessed to take over our entire energy economy—as some analysts are predicting it will—it will be a dramatic transforming event, freeing us from oil dependence and its attendant pollution, spills, and skewed geopolitics. Fuel cells may well power every mode of transportation in the near future: trains, buses, ferries, and personal vehicles, too. "It's a potentially game-changing situation," said Bill Wicker, a Texaco vice president.[1]

Four factors make a hydrogen-based energy economy likely in the near future: pollution associated with fossil fuels and production-based oil scarcity; state, national, and international regulation; the specter of global warming; and evolving technological superiority. The Department of Energy estimates that if only 10 percent of the cars currently on the road in the United States were powered by fuel cells, oil imports could be reduced by 800,000 barrels a day. And the decentralized power generation promised by home-based fuel cells has the potential to mothball the nation's outdated power plants, especially the very polluting coal burners.

Fuel-cell advocates have to be careful, however, not to be too optimistic about the time frame in which all this will happen. While the cells themselves have reached a high level of reliability and production readiness, major questions about infrastructure remain. Will fuel-cell cars run on pure hydrogen gas—the cleanest option—or on a fossil fuel, which means they'll have to carry a heavy onboard "reformer" that will extract the hydrogen? And how will we build a national network of hydrogen-pumping stations to rival the existing network for gasoline? It may take another ten years to arrive at answers to these questions. In the meantime, we have to deal with the automobile industry as it is today. The short-term trends, unfortunately, are not positive.

SUVS AND HYBRIDS, TOO

The introduction of the fuel-efficient Toyota Prius and Honda Insight "hybrid" cars made headlines, and the technology—combining a very small internal-combustion engine with an electric motor—is here to stay, serving as a very useful bridge to the coming age of the fuel cell.

But sales numbers of Japanese subcompacts like these (the Insight seats only two) are likely to remain small.

The Prius and Insight have already proven a hit with environmental "early adopters," who are anxious to publicize the benefits of their advanced technology. I enjoyed a brief test ride in a Prius belonging to Fred Krupp, the founder of Environmental Defense, the New York City–based national conservation group. Krupp is a good citizen who practices what he preaches: he takes the train into Manhattan from his home in Connecticut. But like most suburbanites, Krupp *does* drive, a fact that has obviously been gnawing at him. No matter how he tries, Krupp hasn't escaped auto dependence.

"The car feels very advanced," he said as we drove around the suburbs. "I think that we're at the beginning of a whole new automotive era. There is rising consumer demand for clean cars, and I wanted to be part of it. It's the new new thing."

Krupp cautioned, however, that clean cars aren't the whole picture. "We need to design livable cities with subways, light rail, bikeways," he says. "It's a big priority for us." Later, Krupp's office faxed me a summary of the energy and emissions savings inherent in his commute in the Prius: "Fun Facts," it read, "Driving with Fred in his new Prius." In addition to his daily ten-mile round-trip, Krupp drives another ten miles a week for grocery shopping. That's approximately sixty miles, during which the Prius will consume a mere 1.2 gallons of gasoline. Krupp's old car got twenty-two miles to the gallon, which means it would consume 2.7 gallons each week to travel the same distance. Using the Prius instead of his old car means Krupp will cut emissions of nitrogen oxides and hydrocarbons by 97 percent, his carbon monoxide emissions by 76 percent, and his carbon dioxide emissions by over 50 percent.

Those statistics seem a bit suspect: Doesn't Fred ever go out to dinner? Take in a movie? But the point is there. A stunning statistic I saw pointed out that if every driver in America switched from their current commuter vehicle to a seventy-miles-per-gallon Honda Insight gas-electric hybrid, the fuel savings would wipe out our foreign oil dependence.

Honda and Toyota have adopted their hybrid technology to fit their mainstream product lines, including Honda's Civic and Toyota's Estima minivan. U.S. carmakers are building hybrids, too, but their model is that of the very profitable sport-utility vehicle (SUV) or pickup truck. American auto companies make a profit of as much as $8,000 on an SUV, so they're highly unlikely to stop producing them, no matter what the environmental imperatives. The big hybrids they'll start producing in 2003 may get better gas mileage and produce fewer emissions, but they'll still be heavyweight behemoths taking up critical space on our gridlocked highways.

Accepting American SUV fever and auto dependence is hard enough, but environmentalists have at least been able to point to Europe as a sane alternative, a place where cars are smaller and used less. Only now, even in sensible Europe, where people pay at least $4 a gallon for gasoline, take only half as many car trips, and walk or bicycle five times more, the SUV is making inroads. Normally truck-phobic Europeans, reports the *New York Times,* "are taking to the vehicles in a big way, moving up from their midget Fiat Cinquecentos and Renault Twingos."[2] In 1998, SUV sales jumped 26 percent in Europe, four times the growth rate of the overall passenger car market. That has to be put in perspective, however: SUVs and light trucks are still only a relatively insignificant 3.7 percent of the mix on European roads, compared to more than 50 percent in the United States.

On a recent trip to India, I saw Suzuki-built SUVs everywhere, proof that these off-roaders have permeated the Third World also. I admit to a deep personal prejudice against SUVs, whose larger variants have half the fuel efficiency of the average four-door sedan and produce five times the amount of smog-causing nitrogen oxides. Switching from an average car to a thirteen-miles-per-gallon SUV wastes enough energy in a year to keep a bathroom light burning for three decades. A loophole in federal laws allowed automakers to dodge more than $10 billion in gas-guzzler taxes on these road hogs. A friend of mine prints up bumper stickers that read SUV SUX, and I've been tempted to plaster them on half the vehicles in my office parking lot.

And all the off-road vehicles aren't SUVs, either. We're also being assaulted by all-terrain vehicles, motorized single-rider four-wheelers that have been invading our parks and recreational areas since the early 1980s. There were an estimated 28 million of these trail-chewing beasts in the United States by 1995. And according to a White House Council on Environmental Quality report entitled "Off-Road Vehicles on Public Lands," the little recreational vehicles have damaged every kind of ecosystem found in the United States.

I loathe any form of off-road vehicle. I've never ridden a skimobile, Jet Ski, all-terrain vehicle, or even a motorcycle with knobby tires. The idea of swamping rowboaters, colliding with manatees, or terrorizing deer does not turn me on. The funny thing is, though, that I do drive SUVs, and quite a lot. One of my incarnations is as an automotive journalist, and test cars (or trucks) are delivered to me weekly. Since more than thirty carmakers produce SUVs, that's what I get to try out.

So I'm not looking at SUVs from the outside—I've driven almost all of them, and an uncomfortable, impractical lot they are, too. I've got two thumbs, and they both go down when it comes to reviewing SUVs. Recently, I had the dubious honor of driving the ultimate SUV, the Hummer, a demilitarized version of the army's jeep replacement that blitzkrieged through the Persian Gulf in Operation Desert Storm. Early civilian versions of the huge SUV are relatively rare, seen only in the garages of well-heeled and ultramacho celebrities like Arnold Schwarzenegger. But General Motors, which recently acquired the Hummer brand from AM General, refused to see limitations. The company, whose surveys reveal that the vehicle is an icon for teenage boys, jumped in immediately with a plan to market a cleaned-up Hummer for mass consumption.

There's a psychological dimension to this. Caught unawares when the SUV craze began with an uptick in sales of the (since discontinued) Jeep Cherokee in the mid-1980s, automakers are now doing considerable market research to understand why people buy the cars and trucks they do. Going "off road," which only a tenth of four-wheel-drive owners do, is hardly a factor. SUV buyers, it turns out, aren't sure they're ready for parenting and don't like the image a minivan projects. They want to be "in control," sitting "above the traffic."

There's a social dimension, too. According to Strategic Vision, a San Diego–based research company, "[A] greater percentage of mini-van buyers than sport-utility buyers are involved in their communi-ties and families. Minivan buyers are more likely than buyers of any other kind of vehicle to attend religious services and to do volunteer work, while sport-utility buyers rank with pickup truck buyers and sports car buyers as the least likely to do either."[3] SUV people are also more likely to indulge in expensive restaurants, sports events, and fit-ness clubs.

I discovered that a Hummer attracts attention. Swing it down a suburban street and heads swivel, followed by broad grins. I'm not sure what the onlookers are so happy about, unless it's the sight of a vehicle so unlikely, so huge, so inappropriate for soccer-dad duty. Here's an urban assault vehicle that's more than seven feet wide but seats only four, with less usable interior space than a New Beetle. I drove my Hummer down Round Hill Road, the toniest street in Greenwich, Connecticut, and another one, in bright yellow, passed me going the other way. The driver waved. I was appalled.

For making a statement, the Hummer is unparalleled. For any-thing else, however, it's useless. Unless your lifestyle includes serving on a commando squad, this vehicle is like a fish out of water or an air-liner on the ground: it moves, but not gracefully.

I offered to pull my neighbor's house down with the Hummer's winch, but he selfishly declined. I volunteered to "blaze a trail" through the community wilderness area, but the rangers lacked enthusiasm for the plan. I wanted to test the fording capability in the family swimming pool, but my wife vetoed the idea. The kids' school refused to allow me to try out the sixty-percent-grade capability on the side of their building.

For the most part, I just drove the behemoth to work and used it as a school bus. And I suffered oceans of embarrassment when circum-stances forced me to drive to a signing for my first book (which is about hybrid and fuel-cell vehicles) in the Hummer. Two other people arrived there in zero-pollution battery electric cars. After a week with the Hummer, I was convinced that this thing doesn't belong in civilian guise. Assault vehicles shouldn't be picking up kids.

The auto industry is beginning to listen to environmental critiques of the SUV. In part because of increasing awareness of an SUV's rollover risk, carmakers are less likely to build them on unstable truck chassis. Minivan- and car-based SUVs are not only less dangerous but more fuel-efficient. In 1999, I was sitting in the penthouse office of William Clay Ford Jr., chairman of the Ford Motor Company, when he himself brought up the satirical name bestowed upon the company's largest SUV, the Excursion, by the Sierra Club. "They're calling it the '*Ford Valdez,*'" he said with something of a forced chuckle. Ford surprised and delighted the environmental community when, in the spring of 2000, it candidly acknowledged some of the SUV's inherent environmental and safety problems. It pleased them even more several months later when it announced that it would voluntarily make its SUVs 25 percent more fuel-efficient. (General Motors quickly said it would exceed Ford's gains.)

The SUV will be cleaned up, at least a little. And part of the impetus may be coming from the universities. I visited Mesa, Arizona, for the first round of FutureTruck, a college-based competition cosponsored by the U.S. Department of Energy, GM, and Yahoo! that tests the ability of fifteen groups of engineering students to build a cleaner SUV. Six months before the competition, the teams were issued identical, off-the-line, full-sized Chevrolet Suburban SUVs. These are big trucks, gas guzzlers that arrived complete with big V-8 engines, three rows of seats, and all the trimmings.

The vehicles the students built (with one exception) were hybrids, meaning that they have electric and internal-combustion engines, plus the computer controls to operate the package efficiently. Most of these experimental trucks shaved at least ten miles per gallon off the performance of the standard Suburban and considerably reduced emissions, too. The students' efforts paralleled Detroit's own. GM will put a hybrid version of its Silverado/Sierra pickup truck into production by 2004, complementing hybrid SUVs coming in 2003 from both Ford and DaimlerChrysler.

On the road, with GM engineer-judges at the wheel, the trucks showed off their hurried preparation. I was stranded on three out of four test rides, and none of the vehicles performed flawlessly in the 112-degree heat. Cheers went up when the competitors made it through the sand course, however. The joint winners, as it turned out, were the teams from West Virginia University and the University of Maryland. The contest will be held annually until 2003.

FutureTruck was heartwarming in the same way a tear-jerking movie is, but a cleaner SUV doesn't make much difference in the automobile's grand march toward world domination. Even hybrid SUVs use a lot of gasoline and produce emissions, contributing to the increasingly daunting problems caused by global oil dependence.

THE BATTLE OVER OIL

Worldwide, oil use is the primary cause of increased emission of carbon dioxide, the primary global-warming gas. Burning fuel adds 6 billion tons of carbon to the atmosphere every year, and 17 percent of that comes from internal-combustion engines in transportation vehicles. In the United States, that percentage is much higher: at least 30 percent of our carbon emissions can be blamed on our more than 200 million cars and trucks, with much of the rest coming from power plants and other human factors.[4]

One of the wonders of the fuel cell is its infinite scalability. Cells can, in fact, take the place of nearly every use we have for fossil fuels today, and that's a good thing, not least because the oil option is expiring. Oil is the engine of our economy, but it won't be for much longer.

The chorus agreeing with that assessment is growing, and it's not just wish fulfillment on the part of some oil-hating environmentalists. No less an authority than Ahmed Yamani, Saudi Arabia's oil minister from 1962 to 1986—the man most directly responsible for setting Organization of Petroleum Exporting Countries (OPEC) prices after

1973—thinks the oil era is ending. Speaking to the British *Sunday Telegraph* in June 2000, Yamani said that he anticipated the widespread use of fuel cells by 2010, with the result that gasoline consumption will be cut by almost 100 percent. Saudi Arabia, he said, will face "serious economic difficulties." By 2030, he anticipates, "there will be a huge amount of oil—and no buyers. . . . The Stone Age came to an end not because we had a lack of stones, and the oil age will come to an end not because we have a lack of oil."[5] Jürgen Schrempp, the chairman of DaimlerChrysler, has said publicly that he expects a full-scale oil crisis by 2015 if alternatives are not developed.[6]

I'm consistently amazed that high oil prices are almost never related to our runaway appetite for the stuff. Even with the series of price shocks that occurred in 1999 and 2000, Americans still pay the lowest oil prices in the world, while using the most energy per capita. In the United States, transportation gobbles up 65 percent of the oil supply.

Because of our insatiable appetite for oil, the traditionally oil-rich United States has become a major importer, dependent on OPEC and its allies for 56 percent of the supply. (At the height of the energy crisis in 1975, we managed to reduce that dependence to 35 percent.) Oil prices aren't going up because we put taxes on it but because we've become hat-in-hand beggars at OPEC's table, asking, "Please, sir, can I have some more?"

There's little realism about oil on the national political scene. During the 2000 presidential campaign, the candidates traded blame for high oil prices and played games about releasing what are largely symbolic amounts from the nation's emergency Strategic Petroleum Reserve. Al Gore portrayed George W. Bush as captive to oil interests, and Bush responded—ludicrously—by blaming the Clinton administration's imposition of clean-air standards.[7] A typical political response was that of Republican Senator Kay Bailey Hutchison of Texas, who called on Congress to suspend the 18.4-cents-per-gallon federal tax on gasoline because of rising prices at the pumps. Very few politicians had the courage to suggest that prices could be lowered through energy conservation on the part of the American people, a strategy that many perceive as having cost President Jimmy Carter reelection.

Both President George W. Bush and Vice President Dick Cheney have backgrounds in the oil industry, and both support more domestic drilling, including drilling in the highly sensitive coastal plain of the Arctic National Wildlife Refuge. Cheney, in fact, was plucked directly into the campaign from the helm of the Texas-based oil services giant Halliburton, Inc., which helped rebuild Iraq's petroleum industry after the Gulf War. In a nice example of circular logic, President Bush pointed to the million barrels of oil a day imported into the United States from Saddam Hussein's Iraq as a reason for drilling in the Arctic Refuge.[8]

As a U.S. senator from Michigan, Secretary of Energy Spencer Abraham not only twice cosponsored bills calling for oil drilling in the Arctic refuge, he also proved his loyalty to his state's auto industry by fighting against increases in federal fuel-economy standards for cars and trucks. National Security Adviser Condoleezza Rice, a former Chevron board member, had an oil tanker named after her. The Bush administration's lone Democratic cabinet member is Secretary of Transportation Norman Mineta, who actually had a good record of support for mass transit and increases in fuel-economy standards during his term in Congress.

According to a study by the Center for Responsive Politics (CRP) of political contributions in the 1997–98 election cycle, 76 percent of the $22 million donated by the oil industry went to Republican candidates considered friendly to industry interests. In 2000, energy and natural-resource-extraction companies were among Bush's largest contributors. Bush raised a record $21.3 million for the presidential race at a single fund-raiser hosted by Kenneth Lay, the chief executive of Enron, the largest natural gas dealer in the United States.

The Bush administration is proving itself to be hostile toward energy conservation in general and tax subsidies for environmentally responsible vehicles in particular. Speaking at a recreational vehicle plant in Washington State during the campaign, Cheney made points with the audience by declaring, "You have a solar panel on your house, you get tax relief. If you drive a solar-powered car, you get tax relief. It's goofy."[9]

The auto industry, which builds "solar-powered cars" only reluctantly, has a direct pipeline to the Bush administration in the person of Andrew H. Card Jr., an early appointment as chief of staff. From 1993 to 1998, Card was the president of the American Automobile Manufacturers Association, "where he oversaw the lobbying against tighter fuel-economy and air pollution regulations for automobiles," as the *New York Times* described it.[10] From there, it was on to a vice presidency at General Motors.

With the United States so dependent on imported oil, supply disruptions and consequent price hikes can easily cause major upheaval. Politicians were at a loss in responding to the spontaneous demonstrations in the fall of 2000 that blocked many wholesale fuel terminals in Europe, virtually closing down the retail sale of gasoline in several countries.

The blockades were led by truckers and farmers, but their civil disobedience against high gasoline prices had widespread public support. As in the States, the main demand was to lower national fuel taxes. Some leaders, in France and Italy in particular, simply caved in and met the demands. But even that stopgap choice will no longer be available when fuel price rises are caused more by true international shortages than by artificial OPEC production quotas and oil company profiteering. We can expect to see many more instances of economies virtually shut down by oil-flow problems in the years ahead.

SETTING THE STAGE FOR HYDROGEN

Oil is a finite resource, and no longer an assured one. The oil companies might be expected to be fierce opponents of hydrogen fuel cells, but there's evidence of some pragmatism in the industry. As they announce their intention to become "energy companies" instead of oil companies, it's easy to be reminded of the merger of Nabisco and R. J. Reynolds. The joint company, now separated again, would just as soon sell crackers as cigarettes. And that may be why U.S. Tobacco formally changed its name to UST.

In 2000, General Motors, partnered with Exxon Mobil in the

development of a gasoline processor for fuel cells, announced a break-through in a design that achieves an incredible 80 percent efficiency. The Holland-based Shell Group launched a division called Shell International Renewables in 1997, exploring such areas as solar power and biomass. Shell Hydrogen is working with DaimlerChrysler on a gasoline processor for the fuel-cell cars the German company plans to introduce in 2004.

Shell Hydrogen's Alastair Livesey, speaking at a Michigan envi-ronmental-vehicle conference in 1999, hastened to assure his audience that Shell does not believe that oil is running out; it is just, he said, being replaced. Curiously, he used the same analogy as former Saudi oil minister Ahmed Yamani. "The Stone Age did not end due to a lack of stones," he said. "It was due to Bronze Age axes being cheaper and better."[11]

Shell Hydrogen is also partnered with a prominent fuel-cell and battery company, Michigan-based Energy Conversion Devices (ECD), in building the hydrogen pumping station of the future. ECD Chairman Robert Stempel, a former chairman of General Motors, told UPI[12] that he's confident that Shell can "provide the hydrogen at the retail level at some kind of [filling] station."

Filling stations are crucial for fuel-cell development in exactly the same way that track is crucial to mag-lev trains and light rail. It's infrastructure again. "If we are going to supply hydrogen and there were no vehicles, it would make no sense," said Don Huberts, presi-dent of Shell Hydrogen. "And if the car companies make the car and there's no fuel, it makes no sense."[13] The fuel-cell car can work flaw-lessly but go nowhere because there's no supporting network of hydro-gen stations or an inexpensive way to produce hydrogen.

Amory Lovins of the Rocky Mountain Institute, who was an early champion of both hybrid cars and fuel cells and is now developing a lightweight "hypercar" of his own, would dispute this. According to the book he co-authored with Paul Hawken and L. Hunter Lovins, *Natural Capitalism,* "Another common objection to hydrogen-fueled cars—that the first such car can't be sold until the whole country is laced with hydrogen production plants, pipelines, and filling stations costing hundreds of billions of dollars—is . . . misplaced."[14] Lovins tends to be an optimist on infrastructure issues and has great faith in decentralization. Fuel-cell cars could get their hydrogen directly from office and apartment buildings with power-generating cells of their own, he says. He also thinks we can turn our fuel-cell cars into minia-ture power plants. The cars could generate electricity in the 96 per-cent of the time when they're not in use, then upload that power back into the grid. Ultimately, Lovins says, "the U.S. Hypercar fleet could have five to ten times the generating capacity of the national grid."[15]

Lovins may be right, but the hydrogen infrastructure is not unfolding that way. Filling stations are very much part of the picture. I visited Dearborn, Michigan, in 1999 for the unveiling of Ford's first pumping station for both liquid and gaseous hydrogen and was grati-fied to see how easy the procedure was. If you can pump gasoline, you can pump hydrogen. But Ford's station was only the third built in the entire world.

The hydrogen-production problem remains a serious obstacle. Current methods, used only on a small scale, involve steam reforming of natural gas or the electrolysis of water. They make expensive hydro-gen. Producing the gas with photovoltaics is also possible and could even be cost-effective, given enough land for a large-scale "farm" of solar arrays. Those methods will become obsolete if scientists can develop a low-cost method for isolating hydrogen from tap water (which is two parts hydrogen and one part oxygen). A Canadian com-pany called Xogen Power announced in 2000 that it could do exactly that, producing a pleasant vision of cars driving around with nothing but water in their tanks. You'd be able to fill them up from the gar-den hose. And the water wouldn't be consumed, either, because fuel cells produce water vapor as their end product. Xogen says its proto-type system is powered by a single twenty-four-volt battery, which can be kept charged through use of an onboard solar panel. Hydrogen developments are followed closely by the stock market, and Xogen's announcement sent shares of major investor Tathacus Resources soar-ing more than 400 percent.

Yet another approach came to light early in 2000, when Tasios

Melis, a University of California at Berkeley biologist, announced that he and his team had successfully produced large volumes of hydrogen gas from what is, in effect, pond scum. When the green algae that forms on stagnant lakes and ponds is deprived of sulfur, Melis said, it produces significant quantities of hydrogen, enough to be commercially viable. "I guess it's the equivalent of striking oil," he declared, adding that considerable work needs to be done before any actual production can begin.[16] In an e-mail, Melis told me that an Olympic-sized swimming pool full of treated green algae could theoretically produce enough daily hydrogen to drive a Ford Taurus fuel cell car about five thousand miles. But Melis's algae method would probably produce less hydrogen per acre than a state-of-the-art photovoltaic installation.

The fuel cell was invented by William Robert Grove in 1839. He lectured on its properties in London three years later, and nobody doubted him. And yet the invention, which predated the internal-combustion engine, sat on the scientific shelf for 160 years. Unfortunately, ideas aren't enough. The hydrogen community makes a "breakthrough" at least once a month, and the technology of the fuel cell in 2000 was dramatically better than it was even a year before. The cells fit under the hood of a car. The cars run well, and they even start in cold-weather conditions. Their range is approaching three hundred miles, a threshold most Americans will accept. They can be refueled easily. But that doesn't guarantee a fuel-cell car in every garage.

CLEAN CARS IN CALIFORNIA

The future of the electric car, the fuel cell, and, indeed, the hydrogen energy economy is being decided in California. The whole world is watching as an important demonstration project, the California Fuel Cell Partnership, puts fuel-cell vehicles to work in the real world. At the same time, California's Air Resources Board (ARB) has imposed a mandate on carmakers that requires them to get into the electric-car business and spurs development of the fuel-cell vehicle.

"A whole group of auto companies, fuel-cell companies, and hydrogen suppliers, under ARB's direction, are working together on the questions of refueling and safety," ECD's Robert Stempel told me. "Each of the major oil companies is working both independently and as a group on standardizing the fuel system they're going to use. The auto companies likewise are looking at the tank design and the interconnect design. Obviously, you want to be able to pull into any station with any car or any truck and refuel. You don't want a whole group of different systems."

What Stempel is talking about is the hard and not necessarily glamorous work of actually making the fuel-cell vehicle practical, and not another transportation also-ran. The California Fuel Cell Partnership could help make that happen. Launched in 1999, the partnership has a diverse membership that includes carmakers General Motors, DaimlerChrysler, Ford, Honda, Toyota, Nissan, and Volkswagen; major fuel-cell producer Ballard Power Systems; oil companies Arco, Shell, and Texaco; state regulators, California's Air Resources Board, and the California Energy Commission; and the U.S. Department of Energy. California transit agencies are involved with the partnership, too, including the Alameda–Contra Costa Transit District, which operates seven hundred buses in the San Francisco Bay Area, and SunLine Transit, which runs alternative-fueled buses in Palm Springs.

Operating out of a west Sacramento hydrogen filling station near the state legislature, the partnership is putting rubber on the road: sixty fuel-cell cars, trucks, and buses in test fleets that will operate until 2003. Fifteen fuel-cell cars have emerged from the collaboration between Ford and DaimlerChrysler. Twenty-five buses, equipped with Ballard fuel cells, are being tested by the California transit agencies.

DaimlerChrysler, in collaboration with Ballard, has developed the world's most advanced fuel-cell cars in its NECAR series. Dr. Ferdinand Panik, who heads the company's Fuel Cell Project from a base in Germany, is keenly aware of the on-the-ground problems. In announcing the company's work with the partnership, he said, "Until now, we haven't had the critical support of the fuel industry and government

partners to examine all the infrastructure issues."[17] In addition to its
work in California, DaimlerChrysler is also testing fuel-cell buses in
Iceland with such partners as Royal Dutch Shell and Norsk Hydro of
Norway. There will be three Mercedes fuel-cell buses plying the
streets in Reykjavík, the country's capital, by 2003, paving the way
for the world's first hydrogen-based energy economy. Why Iceland?
The tiny country, with a population of only 276,000, already produces two-thirds of its energy from clean hydroelectric and geother-
mal sources. Professor Bragi Arnason of the University of Iceland has
been campaigning for twenty years to convert the remaining fossil-
fueled third to hydrogen. By 2030, Professor Arnason says, all of
Iceland's cars and buses—and even its fishing boats—will be powered
by fuel cells.[18] Eventually, Iceland's electricity and home heating will
be fuel-cell generated.

DaimlerChrysler, though it is exploring gasoline processing, has
been proceeding on the assumption that its first fuel-cell cars will run
on methanol. An onboard chemical factory called a "reformer" would
extract pure hydrogen to run the cell. Methanol has the advantage of
being easy to pump, transport, and store. But it's also, like the gasoline additive MTBE, a nasty groundwater pollutant. Meanwhile,
General Motors, with its own oil company partners, is increasingly
drawn to the easiest possible option—gasoline reformation—which
would require absolutely no infrastructure changes. We already have
gasoline filling stations.

Many environmentalists are urging the players to skip the pollution-
producing reformation stage altogether and proceed directly to onboard
hydrogen gas, which is by far the cleanest option in terms of emissions. (A fuel-cell car running on hydrogen gas produced from renew-
able energy, such as photovoltaics, is a zero-emission vehicle, or ZEV.)
Part of the partnership's goal is to resolve such differences whenever
possible and produce international standards.

The partnership will put only sixty vehicles on the road; the 2003
ARB mandate will put thousands there. Never has a single state's
law been so hotly debated or had so many dramatic consequences
for international industry. The ARB mandate was enacted in 1990,

designed to gradually introduce electric vehicles (EVs) into California's automotive fleet. The reason for it was obvious: California has the dirtiest air in the nation. (Los Angeles has recently been seesawing with Houston in a dubious race for the "dirtiest city" distinction.)

The auto industry has been a reluctant partner in making the mandate happen, especially the provisions for zero-pollution cars. For the most part, that means electric cars with rechargeable batteries. Never much of a believer in battery-powered cars, the carmakers joined with a spooked oil industry in mounting a multimillion-dollar public relations campaign against the mandate through much of 1995.

Though ARB would deny that it was influenced by anything other than technological and economic factors, an initial 1998 mandate that would have required the industry to produce 2 percent of its fleet as "clean cars" was canceled. There definitely *were* technical challenges in producing electric cars that consumers would accept, but the campaign helped poison the waters. In 1996, in lieu of accepting the part of the mandate that addressed 1998 to 2002, the major carmakers (with sales of more than 35,000 annually in the state) agreed to a more limited "Memorandum of Understanding" that allowed them to place small numbers of EVs in test fleets.

Carmakers lobbied almost as hard against the 2003 standards as they had against the 1998 rules. Supporters of the standards lobbied, too, using an electric postal van to deliver more than 50,000 letters from California consumers supporting ARB. The agency responded with a new set of 2003 rules that fell carefully in the middle. Although it modified its rules in late 2000 to be friendlier to hybrid and fuel-cell cars, a 2 percent zero-pollution mandate for 2003 remained in place. That mandate requires the largest auto manufacturers to build and either sell or lease an estimated 4,650 EVs annually (down from 22,000 before the rule change). The mandate, affecting 10 percent of the state's new cars overall, allows 2 percent of cars offered for sale to be hybrids and 6 percent to be various types of low-emission vehicles, including very clean gasoline vehicles. The modified rules were hailed as a victory by the auto industry, but some environmentalists supported the changes as well because of doubts about battery technologies. Whichever way it's interpreted, the board's vote made a substantial increase in California's clean-car fleet inevitable. The cars will be on the lots; whether they will be a hit with consumers is another story.

In 2000, there were only about 2,000 zero-emission cars on the road in California. Even taking into account the burgeoning sales of the hybrid Toyota Prius and Honda Insight, there were still considerably less than 10,000 "clean cars" in the whole country then. In the four years between 1996 and 2000, automakers sold or leased only 3,300 EVs.[19] So the mandate represents a real departure and a goad to bringing clean cars to market. "Conventional fuels and technologies are clearly not enough," said ARB president Alan C. Lloyd at the 2000 Future Car Congress in Washington. "We need to push further." Lloyd noted that California's population increased 41 percent from 1980 to 2000 and its vehicle miles traveled jumped 81 percent, yet ground-level ozone levels have actually improved. It's proof, he said, that the policy of requiring cleaner tailpipes is working.

ARB's ruling has repercussions well beyond California's borders. The federal Clean Air Act gives states the option of adhering to national emissions standards or matching California's requirements. Four states—Massachusetts, New York, Maine, and Vermont—have gone with California, and so will have clean-car fleets as well.

The next few years should be highly interesting in determining just how large the market for "clean cars" in California is. As Bill Moore puts it in his on-line newsletter *EV World*, "When ARB asked each manufacturer to report on its estimate of the size of the EV market in California, several of them disdainfully reported 'zero,' a childish response that clearly belies the situation."[20] But the leasing programs of such battery vehicles as the General Motors EV-1, Ford Ranger, and the Honda EV Plus did indeed produce pitiable results, with no car company putting more than 700 cars on the road. The results contrast sharply with early sales figures for hybrid cars like the Honda Insight. A huge wave of interest caused Honda to increase imports of the gas-electric car from 4,000 to 6,500 in 2000. That's more than the combined lease programs of almost all the battery EVs over several years.

Automakers were gleeful at the results of a study prepared by Professor Kenneth Train of the University of California at Berkeley that claimed that state consumers would refuse to buy a battery EV unless it was sold for $28,000 less than a comparable gas car. "Since the average retail transaction price of an internal-combustion Toyota RAV-4 is about $21,000, this would mean that, in order to meet California's EV mandate, Toyota would have to give the average consumer a free RAV-4 plus a check for approximately $7,000," Train claimed. Toyota liked the study so much it e-mailed the results to reporters.[21] Environmentalists dismissed it as ridiculous. A competing study, commissioned by the California Electric Transportation Coalition in 2000, found that one in three state residents would be willing to buy an EV if its price was comparable with that of a conventional car.[22]

For carmakers, the environment is a war with many fronts. General Motors, for instance, introduced the EV-1 electric car and agreed to spend $2.5 million in California to help reduce emissions from diesel school buses, but it also continued with spirited opposition to the ARB mandates. The companies together have lobbied heavily against the Clinton administration's tighter national air-quality standards and tenaciously battled any change in corporate average fuel economy (CAFE). The federal CAFE standards determine the fuel performance of an automaker's whole fleet, and they've been stagnant since 1975 at 27.5 miles per gallon.

At a Washington press conference in June 2000, Daniel Becker of the Sierra Club asked those gathered to remember what they were doing in 1975. "Gerald Ford was president of the United States," he said. "Bill Gates was twenty years old. *Jaws* was playing in movie theaters. KC and the Sunshine Band was atop the pops. And Congress set CAFE standards for cars at 27.5 miles per gallon."

The conservative Competitive Enterprise Institute countered with a weakly reasoned report claiming that the fuel standards, limited as they are, kill up to 4,500 people a year by requiring the sale of small cars.[23] The standards remained unchanged, and in 1999 "U.S. fuel economy overall dropped to its lowest value in 20 years," reported the Union of Concerned Scientists.[24]

While gradually accepting the reality of global warming and symbolically dropping out of the industry-supported naysayer group, the Global Climate Coalition, the carmakers are also creating more greenhouse gas than ever. With the exception of BMW, every carmaker's fleets emitted more global-warming gas in the 2000 model year than they did in 1990.[25]

Especially when set against the typical CAFE-frozen, carbon-emitting car of today, battery EVs have many important advantages. They're easy to drive and to recharge, very quiet, and reliable, too. And there's no polluting tailpipe. The main challenge remains the batteries themselves, which struggle to give the cars a range of more than 120 miles. It's unlikely that battery cars will have much effect on the overall transportation picture, even under the rosiest sales projections. There are more than 200 million cars in the United States, and no one has yet advanced a workable strategy for bringing the battery-powered EV to the mass market. Environmentalists and early adopters will readily see the appeal of a zero-pollution vehicle, but most Americans will buy one only when it's as good in every way— price, performance, versatility, range—as the car they're already driving. And that's where fuel-cell cars come in. They *are* as good.

FUEL-CELL CARS: WHAT'S COMING

When they're not fighting against environmental regulations, carmakers do a pretty credible job of building cars. The dream that independent start-up companies could challenge Detroit with competitive EVs has largely died, and most cutting-edge fuel-cell development is located in the auto capitals of Tokyo, Stuttgart, and Detroit (with Vancouver, British Columbia, home of fuel-cell maker Ballard, thrown in for good measure). Here's a look at what three automakers— General Motors, Ford, and Honda—are planning.

GENERAL MOTORS: THE SLEEPING GIANT AWAKES

"The General Motors Corporation has developed an emissions control system," read the excited front-page *New York Times* story. "If the system works as well as GM believes it will, the automobile will be removed as a pollution problem."[26] Who wouldn't celebrate such news? The problem is that the story ran in 1972, and GM's system—the catalytic converter—did not end pollution as we know it.

In the early race to develop a fuel-cell car, GM was an also-ran, displaying a nonrunning prototype that was little more than a stretched EV-1 at shows in 1999. GM reacted petulantly when Ford announced in 2000 that it would improve the gas mileage of its sport-utility vehicles 25 percent by 2005. "GM will still be the leader in five years, and in 15 years for that matter," sniffed Harry Pearce, GM's vice chairman, at a Detroit news conference.[27]

But then GM showed a more impressive hand. The company quietly announced a joint venture with Giner Inc., a fuel-cell pioneer, and new alternative-energy alliances with frequent partner Toyota. It then released a flood of impressive technology announcements, including the new and remarkable capability of compressing hydrogen gas to 10,000 pounds per square inch. The most significant achievement, unveiled in the summer of 2000, was HydroGen1. Based, like previous GM fuel-cell vehicles, on a German Opel Zafira minivan, HydroGen1 achieved an impressive 53 to 67 percent efficiency in operation, much better than any previous car-based fuel cell. The best internal-combustion engines achieve only 15 percent efficiency burning gasoline.

HydroGen1 ended all speculation that fuel-cell cars can't operate in cold temperatures (a continuing problem with battery EVs) by generating electricity, starting up, and driving in below-zero conditions. "But it is its compactness that really makes it look a plausible predecessor to a production version," wrote the *Economist.*[28] In the earlier version of the Zafira fuel-cell van, the cell took up not only the engine compartment but everything behind the front seats. In HydroGen1, it all fits under the hood and under the intact passenger compartment. The vehicle can carry enough liquid hydrogen in its tanks to travel 400 miles—satisfactory to any consumer. Running the van on liquid hydrogen makes it easier to save space, but GM's engineers will face considerable challenge in achieving the same fit with a bulky hydrogen gas tank or a heavy chemical reformer. An earlier GM fuel-cell car, shown off in the company's high-tech (but ugly) Precept concept car, used hydrogen stored in a solid hydride form.

GM's fuel-cell work is proceeding in Rochester, New York, and in Germany, at Mainz-Kastel, under the direction of Dr. J. Byron McCormick. While at Los Alamos National Laboratory in the 1970s, McCormick was part of the team that developed and ran a fuel-cell vehicle on liquid hydrogen. With the energy crisis as an impetus, McCormick created a fuel-cell program at Los Alamos that achieved a significant breakthrough during the 1980s: a design for the proton exchange membrane (PEM) fuel cell that reduced the need for expensive precious-metal catalyst by 90 percent. In the HydroGen1, the platinum catalyst is half as large as in the previous Zafira, bringing costs down considerably.

"When I first came to GM," McCormick told me, "fuel cells were my avocation while I worked on other business. I was convinced that there were no breakthrough batteries on the horizon, and that fuel cells were the key." He talked about them so much that, in time, GM let him work on them full-time. "We have a very orderly development program aimed at really solving problems that will make the fuel-cell vehicle have a utility as good or better than internal-combustion," McCormick said. He's confident that the company will have a production-ready fuel-cell car by 2004. "We could be off by a year or two," he said.

The major issue facing McCormick's team is achieving the kind of quick start, in all weather, that drivers are used to. Since fuel cells produce water as a by-product, keeping that water from freezing and incapacitating the system is still a challenge.

Larry Burns, GM's vice president for research, expresses the hope that the company can achieve high-volume production of hundreds of thousands of fuel-cell vehicles annually by 2010. "Leading companies like GM and Toyota have to have the courage to step out and lead," he said.[29]

FORD: GREEN ON TOP

I spent a good deal of effort in 1999 trying to arrange an interview with Ford's chairman, William Clay Ford Jr. I finally got one, and took in the view from Ford's office atop the worldwide headquarters in Dearborn, which has the iconic address One American Road.

It's unusual, if not exactly unknown, for a maverick to survive in the conformist culture of the automobile industry. Think of John DeLorean's early days at Pontiac, during which he shocked tradition by wearing blue jeans and creating the GTO. But it's unprecedented in the modern era for a maverick to also be chairman. William Clay Ford Jr., whose great-grandfather founded the company that bears both their names, became chairman of Ford in early 1999, and he has shaken up the industry with his environmental makeover plan. Ford's vision includes not only clean cars but, in the company of celebrated ecology-minded architect Bill McDonough, a top-to-bottom green renovation of the company's sprawling Rouge assembly complex in Dearborn. In partnership with Ballard Power Systems and DaimlerChrysler, Ford is also emerging as the world leader in getting a fuel-cell car to market.

"Bill Ford is having a profound effect on the behavior of the company," said Maryann Keller, author of *Collision: GM, Toyota and Volkswagen and the Race to Own the Twenty-first Century.* "They're becoming proactive on environmental matters, instead of having to be dragged kicking and screaming." It's a good thing he's there. He almost wasn't. Ford has said that, on several occasions, he nearly left the company to start an environmental group. "My friends and my wife always convinced me that the impact I could have would be far greater if I stayed," Ford said.[30]

The forty-four-year-old Ford has a very sincere manner and looks directly at his interviewers. I asked him about fuel cells right away. "We'll have vehicles for sale and on the road by 2004," he said. "But the critical issues are manufacturability in high volumes, cost, and the real unknown of infrastructure, something we can't control. Those questions are going to drive the timing in acceptance of the vehicle. The manufacturers are going to have to show that we can build these cars in volume, that they're viable, that they're no-trade-off vehicles for the customer in terms of performance and range. When we've demonstrated that, then I think the fuel companies will get serious about providing the infrastructure."

I asked Ford if he personally would prefer to see fuel cells powered directly by zero-polluting hydrogen gas, rather than the methanol or gasoline that carmakers have championed as easier on the infrastructure. "Yes," he said, "because when you use methanol or gasoline there are trade-offs. Direct hydrogen is the cleanest and simplest way to get the fuel cells powered and running. It's not inconceivable that there will be interim steps—that we'll launch with methanol and then, in time, go to direct hydrogen."

Bill Ford is convincing in demonstrating the company's sincerity with actually producing a high-volume, no-compromises fuel-cell car. To be a success in the market, he says, Ford "will hit the heartland of the market instead of playing on the fringe." And that means a popular four-passenger car platform, not an exotic two-seater or specialty vehicle.

Ford's first production gas-electric hybrid vehicle will be an SUV, a 40-miles-per-gallon, 500-miles-range version of its small Escape, on sale in 2003. The Escape will have double the fuel economy Daimler-Chrysler is able to wring out of the 2003 model Dodge Durango hybrid (which, at 18.6 miles per gallon, improves fuel economy performance only 20 percent over the standard Durango; you have to ask why the company bothered). Beginning in 2004, Ford will offer new technology on its Explorer SUVs that will save fuel by shutting the vehicles' engines off at traffic lights. With that option, similar to systems in the Honda and Toyota hybrid cars, the Explorer's fuel economy will increase 42 percent, from 19 miles per gallon to 27.

Ford also plans to produce a range of battery-powered electric vehicles under the TH!NK brand, including small plastic-bodied battery cars (the TH!NK City) and low-speed community EVs (the TH!NK Neighbor). There are TH!NK electric bicycles, too. Plans to market these small EVs may run into trouble in California, where the state's Air Resources Board is trying to encourage carmakers to produce family vehicles. According to Jerry Martin, the air board's director of communications, "The fear is that the market will be flooded by vehicles with low range that aren't freeway capable. Then the car companies can say, 'See, there's no market for EVs.'"

Ford's ultrasleek Prodigy hybrid was the company's entry in the federal Partnership for a New Generation of Vehicles program, which aims to produce an 80-miles-per-gallon car. It isn't likely to become a production car. The Prodigy, a direct-injection diesel, isn't quite there—it gets 70 miles per gallon—but it would provide an excellent platform for the kind of high-volume, no-compromises fuel-cell production car Bill Ford talks about. The sleek Prodigy shape is both very lightweight and aerodynamic. It uses rearview cameras instead of mirrors, a detail that very likely would *not* go into production.

A lightweight Ford P2000 is the most credible fuel-cell car I've driven, on a test track in Dearborn. While not quite as high-tech as the Prodigy, the P2000 felt like a real automobile. As I tested it, the car, running on hydrogen gas, delivered the equivalent of 100 horsepower and a range of 100 miles. Ford is a close partner with Ballard Power Systems, the world's leading fuel-cell manufacturer, and a Ballard cell was installed in both the P2000 and Th!NK FC5, the next generation of Ford fuel-cell car.

The FC5, which is powered by methanol and based on a four-door Focus sedan, has a single, very compact fuel-cell stack. All of its components, including the latest Ballard fuel-cell stack, fit under the floor. John Wallace, the executive director of the TH!NK Group, told me that the FC5 is "awfully similar" to the car that the company will actually put into limited production in 2004. "I think consumers will find it very acceptable," he said, adding that research on direct-hydrogen power is continuing. As with nearly all fuel-cell-car programs, no price is yet available—whatever it is, Ford will be sure to lose money on its early vehicles.

In 2000, Ford made headlines more for its truth telling than for its engineering feats. In a book prepared for its annual meeting,

Connecting with Society, Ford admitted that SUVs burn more gas and produce more emissions than other vehicles, and can impact heavily on smaller cars in crashes. "[S]ustainability concerns associated with SUVs raise issues relative to Ford's corporate citizenship commitment," the document noted candidly. "SUV owners who use their vehicles for off-road recreation can damage the nature they and others seek to enjoy." The company, whose gas-guzzling Ford Expeditions and Excursions helped it make $7.2 billion in 1999, admitted that its products "are not industry leaders in fuel economy." It was certainly all true, but not the kind of thing automakers ordinarily acknowledge. Spin control started almost immediately. "It was a modest attempt to start a dialogue, but it triggered an avalanche," said Ford spokesman Jason Vines in a letter to journalists.[31] "The uproar created some confusion about the company's position on SUVs. Ford was portrayed as either 'attacking' its own vehicles or 'admitting' they are bad. It did neither." But, of course, in a very real way, it had done both, and the company deserves to be commended for it. "We take our social responsibility seriously," said Bill Ford after the annual meeting.

I asked Ford during our interview if he believed that the hydrogen-based energy economy would come about in our lifetimes. "I don't have any reason to disbelieve it," he told me, "but I can't control the infrastructure. If we were to go to a 100 percent hydrogen economy, I like our chances of being well positioned to serve that economy."

HONDA: A CLEAN AGENDA

In 1999, Honda's U.S. fleet was the cleanest on the market for both global-warming gas and smog-forming emissions, according to the Union of Concerned Scientists report "Pollution Lineup: An Environmental Ranking of Automakers."[32] Its cars also had the best overall fuel economy at 31.8 miles per gallon. Honda was the first automaker to sell a hybrid gas-electric car in the United States, and the first to turn a significant portion of its cars and trucks into low-emission vehicles, or LEVs, a standard 57 percent more stringent than the then-current national requirements.

Honda's Insight is a great achievement, with an EPA rating of 70 miles per gallon and a 700-mile cruising range. It's one of the world's lightest cars, with an all-aluminum body and chassis. Its sleek, CRX-like body has an extremely aerodynamic shape, achieving a world-class .25 coefficient of drag. And it employs a super-thin 2.3-inch electric motor to help the ultracompact three-cylinder, one-liter engine power up hills. When I first drove one, on a long cruise around the picturesque Maryland countryside, I was most impressed by the Insight's gas-saving idle-stop ploy of shutting down completely when stopped at traffic lights. On manual-transmission versions of the car, a restart in a tenth of a second occurs as soon as the driver's foot hits the clutch.

Insight owners are fanatical about their cars. U.S. Senator Bob Bennett of Utah owns one, and so do many environmental leaders. John Wayland, a California-based electric drag-racing guru, souped his up. Though as a two-seater the Insight may never become a mass-market car, Honda adopted its Integrated Motor Assist hybrid technology to the very popular Civic and first offered the car on the Japanese market in 2001. That car will go worldwide, bought by people who are only dimly aware of what's under its hood. Honda's entire range of four-cylinder cars will have super ultra-low emission vehicle (SULEV) status by 2005.

Honda is a member of the California Fuel Cell Partnership and has tested cars with both methanol power and metal hydride storage. It builds its own fuel cells but also works with Ballard. I briefly drove a whirring and hissing fuel-cell Honda, the Ballard-powered FCX-V1, during a whirlwind visit to the company test center in Motegi, Japan, in 1999. It was not particularly impressive, but the ride was for only a few hundred yards. Since then, Honda has unveiled FCX-V3, a more accomplished vehicle with 22 percent more power and a quicker startup than its predecessor. Honda's fuel-cell cars have also acquired a new, more aerodynamic body that may reflect the look of the fuel-cell car Honda plans to market in 2003.

Motegi is a large campus, and employees get around using the Intelligent Community Vehicle System (ICVS). The ultrasmall one- and two-passenger transporters, with both electric and hybrid-electric drive, look weird at first, but one soon adapts to their undeniable logic. Employees "rent" the vehicles using cards that double as ignition keys. I took a spin in a one-seater Step Deck hybrid. It was great fun and practical, too. The electronic smart-card part of ICVS was adapted to a program undertaken by Honda in 1999 at the University of California, Riverside. Some two hundred students share fifteen Honda EV Plus electric cars. Similar to fast-access rental programs in Europe, students enter information about their planned trip in a kiosk that doubles as a charging station and are issued a vehicle.

Honda is deeply involved with intelligent vehicle technology, including automated highway demonstrations in 1997 and its own versions of adaptive cruise control, collision avoidance, and lane retention. If any company is going to build the hands-free, emissions-free, fuel-cell car that can fold into a suitcase like George Jetson's space car, it's Honda.

The hydrogen energy economy is not around the corner, and it won't have any immediate effect on our highway pollution problems. We can expect to endure quite a bit more heartache and trade a lot more blood for oil before that transition is made. But the fuel-cell partnership's efforts now under way in California and the fast-moving work in such car capitals as Tokyo, Detroit, and Stuttgart are a good start. There is every indication that the experimental programs will grow into actual limited production of fuel-cell cars by 2004 or 2005. The use of fuel cells for decentralized home power generation is also proceeding, and fuel-cell appliances are already entering the market.

Technology *does* make a difference, and hydrogen power will have profound clean-air benefits. But it won't fundamentally change the automobile or our dependence on it for primary transportation. Surprisingly, the transit mode that has the best chance of doing just that is the one most often overlooked: the humble but popular bus. And while the transit bus, with its clouds of diesel smoke, is for many a symbol of the polluting past, there is very real promise not only for a cleaner bus but for a bus traveling in its own exclusive high-speed corridor.

7

GREENING THE BUS: NEXT STOP, SUSTAINABILITY

EVERY WEEKDAY MORNING, I let go of my seven-year-old daughter's hand and watch as she boards a bright yellow school bus for what is, in effect, her morning commute. I wave, she waves, and soon there is nothing there but the smell of diesel exhaust in the air. My daughter's diesel school bus is not appreciably different from the one I rode in myself in the 1960s. Or much cleaner.

Like coal-burning power plants, diesel-powered buses and trucks are a seemingly immutable part of our national landscape. Trucks, having triumphed over the freight train, carry the nation's goods on highways big and small. Transit buses are, if not America's favorite form of mass transit, at least the one it relies on most to get to work.

Diesel engines, developed in 1892 by Rudolf Diesel as a more efficient competitor to the steam engine, work by compressing fuel in a cylinder with air that is hot enough to ignite it. Instead of gasoline, diesels burn the equivalent of home fuel oil. "The oil base of the diesel fuel makes the fuel heavier, oilier, and full of more dangerous contaminants than gasoline," write Angie Farleigh and Leah Kaplan in "Dangers of Diesel," a report by the U.S. Public Interest Research Group.[1]

Unfortunately, diesel's very familiarity helps put a friendly face on a decidedly toxic technology. According to "Rolling Smokestacks: Cleaning Up America's Trucks and Buses," a Union of Concerned Scientists report by Jason Mark and Candace Morey, the average 2000 model transit bus spews out the equivalent soot emissions of 279 cars, and creates as much smog as 50 cars.[2] The big problem with diesel engines is their production of tiny particles, variously known as soot, particulate matter, or simply particulates, that collect in the eyes and nose and worsen respiratory problems, especially in children, the elderly, asthmatics, and people with heart or lung disease.

Diesel-powered buses and "big-rig" trucks make up only 2 percent of vehicles on the road, according to that report, but are responsible for a quarter of all smog-causing pollution, half of all highway-generated soot, the majority of cancer-causing air pollution in some cities, 6 percent of U.S. global-warming pollution, and a tenth of American oil consumption. A British study commissioned by the Department of the Environment estimated that the actual external cost of a single heavy-duty diesel vehicle (in terms of public health, noise, and wear and tear on the roads) could reach £28,000 a year ($43,000).[3]

Federal regulation of diesel exhaust has been consistent in its weakness. As the Natural Resources Defense Council described it in a report entitled "Exhausted by Diesel," the Environmental Protection Agency created the Clean Fuel Fleet program as part of the 1990 Clean Air Act amendments. Setting exhaust standards for both private and public diesel fleets in twenty-two metropolitan areas with poor air quality, the Clean Fuel Fleet program was a milestone in effective federal legislation. "Since 1993, though, the EPA has been backpedaling on this program, each year further weakening its provisions," said the council report. "This weakening of the standard to further continued diesel use runs counter to the basic premise of the entire clean fuel program—to push the market toward clean fuel technologies." In addition to pulling the teeth of its own requirements, the EPA also allowed the regions covered by the program to escape the regulations if they could demonstrate that they were reducing emissions elsewhere. Sixteen of the twenty-two regions promptly took the escape hatch. Los Angeles and Houston may have the dirtiest air in the United States, but they met the weakened requirements and are no longer in the Clean Fuel Fleet program.

In the spring of 2000 the EPA did crack down on dirty diesels with proposed emissions standards for heavy-duty vehicles. The big-rig standards cut smog-forming pollution by 95 percent and soot pollution by 90 percent. Diesel's high sulfur content, which leads to higher levels of particulate matter and hampers efforts to clean up exhaust, was reduced by 97 percent in the proposed regulations, which were left in place by the incoming Bush Administration.

So what is the effect of all the diesel exhaust we breathe in as part of our daily routines? An analysis done jointly by the State and Territorial Air Pollution Program Administrators and the Local Air Pollution Control Officials concluded that more than 125,000 Americans—mostly in urban areas—may get cancer just from inhaling diesel fumes.[4]

The EPA says that its proposed tightening of diesel standards could, by 2030, reduce particulate emissions by 110,000 tons per year. If its heavy-duty rules go into effect, it said, there would be dramatic public health benefits: every year, more than 4,000 premature deaths, 3,000 hospital admissions, 6,300 respiratory emergency room visits, 5.6 million restricted-activity days, and 650,000 work-loss days would be avoided. Just the regained work time alone would save $67 million a year.

The trucking industry, which operates on thin profit margins, is vigorously opposed to tighter restrictions on engines and fuels. The fight over federal standards is likely to be protracted, and even under ideal circumstances the new rules would not begin to take effect until 2007.

Some observers doubt that the diesel industry will abide by the rules even if they are put in place. In 1998, the EPA and the Justice Department reached a $1 billion settlement with seven diesel engine makers that, the government charged, had intentionally installed "defeat devices" on more than a million diesel vehicles. The devices worked by altering the trucks' fuel-injection systems to produce more emissions on the open road than during stationary testing. Trucks so equipped got better fuel economy but also produced a cloud of "real world" emissions that didn't show up on diagnostic equipment. The diesel makers, representing about 95 percent of the industry, admitted no wrongdoing but paid the largest civil penalty ever imposed for violation of an environmental law.[5]

Further, some environmental groups, including the Washington, D.C.–based Clean Air Trust, have charged that diesel makers have dragged their feet on some provisions of the consent agreement, especially a condition that would have them develop emissions-testing procedures that mimic real driving conditions.[6] The EPA has not rigorously enforced its ruling, which would have seen emissions benefits as early as 2002.

Because federal action is so slow and uncertain, thirteen states joined together in late 2000 to impose joint diesel standards of their own. California has led the way with the country's strictest emission laws for buses; its regulations, to be phased in over ten years, beginning in 2002, will affect 8,500 buses operated by seventy-five transit agencies. A drastic cut in diesel sulfur content will be followed, in 2004, by a 75 percent emissions cut for trucks and buses. Joining California in regulating diesel tailpipes are Nevada, Texas, Georgia, North Carolina, New York, Massachusetts, Connecticut, New Hampshire, Maine, Vermont, Rhode Island, and New Jersey.[7] Not surprisingly, environmentalists applauded the states' initiative, which could increase costs for each truck or bus by $700 to $800. "For over a decade, Americans have breathed unnecessarily high levels of toxic diesel pollution, thanks to the diesel makers' refusal to clean up their products," said Richard Kassell, a senior attorney at the Natural Resources Defense Council. He added that the states' action means that "loopholes that would allow this situation to continue will soon be closed."[8]

TAKING THE BUS

So diesel is dirty. It's also pervasive as a people and freight mover in America. In fact, as a mass-transit option, buses (more than 92 percent of which are diesel-powered) are the overwhelming choice of most Americans. That's true mainly because they are less expensive to ride and offer far more comprehensive routes and schedules than light rail or other more glamorous options. Buses have a built-in cost advantage because they use the existing public streets rather than an expensive dedicated track. For transit officials, adding a new bus route involves creating unobtrusive stops (often nothing more than a small traffic sign), hiring a driver, and assigning a bus. The comparable addition of a light-rail route is a nightmare of logistics, encompassing public hearings, lawsuits, and hundreds of millions of dollars in land acquisition.

In 1998, according to statistics provided by the American Public Transportation Association (APTA), U.S. transit riders made 8.7 billion trips. A staggering 62 percent of those trips were made on transit buses, compared with just 4 percent on commuter rail and 3 percent on modern transit's technology of choice, light rail. Add trolleys, van pools, ferryboats, and "demand-response" rides together, and they account for less than 4 percent of transit trips. Here's an even more dramatic way of looking at the numbers: buses make more than 18 million trips on the average workday; van pools (once considered the best way to reduce corporate auto dependence) make just 43,000.

The situation today is a dramatic reversal from the early days of motoring, when early, unreliable buses were mired on muddy roads as electric transit rode smoothly on steel rails. The triumph of the transit bus over the streetcar and the nation-spanning "interurban" rail lines makes an interesting story. As related in Stephen Goddard's *Getting There,* the trolleys, without significant competition, were in robust good health in the early 1920s. But the rigidly regulated firms, with fixed fares and routes, were in no position to compete when an emerging public zeal for subsidized road-building opened the door to trucks and buses. Automotive magazine ads of the period actually focused on ruining the streetcar's image. A Willys-Overland promotion, showing a sad family boarding a down-at-the-heels, crowded trolley, claimed that subjecting loved ones to such an indignity was "not fair to your children, your wife or yourself."[9]

The four Fitzgerald brothers of Minnesota, who started out hauling miners to the Mesabi Range in a pair of rickety buses, were typical of the self-taught entrepreneurs who spotted a transportation opportunity. By 1925, through a seat-of-the-pants business that saw them converting old Packard limousines to fifteen-passenger buses, they had a fledgling network of routes. Their timing was excellent, because governments across the country were pouring money into paved highways that connected once-isolated villages and towns.

The Fitzgeralds expanded their business rapidly and soon found themselves in an alliance with none other than General Motors, which was having trouble selling buses because of the ubiquity of urban trolley systems. Together with GM, Standard Oil, and Firestone Tire and Rubber Company, the Fitzgeralds were party to the takeover—and dismantlement—of more than one hundred electric trolley systems between 1936 and 1947. Where the trolleys died, bus systems immediately took their place. "Motorization" it was called, and the public applauded. The rapid-fire acquisitions could not have occurred if the trolley systems were not already ailing. "Although these companies may have speeded the decline of trolley systems, the same result would have occurred regardless of the validity of the conspiracy argument," writes transportation analyst Deborah Gordon in her book *Steering a New Course.* "Transit-system managers wanted buses because they were less expensive to purchase and operate."[10] The relative positions of those modes of travel shifted rather rapidly. It took until World War II for bus ridership to equal that of streetcars, but by the mid-1950s buses had six times more riders. By then, however, both buses *and* streetcars were quickly losing riders to the private car.

Buses today don't get a lot of respect: "loser cruiser" is just one of the unfortunate tags that sticks to the municipal and intercity bus like a scarlet badge of shame. Not only are bus passengers generally poorer than commuter-rail passengers but bus services are also treated like poor stepchildren. APTA estimates that low-income riders (those with a household income below $15,000) make up 28 percent of all transit riders (twice the percentage of Americans living in poverty); the number zooms to 38 percent if you exclude New York City, where transit is used by all income levels.

Of necessity, the poor embrace municipal bus systems. In Chicago, for instance, only 18 percent of the city's poor have access to cars, according to the National Center for Neighborhood Enterprise. But the systems don't embrace them back. Buses are, for the most part, overcrowded, poorly maintained, and underfunded. A 1996 study by the Greater Richmond Chamber of Commerce in Virginia noted bluntly that race plays a part in city transit bus planning. "As a result of over four decades of public policy decisions at all levels of government," the report said, "transit is too often viewed and judged as an inefficient social welfare program designed to accommodate the needs of the urban underclass. In most Metro Richmond jurisdictions, transit is thought to be a political liability."[11] Richmond resident Barbara Johnson, who rides the bus to two jobs daily, had just two words to sum up city transit service. "It stinks," she said.

Her words would undoubtedly have resonance in Los Angeles, where crowded highways are just one factor in the deteriorating service. In 1991, an afternoon bus ride from Santa Monica to Los Angeles took thirty-nine minutes. In 2000, congestion meant that the same ride took exactly double that, seventy-eight minutes.[12] Environmental Defense reports that the poorest fifth of urban residents in southern California receive only 4 percent of the area's transportation benefits. Citing 1993 figures, the group added that Los Angeles's Metropolitan Transportation Authority (MTA) spent forty-three times more on per-passenger security for its rail lines ($1.29) as for its bus passengers (3 cents). Overcrowding of 140 percent is typical for MTA bus lines, but such tight conditions are unknown on the city's light rail.

For poor and minority urban dwellers who are also disabled or elderly, bus systems can be especially difficult. A comprehensive study conducted in Houston by Dr. John I. Gilderbloom found that three out of five disabled and elderly residents did not have sidewalks between their homes and the nearest bus stop. An even higher number, 76 percent, lacked bus shelters, making the system all but unusable. Dr. Gilderbloom concluded that even though 50 percent of the people interviewed lived within two blocks of a bus stop, fewer than 10 percent were able to actually ride on the buses.[13]

In an emerging trend, bus passengers are fighting back at what they perceive as transportation discrimination. The landmark 1996 *Labor/Community Strategy Center, et al. v. Los Angeles County Metropolitan Transportation Authority* case, which alleged that city bus passengers are second-class citizens, was settled with a $1 billion consent decree that should equalize conditions for all mass-transit riders in the region.

In the South, where bus discrimination became a rallying cry for the civil-rights movement in the 1960s, unequal treatment continues. In Montgomery, Alabama, for instance, where in 1955 Rosa Parks refused to give up her bus seat, the struggle today is to even keep the bus lines open—in 1998, 50 percent service cuts were paired with 50 percent price increases.

The population of Macon, Georgia, is evenly divided between blacks and whites, but 90 percent of the city's bus riders are black, and some of them joined in a 1994 class-action lawsuit charging transit discrimination in the region's use of federal money. In 1993, according to Mercer University law professor David Oedel, the two counties in the metropolitan area spent more than $33 million on road construction and only $1.4 million on public transportation. Some 28 percent of Macon's black population is carless, but only 6 percent of the white population is.[14] "It is well known locally that while the white population generally travels in private vehicles, fixed-route buses are generally reserved for African-American residents," says the civil-rights complaint.

Minority communities are also fighting back against a form of environmental racism: the siting of polluting transit depots in their communities. In Seattle, a federal lawsuit seeks to stop the city's $3.5 billion light-rail system because the proposed layout would impose "disproportionately high and adverse environmental and safety harms and housing burdens on the low-income and minority residents of the Rainier Valley." And in New York City, West Harlem Environmental Action filed a federal complaint in late 2000 with the Department of Transportation, citing the city's location of most of its diesel bus facilities in minority neighborhoods. The complaint was undoubtedly the first citing transit-facility discrimination filed under Title VI of the Civil Rights Act.

The director of the Harlem group, Peggy Shepard, said that six of Manhattan's eight bus depots are located in communities of color on the northern end of the island. The buses, she said, are "idling on our curbs, idling outside our schools, idling outside our public swimming pools." She added that she wants the city's Metropolitan Transportation Authority to increase air-quality monitoring and to replace diesel buses with those fueled by natural gas.[15]

Intercity buses, once seen as a way to "leave the driving to us," have declined in both routes and service since the industry was partially deregulated in 1982. Deborah Gordon has noted that the carriers that once linked urban and rural America "have dropped many routes that they considered unprofitable. While all carriers are undertaking cost-cutting measures to improve their competitive positions, their actions have not been enough to reverse the trend of decreasing profits. As a result, much of rural America, already without train service, is being cut off as it loses bus service."[16]

Trailways, for one, went through bankruptcy after deregulation left it in an unfavorable competitive position with its chief rival, Greyhound. As Trailways puts it in the official company history, "For an organization that was not only driven by competing equally with Greyhound, Trailways also had to face other harsh industry realities, such as the decline of intercity bus travel and the increased competition from other modes of travel."

A few years ago, I got a chance to experience the "modern" intercity bus from the passenger seat. My wife and I traveled from Washington, D.C., to Raleigh, North Carolina, by motor coach and found it a horrifying experience. Washington's bus terminal was filled with a mass of confused, milling passengers, many of whom were waiting for scheduled buses that simply hadn't shown up. Despite the fact that we had purchased tickets well ahead of time, "our" bus had loaded up with the first passengers to arrive and had taken off. The line's standard procedure with stranded travelers was simply to wait for a sufficient number to accumulate, then draft another overworked driver into service. Ours proved to be both cheerful and talkative when we finally left, two hours behind schedule. After getting lost somewhere in rural Virginia—and asking passengers for help with directions—he confided that he had come straight from another overnight run and hadn't slept for twenty-four hours.

I don't think this was an isolated bad experience: intercity bus travel is one of the many forms of transit to be neglected during the rule of the car. Traveling by bus, once a respectable option for middle-class Americans, has become the mode of last resort.

A CLEANER ROUTE

Can the humble transit bus go through a makeover and emerge as a crown jewel of the nation's public transportation fleet? The raw statistics certainly don't indicate that any such transformation is under way. In 1999, according to APTA, there were 47,745 diesel buses operated by the top three hundred transit agencies in the United States. Contrast that with a relatively paltry 2,495 buses operating on compressed natural gas and a mere 41 that were either battery electric or hybrid-powered, with both an electric motor and a gasoline engine.

But such business-as-usual data hides the dramatic experimentation going on at the edges of American transit. While they've yet to have any real impact in the big transit districts, there actually are a growing number of electric and electric-hybrid buses plying the public roads from Santa Barbara to Miami Beach. According to the Electric Transit Vehicle Institute (ETVI), battery electric buses reduce pollution by more than 98 percent over exhaust-heavy diesels. The savings from hybrid buses—many of which have small diesel engines—are more ambiguous, but ETVI says that the Orion diesel hybrid buses operating in New York City "are as clean, if not cleaner, than similar buses operating on compressed natural gas."[17] Even cleaner are the dozen electric transit buses powered by hydrogen fuel cells. In demonstration projects in Chicago; Vancouver, B.C.; Washington, D.C; and other cities, fuel-cell buses carrying tanks of hydrogen gas have proven not only very reliable but also nonpolluting—that is, their emissions level is zero.

The clean transit-bus movement got under way in 1991 when the California city of Santa Barbara began operating a pair of twenty-two-foot open-air electric trolley buses. Not only were the buses quiet and emission-free but they also proved a public relations bonanza for Santa Barbara, prompting other cities to follow its lead.

One of the cities that sent representatives to Santa Barbara to see the electric trolleys in action was Chattanooga, Tennessee, which in 1991 was in the process of transforming itself along sustainable lines as part of a process called Vision 2000. Downtown Chattanooga was then a gridlocked mess, with overloaded parking lots and three jammed through streets. Despite the fact that 65 percent of the downtown land area was dedicated to cars, traffic inched along. Shoppers avoided the area, hurting business revitalization.

The Chattanooga Area Regional Transportation Authority (CARTA) developed plans for what it called a downtown circulator, a public transit loop that could service satellite parking lots and keep traffic out of the downtown grid. The shuttle was envisioned as a free service from the beginning.

The Santa Barbara experience convinced CARTA that the shuttle buses should be battery-powered electrics. The long, flat floor of the transit bus makes a perfect platform for batteries, and the short downtown loop posed no problem to the buses' limited range. What's more, the buses could be quickly recharged and maintained in a central CARTA-operated garage.

Chattanooga officials couldn't find the buses they wanted on the open market, so Joe Ferguson, who had been a consultant on the shuttle project, decided to make them himself, in Chattanooga. He created Advanced Vehicle Systems (AVS) specifically to build buses for the shuttle, and for outside customers, too.

With state and federal funds, CARTA launched the $19.6 million project in 1992. The shuttle was begun with the purchase of sixteen electric buses to serve three interceptor parking garages built for that purpose (which also provided revenue to keep the shuttle self-sustaining). Chattanooga was soon operating not only the country's largest electric bus fleet but also the busiest electric-vehicle battery-charging station in the United States.

The shuttle is a popular tourist attraction in Chattanooga now, but it's also the primary transportation for people who work downtown. I rode the shuttle myself on a visit to Chattanooga and was impressed not only by how quiet it was but also by the fact that, on a weekday afternoon, it was packed with passengers. Despite the opening of some major tourist magnets, like the Tennessee Aquarium and the riverfront entertainment district, traffic downtown has eased considerably. Complementing the shuttle is the Walnut Street Bridge, which once funneled traffic into the city; now it's for nonmotorized travelers only and brings in cyclists and pedestrians.[18]

The concept of the electric shuttle has spread far and wide. At last count, Miami Beach operated seven AVS buses; Norfolk, Virginia had eight; and Bremerton, Washington, four. The transition to electric power has not been without bumps in the road, however. Paul Griffith, president of the Santa Barbara Electric Transportation Institute, cautions that transit agencies whose usual modus operandi is buying big batches of diesel buses from large manufacturers may experience a rude awakening when dealing with tiny enterprises that essentially build to order. In some cases, he said, "bus operators have presumed that they will receive a 'turn key' product that will perform with the same reliability as the diesel bus."[19] Instead, Griffith added, agencies should expect something akin to a "prototype" that will need a certain shakedown period. In his experience, electric buses are a "rolling energy crisis" whose most common breakdown is related to battery failure.

Electric-hybrid buses are also entering transportation fleets. Chattanooga, for instance, was operating three in 2000 and had more on order. The hybrids offer greatly extended range, a major advantage for cities where short loops are not practical.

While the transit bus is making some startling progress, the diesel-fueled school bus has lagged behind. Part of the problem for most school boards is a lack of funds to buy new vehicles. In California, for instance, 9 percent of the school buses in the state's 24,000-bus fleet were built before 1977, when the first antismog devices were installed. State and local legislation, backed by the new federal diesel rules, could make a big difference in cleaning up school-bus exhaust. California's Air Resources Board held hearings in late 2000 to determine how to spend $50 million reserved for new bus purchases. Although the diesel industry says that its latest engines run cleanly on low-sulfur fuel with particulate traps attached to their exhaust systems, many of those who testified spoke against any role for diesel in the state's fleet.[20]

In early 2001, the Natural Resources Defense Council caused a stir by releasing a study showing that fumes *inside* the four Los Angeles–area school buses it tested could be exposing children to a cancer risk forty-six times higher than the Environmental Protection Agency's "safe" standard. A San Francisco–based environmental group, As You Sow, sent notices to twelve bus manufacturers, dealers, and distributors in February 2001, proclaiming them to be in violation of Proposition 65, which regulates toxic emissions.

California's first natural gas school bus made its debut in 1991, promoted by the state's Air Resources Board. The Los Angeles school district now owns thirty-three natural gas buses and is testing six diesel buses with particulate traps. General Motors introduced a hybrid electric bus for school use in 2001 and has contributed $250,000 to the South Coast Air Quality Management District's Adopt-a-Bus program. The money will be used to retrofit existing buses with particulate traps. Making those changes fleetwide, in California and across the nation, will take some time. A single trap retrofit costs $7,500, and GM's new emissions-reducing hybrid buses are $50,000 each.[21]

GETTING OUT OF THE TRAFFIC STREAM

Cleaning up diesel exhaust is only part of the challenge, however. The Chattanooga experience is useful because the electric buses didn't simply banish the exhaust pipe; they also provided a way to reduce city traffic. The best of the new bus systems present novel ways to get these transit vehicles off the main thoroughfares, which not only eases gridlock but also leads to a much more satisfying bus experience.

Inspired by Curitiba, Brazil, which bans traffic downtown and puts its buses on dedicated guideways or busways that shun all other vehicles, a host of North American cities are following suit. Busways offer the speed and gridlock-free commuting of light rail without the crippling per-mile construction costs or expensive equipment. Buses on dedicated routes can regularly travel at thirty-five miles per hour, with both local and express service. Though the rolling stock is in every way a transit bus, it behaves much more like a light-rail car in its swift progress and adherence to a schedule.

One of the best systems that's up and running is in Ottawa, Canada, perhaps not coincidentally also a center of car-free activism. Robert Cervero's book *The Transit Metropolis* reports that Ottawa's bus-only guideway carries 200,000 passengers daily, producing the spectacular result that three-fourths of all peak-hour trips into downtown are by transit.

Ottawa has long gone against the tide. As Cervero points out, the city "opted for a busway at a time when every other medium-size North American metropolis investing in new transit systems selected the eminently more popular light rail transit technology."[22] Ottawa can also boast of a greenbelt like the one that protects Portland, Oregon, from runaway sprawl, but Ottawa's development-free zone was put in place in 1959.

Called the Transitway, Ottawa's system of dedicated bus routes was adapted in 1974 as part of a far-reaching and well-thought-out development plan. Ottawa's regional council envisioned reducing traffic and car dependence by locating 40 percent of regional jobs within walking distance of the bus line. The plan is working. By 1996, 32 percent of all jobs could be reached on foot from a bus station.

The Transitway is spectacularly successful, even when compared with higher-profile light-rail systems like Vancouver's SkyTrain. It averages more riders per capita than any other transit system of its size in North America, even though it was 30 percent cheaper to build and is 20 percent cheaper to operate than a light-rail system.[23]

Transitway covers four times as many passenger miles as the similar busway in Pittsburgh does. But busway development in the United States is just getting started. In 1999, according to APTA, there were 1,269 miles of fixed bus guideways in the United States and 131 miles under construction.

Detroit, which was briefly in the vanguard of American mass transit with an ultimately ill-fated monorail system, may be the next U.S. city to see a dedicated busway. The city's Metropolitan Affairs Coalition has teamed up with Detroit Renaissance, the Greater Downtown Partnership, and the Detroit Regional Chamber to envision a three-tiered system that would include SpeedLink, a "train on tires." As on other busways, traffic would be speeded up with pre-boarding fare collection, fast loading and unloading from sheltered stations, and color-coded routes.

Detroit's busway would be complemented by InterLink, a traditional bus system for longer trips, and HomeLink, a neighborhood-based "paratransit" network consisting of small vehicles that can be dispatched by telephone for trips to stores, schools, and medical facilities.[24]

A variation on the fixed-guideway bus system is the "signal-priority" technology used by Los Angeles's Metro Rapid, which began limited service in June 2000. Signal priority is a high-tech approach to speeding up a slow-moving transit bus. Antenna loops are buried in the pavement to communicate with transmitters mounted in the bus. When a bus approaches a traffic signal, it triggers the light to remain green for an additional ten seconds. To prevent bunching up, buses arriving ahead of their scheduled time get no assistance from the signals.

An added benefit of the low-floor buses used by Metro Rapid is that they are fueled by compressed natural gas. In the first few months of operation (until service was interrupted by the city's transit strike in September 2000), the system averaged 100,000 passengers a day on two routes, Whittier–Wilshire Boulevard and Ventura Boulevard. As noted earlier, L.A.'s gridlocked streets have doubled travel time on some bus routes, but Metro Rapid has lived up to its name by cutting elapsed times by 25 percent.[25] The signal-priority system may be implemented on an additional twenty bus lines, and an expansion to dedicated busways is being considered.

Chicago, the first American city to put a fuel-cell bus into regular service, is trying to get its buses moving with six express routes that will be part of the existing street grid. Most of the elements of the Los Angeles plan are included: low-floor clean-fuel buses, signal priority, preboarding fare collection, and stop improvements. Busways are under investigation.

One of my personal favorite approaches to updating the transit bus is Civis, an ultra-high-technology electric bus designed by the French company Matra Transport International. Civis was adapted by the city of Las Vegas, which received $4.5 million in federal funds to run the buses in a pilot project announced in 2000.[26] Although it runs on rubber tires, Civis closely resembles a light-rail car and features huge wraparound windows. A highlight is its optical guidance system, in which a camera mounted behind the windshield reads coded marks on the dedicated roadway. The system is very accurate, allowing the bus to follow a route with only a fraction of an inch of course deviation. Civis is relatively slow, operating at eighteen miles per hour on a two-mile route in North Las Vegas, but it's designed with only a three-minute gap between vehicles.

ONE BUS AT A TIME

Making bus transit work involves more than improving the technology and cleaning up the exhaust. The driver is a vital link in the chain. In some cities, such as Portland, Oregon, "reimagining" bus service includes new rules for drivers regarding elements of common courtesy: helping with directions, saying "good morning," assisting with change. No such rules are necessary for Rod Parlee, a

Connecticut bus driver who's that way naturally and has a raft of dedicated passengers to show for it.

Parlee, a trim fellow in his mid-forties with sandy-colored hair and a mustache, doesn't look like a radical, but that's what he is. Driving a bus between Manchester and Hartford, the state capital, isn't just a job for him; it's a mission. He's been plying the route for more than fifteen years but doesn't get bored because, at every stop, new passengers get on. Parlee talks to them: about energy conservation, global warming, sustainable transportation. If they're lucky, they'll get a free copy of Parlee's environmental newsletter, *Tundra Talk,* written by his family and friends. If they throw away a fast-food wrapper, what they'll get is a lecture.

I boarded Parlee's bus in Manchester just before the first passenger of the day climbed on board. He was one of Parlee's regulars, Joseph Gately. Joe is chairman of Bolton's Republican Town Committee but is not, as you might expect, Parlee's foil on environmental issues. They actually agree on most things, especially public transportation. Gately has a car but doesn't see why he should drive it through the congestion to Hartford when he can get a bus passenger's senior citizen discount. The bus, said Gately, "is always on time. We're big supporters on the Republican Town Committee."

Another regular, Kellie Dietz, got on. Like many capital commuters, she works at a Hartford insurance company. "I own a car, but the bus is more economical and more convenient," she said. "And it's partially subsidized by Travelers, so instead of paying forty-four dollars a month I pay twenty-two."

The third regular, Gary Vanassel, walked on wearing shorts and a Hartford Steam Boiler cap. The company does not make steam, he explained, but instead insures steam boilers. It's one of Hartford's oldest businesses, dating back to 1883. "Riding the bus, there's something new every day," he said. "Rod's a toastmaster. When he's not driving, it's just a ride to work."

The bus wound its way through East Hartford, a rather gray town lined with auto dealerships. Parlee explained that he's trying to raise money to connect Bolton's bicycle path with the existing trail through East Hartford and Manchester. He started talking to the passengers, as a group, about the need to get environmentally involved and protect "our right to breathe clean air and drink clean water." He added, "Right now, the corporations are abusing that right, using loopholes in the law to get around environmental laws. Energy conservation is important, too. There are lots of other things you can do besides ride the bus. Support the candidates who share your views about conservation."

"One of these days he's going to stop this bus and give us a test," Vanassel said. We crossed the Connecticut River into Hartford, and Parlee pointed out the peregrine falcon nest on the roof of the Travelers tower. The falcons are stars of their own Webcam movies, he said. Most of the passengers got off in Hartford's busy and slowly gentrifying downtown, and a small knot of reverse commuters took their place.

"How did the Red Sox do?" asked a young black man in shades, a Yankees cap, and a Hoop It Up Tour 2000 T-shirt. Parlee told him. "If you're not a Celtics or Red Sox fan, Rod doesn't want to know you," said the young man, noticing my notebook. He asked to be called "Bob," though that was not his name.

Bob, who is studying computers at Goodwin College in East Hartford, was carrying a much-underlined copy of *A Guide to Windows NT.* He went back and forth between looking at the book and making wisecracks about Parlee, whom he obviously holds in high esteem. "This guy here," he said, "pushed an old lady out of the bus because she was short a nickel. Then he ran over her bag. See that number on his uniform, No. 914? That doesn't really exist." There was mention of "the underwear incident," and all the regulars nodded. "I feel like I'm getting roasted here," said Parlee.

The bus knelt down to help an elderly passenger at the curb. Parlee pointed out the fully functional wheelchair seat behind wisecracking Bob, who got off with a wave. Parlee told a long story about a town selectman somewhere who got the boot because he was too cozy with developers, and before I knew it, we were back in Manchester.

Parlee would do the route three more times that day, then take off on a canoe trip. In 2007, he'll retire and become a full-time environmental activist, maybe even a writer. He certainly has stories to tell.

I started this chapter with a description of my daughter's morning ride on a diesel-powered school bus. She may not have to ride that bus much longer. We live only about half a mile from her elementary school, and that makes us prime candidates for a Walking School Bus, the charming proposition of British "street-reclaiming" advocate David Engwicht. The bus is a virtual one, "driven" by a walking adult whose job it is to get the kids in his wake safely across intersections. In one version, the adult pushes a gaily painted cart that not only helps motorists understand the concept but also stores school packs and weather gear. Since Engwicht first proposed the idea in 1992, it has been adopted internationally, most concretely in Canada (where there's government funding). The Walking School Bus can't take the place of every dirty diesel, but it's a gutsy grassroots response to an overdose of exhaust fumes.

I recently came across a photograph from the 1920s showing my street, now reserved for automobiles and very brave cyclists, with overhead electric lines and train tracks running down its center. It's hard to believe today, but back in the "good old days," my daughter could have ridden a train to school.

8

ON TRACK WITH
HIGH-SPEED TRAINS

I'M NOT AN OVERLY nostalgic person. I was at the Woodstock Music and Art Fair, but I've never seen the movie. I never listen to "golden oldie" stations, despite what I might have been doing when I first heard hits like "Green River" by Creedence Clearwater Revival. I don't watch Nick at Nite. But in the course of writing this book, I became seriously hooked on the idea of reviving the railroads.

It's hard to imagine the impact the railroads must have had on the world of the early nineteenth century, whose transportation modes were practically unchanged from those of Julius Caesar. Contemporary accounts from the German-language book *The History of Train Travel* show that most passengers were, at least initially, stupefied by fear, which they then sought to rationalize. A German-American passenger on a train from Albany to Schenectady in the 1840s remarked, "If anything draws our attention, the speed is so great that we cannot look at it. Conversation is impossible. We are in the company of other travelers who think of nothing but the end of the voyage." The philosopher John Ruskin remarked at about this time that "a balanced person, with a moderate power of feeling, cannot travel more than 10 to 12 miles per day. A trip becomes stupefying in direct proportion to its speed." The French novelist Gustave Flaubert was also a very nervous rail passenger. "After five minutes in a train, I begin to howl and other people think I'm a lost dog," he said.[1]

To conjure up a time in which trains mattered to just about everyone, I paid a visit, with my wife and children in tow, to the

Shore Line Trolley Museum in East Haven, Connecticut. The Shore
Line is one of no less than two railroad museums in Connecticut, so
curiosity about this form of transportation, which once moved a
nation, remains high.

The trolley museum is not a static display, which wouldn't have
interested my kids for more than two minutes. Instead, its central
attraction is an actual three-mile ride on the remaining track of the
Branford Electric Railway, the oldest suburban trolley line in continuous operation in the United States. It celebrated its one hundredth
birthday in 2000.

Shore Line's story is a typical one, really, but with a happier ending than most. The line started out small, connecting East Haven
with the beachfront community of Short Beach. It then expanded to
serve other beach towns, Stony Creek and Guilford. By changing trolleys four times, a traveler could reach New York City. But service
deteriorated and track disappeared as cars and roads began to dominate transportation in the 1920s. In 1947, with closure imminent,
the diminished line was purchased for its scrap value by the Branford
Electric Railway Association (BERA), a group of railroad buffs who
have operated it as a museum ever since.

Our conductor was Charles Dennis, a friendly older gentleman in
full uniform, with period-looking brass BERA badges. Dennis grew
up in Brooklyn, where as a youth he rode on the last American trolleys, in the PCC cars. "I first came to the museum as a volunteer, and
I really enjoy it," he said.

We boarded the trolley, which was beautifully restored with shin-
ing paint and polished wood. We sat down on uncomfortable but picturesque cane seats. Our fellow passengers included a Korean couple
with a demonstrative son, a tattooed young woman with cornrowed
hair who talked quietly with her daughter, a Moslem couple, and
Dick and Rachel Bauer, a father-and-daughter team from Boston.

We began moving. The air compressor for the brakes made a
pumpa, pumpa sound. BERA had done an excellent job of invoking the
trolley period: ads in the ceiling display space promoted Sloan's
Liniment ("for sciatica, rheumatism and sprains"); B. T. Babbitt's soap

powder, Chesterfield Filters, Arrow Shirts ("starched cuffs are proper and distinctly refined"), and the New York City police ("Robert F. Wagner, mayor").

We moved past an abandoned stone quarry, once served by a lively barge traffic, and through a protected wetland, complete with osprey nests. My girls, who were three and six at the time and indifferent to the history of it all, liked this part. Dennis demonstrated how, in the days before air-conditioning, passengers could keep cool: in summer, the cars rode with their glass side panels off. In winter, the electric heaters under the seats were turned on.

We arrived at the BERA car barns and the trip turned into a rail enthusiast's magical mystery tour. The giant sheds were full of train and trolley cars in various states of restoration, with all the work done by volunteer labor. One team was removing antigraffiti paint from a contemporary Lexington Avenue, New York, subway car. "Here is an old woody, built in 1904 by the Jewett Car Company," Dennis said. "It ran on this very line. And here's a car built in 1939 by the Third Avenue trolley line in New York City. The line built its own cars because it could not get funding from Mayor Fiorello La Guardia, who'd been convinced to get rid of the trolley lines in favor of smelly diesel buses." Dennis used the phrase "smelly diesel buses" several times. He wasn't afraid to let editorial commentary sneak into his monologue.

That same Third Avenue car was operated in both Manhattan and the Bronx before the lines were torn up. After that, it was sent to Vienna, Austria, as part of the Marshall Plan and served for thirteen years more. Any visitor to Europe soon discovers that trolleys are still a vital part of the transportation mix there.

We saw a Blue Car from Staten Island Rapid Transit, a service that went into swift eclipse after a huge fire in 1947. Another veteran, from Johnstown, Pennsylvania, was found by restorers to still contain mud from the famous flood of 1889. A parlor car provided instant nostalgia for the level of service on trains before World War II: it offered linen tablecloths, monogrammed china, and valet service. A sign of the times was a lightweight all-steel "single-truck" model from 1920, designed to save electricity in what were already becoming straitened times for the trolleys. "The problem was that they would derail easily," Dennis said. "After they were put in service in Brooklyn, kids learned that they could bounce up and down on the back until they jumped the tracks." It's easy to imagine the Dead End Kids doing this, because entertainment for poor children was limited in those days before television.

And, finally, we saw a rare PCC car. The old trolley warrior was dusty and battered, but the impressive streamlining shone through, and remnants of the beige-and-red livery remained. The history is rather sad. The President's Conference Committee (PCC), composed of leaders of large streetcar companies, got together in 1929 to try to save what was becoming a lost cause. Unaware that their moment in history was already over, they commissioned elaborate research on wheel trucks and springs to develop a trolley car that the modern train-riding public would accept. The result was the PCC car, five thousand of which were built from the mid-1930s to the early 1950s. The PCC cars represented a huge advance from the rattly iron-and-wood cars of the past, and in 2000 a few were still in service on the Mattapan-Ashmont line in Massachusetts. But it was too little, too late.

Back at the museum proper, I spoke briefly with its director, George Boucher, who was five years old in 1948, when the New Haven trolleys stopped. The museum's paid admissions have been declining in recent years, to between eighty and one hundred on typical summer days. "The younger generation doesn't remember," he said. "So basically it's an amusement ride for them." It certainly was that for my girls, who, alas, had gotten bored by this time and were back at the car.

I walked through a few rooms of exhibits. There was a tribute to Frank J. Sprague, "Connecticut's forgotten inventor," who died in obscurity in 1934. A friend of Thomas Edison's, Sprague reportedly staked his last dollar on installing an electric railway in Richmond, Virginia. His gamble worked. By 1889, his company had equipped

113 of the 200 electric street railways then in operation or under construction in the United States. But who remembered that in 1934, when the trolleys were dying?

I saw a fascinating and evocative photograph, showing revelers packed into an open-sided trolley car. "New Haven had the open cars longer, because they could accommodate the huge crowds for the Yale football games," read the caption. "There were no interstates, so the people came in on trains, and two or three would ride on the running boards. The cars could get so loaded they would sag in the middle." The photo showed a train carrying overflow from the Yale-Harvard game of November 22, 1947, the last Yale football game in which open cars were used.

Through the whole tour, I'd become aware that the Bauers, Rachel and Dick, were no ordinary passengers. Instead of oohing and aahing over the pretty trains, they were exchanging all manner of erudite train lore, historic and modern. We began talking. Dick Bauer, a fit-looking bicycle rider with a trimmed beard, is an attorney with Greater Boston Legal Services. Rachel Bauer, whose wild, frizzy hair belies a very serious demeanor, is a civil engineering major at Cornell.

It was Rachel Bauer who first told me that Robert Moses built his highways too narrow to allow rail lines in their centers, and Bauer again who recommended several of the books I used as reference. She is a dedicated student of the subway lines. Through a book she recommended, *722 Miles,* by Clifton Hood, I learned that New York City had the world's first street railway in 1832, built its first elevated line in 1868, and finished the first portion of its subway in 1904. Mass transit in New York now carries 6.5 million people every weekday, making New York the most transit-dependent city in America.[2]

We continued our conversation via e-mail. I sent a few questions to Rachel, who wants to make a career promoting mass transit and volunteers at a steam railway museum. Her answers were exceptionally well thought out and inspire optimism about a new generation of dedicated transit enthusiasts.

What fueled your early interest in mass transit?

My family's car has generally sat in the driveway except for long trips, grocery shopping, or carpooling. I went to a magnet elementary school too far away to walk to, and live in a city too compact to have school buses (probably the most common form of mass transit), so I, along with most of my classmates, carpooled. My parents always took public transportation to work, until my father started bicycling and my mother started telecommuting. My father has been interested in old vehicles since before I was born, so I grew up being dragged to visit antique train, trolley, and car museums. They were generally interesting, if for shorter time spans.

What do you want to do with your degree?

I want to make transportation available to people who have been left behind by our car culture, particularly people who are too poor to own cars, too elderly to drive safely, or too young to drive. I've become very interested in the field of rural mass transit, probably because it's so new to me. Both rural and inner-city poor have a terrible hurdle in getting to jobs or affordable stores. Of course, I'd also like to get more people out of their cars, working closer to home, and commuting on foot, bicycle, or public transportation.

Do you have hope for a future in which there will be a much greater percentage of people riding mass transit? What could bring that about?

Some thoughts on getting people out of their cars:

- Amtrak has seen very significant increases in ridership in the Northeast corridor already with the introduction of Acela regional service.
- Lots of people choose to take airplanes (a form of public transportation) instead of driving someplace.
- The Internet has already begun replacing trips, both commuter and discretionary, and will replace more in the future.

(Think about working from home on occasion, finding air-plane tickets on-line instead of going to a travel agent, reading the newspaper on-line instead of traveling somewhere to buy it, and checking on-line to see if your library has a book instead of going there to look yourself.)

- In metropolitan areas, groceries can be ordered on-line from any of a number of competing companies, eliminating a major hurdle for outer-city dwellers thinking about giving up their cars. (Grocery shopping on foot anywhere except the inner city is very difficult.)

What will make people choose not to drive someplace? When the comfort and convenience are at least as good. The single biggest thing is scheduling. If trains or buses don't run early enough or late enough, people won't use them because they're not available or they fear getting stranded. If they run too infrequently or don't get close enough to both origin and destination, they become too inconvenient. If they stop too many times, they become slower than driving. This is more of a problem, of course, with buses than with trains. The vehicles and waiting areas need to feel sufficiently clean and safe. We've become accustomed to being insulated and, as a culture, are uncomfortable with the democracy of public buses.

Another big issue is cost. Most of the costs of automobile travel are hidden. What would rail travel cost to consumers if all of the infrastructure and all of the dispatching was provided, as a matter of course, by the government, as is the case for air travel? OK, now what would prices be like if the electricity powering those trains were as subsidized as gasoline? Now, imagine if we were constantly building new rail connections the way we're constantly building new highways, and often building new airports. One more twist: imagine if car owners didn't just accept the costs of buying, insuring, and maintaining a car but mentally added those to the cost of gas for every trip.

I can imagine Rachel Bauer, fresh out of college, getting snapped up by some transit agency. I certainly hope the bureaucracy doesn't drag her down.

Rachel's father was just as stimulating. He calls himself "an amateur transit historian." Because he works in Boston, I asked him about commuting to work from his home in Somerville. "The service on the T is good, but the problem is the feeder bus lines that connect to it," he said. "On a bad day, it can take forty-five minutes to get from my house to North Station. I can walk faster, so I mostly ride my bicycle to work." The irony, as Bauer explained it, is that through the 1920s Somerville had eight to ten trolley stations, which could whisk city-bound workers to Boston in ten minutes.

DEATH AND REBIRTH ON THE RAILS

Luckily, I don't have to write a book of hand-wringing about what happened to the trains—because they're on their way back, and we're slowly rebuilding a national rail network that, at its peak, included 300,000 miles of track. The world that was came vividly to life when I visited Chattanooga, Tennessee, recently. Chattanooga's handsome railroad station has been painstakingly rebuilt—as a hotel. No passenger trains actually visit the city immortalized in the song "Chattanooga Choo Choo," but you can spend the night in a car parked on a siding that leads nowhere. Chattanooga is building a sustainable image through such innovations as a free electric shuttle bus in the downtown area, but it would achieve a major and more than symbolic victory if it reconnected passenger rail to its glorious station.

It's hard to imagine it in this era of widespread complaints about Amtrak subsidies, but in his book *Getting There: The Epic Struggle Between Road and Rail in the American Century,* Stephen B. Goddard points out that railroads of all types once attracted private investment like a magnet. By 1902 investors had put $2 billion into building 22,000 miles of electric trolley lines, which were already carrying 5 billion people a year. "Railroad capital soared from $2.5 billion in

1870 to $21 billion at its peak in 1916, when railroads were handing weekly paychecks to 1.7 million Americans," says Goddard.[3]

But by the 1920s, interstate trucking was a growing field that took business away from the lucrative freight trains in geometric progression. Trucks could deliver their cargo directly to loading docks, without a lengthy and costly reloading process. Interstate road building abetted the process. Cars offered similar convenience advantages over passenger trains. The novelist Edith Wharton, in *A Motor-Flight Through France,* clearly preferred to take her chances in the primitive and breakdown-prone automobiles of the period. "Freeing us from the compulsions and contacts of the railway, the bondage to fixed hours and the beaten track, the approach to each town through the area of desolation and ugliness created by the railway itself, [the automobile] has given us back the wonder, the adventure and the novelty which enlivened the way of our posting grandparents," she wrote. The great crusading novelist Theodore Dreiser agreed: "At best, the railways have become huge, clumsy, unwieldy affairs little suited to the temperamental needs and moods of the average human being."[4]

In an effort to stave off the inevitable, railroads tried desperately to increase service. Streamliners like the *California Zephyr* and *Oriental Limited* offered live bands for dancing, movies, onboard aquariums, and children's playrooms.[5] The *City of New Orleans,* made famous by Arlo Guthrie's hit version of Steve Goodman's song, was launched in 1947 and could boast of a twin-unit diner, two lounges, and a parlor car. Hungry riders could partake of "the King's Dinner," which included seven courses, wine, coffee, and dessert for under ten dollars. Other trains offered horseshoe-shaped bars, dial phones linked to the observation cars, and etched-glass windows.[6]

What caused train ridership to decline so precipitously? Gregory Lee Thompson, the author of *The Passenger Train in the Motor Age,* told me in an e-mail that "passenger service was a sideline to freight service and was not operated in an efficient, profit-making manner. U.S. railroad corporations also were the pioneers of big business institutions, not only in the U.S., but in the world. The cultural legacy of this is that railroad institutions were more primitive in practices and outlook than other big business, certainly when compared to automotive competitors. Another institutional/cultural factor is that railroads were out of step with the American paradigm of transportation provision: government provides infrastructure and makes it available to private operators, both individual and corporate, of vehicles. Railroad corporations never recognized this as a fact of life and instead wasted much of their energies over the past eight decades howling about government unfairness."

The railroad robber barons' high-handed ways didn't help. As noted, railroad owners routinely exercised their will on state legislatures. And railroad tycoons like Jay Gould, who controlled both the New York Elevated Railway and the Union Pacific, were infamous models of excess. A famous hobo song of the period contains these sarcastic lines: "Jay Gould's daughter is a friend of mine / And that's why I ride on her father's railroad line / Jay Gould's daughter said before I die / Fix the blinds so the bums can't ride / If ride they must, let them ride the rods / And put their trust in the hands of God." Like that famously pampered race horse Stewball, Helen Gould was said to never drink water, only wine. The black-bearded Gould was said to have driven an associate to suicide with his ruthless business tactics.

The airplane, too, drew away many rail travelers. Between 1949 and 1967, railroad passenger miles were cut in half, while air travel grew tenfold.[7] It was shortly after this, with the nation's private passenger railroad system in tatters and the rolling stock an obsolete ruin, that Congress came to the rescue with a federal bailout. A new entity, the National Railroad Passenger Corporation, nicknamed Amtrak, was established. As an indication of how little faith there was in the future of passenger railroading, nearly all the railroad executives offered cash or Amtrak stock for their holdings went for the cash.[8] Far from operating in the black, Amtrak consumed more than $3 billion in federal money during the 1970s, when half of all passenger lines were dropped. A companion freight operation, Conrail, swallowed up $4 billion in the first five years after its formation in 1976.

A favorite target of antitax crusaders who pointed to it as a government spending boondoggle, Amtrak slowly lurched forward with the acquisition of shiny new passenger cars and rebuilt tracks on some lines, including the still-popular run from Boston to New York. But a "modernized" Amtrak still offers diesel locomotives pulling steel cars at a speed seldom topping sixty miles per hour, approximately the same service of a hundred years before.

EUROPE AND JAPAN ON THE FAST TRACK

Things are different in Europe and Japan, where trains benefited from the same technological progress that has been the exclusive province of the auto and aviation industries in the United States. In Japan, the sleek Shinkansen (literally, "new trunk line") bullet trains were speeding along at a speed of 137 miles per hour as early as 1963. These trains carry 130 million passengers annually and have never had a derailment or collision accident.

"When the Shinkansen construction project was launched," reports *New Technology Japan* magazine, "the internationally prevailing opinion was that railway transportation was destined to tread the path of gradual demise. What actually happened to the railway in the United States seems to have proved the prediction had some validity."[9] Just as many skeptics claimed that airplanes would never fly, railroad executives around the world asserted that trains would never go faster than 100 miles per hour. Proving them wrong, in 1979 a Japanese bullet train set a national speed record of almost 200 miles per hour. Service, which is extensive and frequent throughout Japan, is also legendarily on time. In 1999 the Tokaido Shinkansen recorded an average lateness of twenty-four seconds. The trains are also exceptionally popular, with many of them running at 200 percent capacity (which means more than one hundred people standing in each car) during holiday runs.[10]

The 700 series bullet train, which looks like something out of a *Star Wars* movie and makes the heralded three-hundred-mile Tokyo-Osaka run at 156 miles per hour, entered service in 1999. An even faster train, the 218-mile-per-hour 900 series, is scheduled to start the run in 2007. Because most of the U.S. railway system is not electrified, trains in most places are limited to the pulling speed of diesel locomotives. But every car on the bullet trains is electrified through overhead wires and helps pull the train. Decentralized power is an advantage on Japan's constantly curving tracks because the electric motors act as individual brakes and stabilizers.

Europe is full of fast trains, but the French Très Grande Vitesse (TGV) is a standout. TGV is part of the state-owned Société Nationale des Chemins de Fer Français (SNCF), but it operates at a profit. TGV trains run regular long distances at a speed of 186 miles per hour and travel to every corner of France. Service, which began with a high-speed line between Paris and Lyon in 1981, has also been extended into Belgium, Germany, Switzerland, and Italy. The entire European TGV network will offer 9,700 miles of track when it's completed in 2005.

Like Japanese trains, the TGV is electrified, but it differs in that only the locomotive has power, a sobering 8,800 kilowatts (the equivalent of 11,800 horsepower). The trains incorporate many advanced electronic-control devices, including fully automated predeparture checking sequences. A sign of the TGV's popularity is that many of the cars are double-decker Duplexes, similar to the Bombardier Metrolink trains I saw in Los Angeles. Passenger travel increased 4.8 percent in 1998, when the SNCF carried 823 million people (including 528 million in the Paris area alone). In contrast to Amtrak's meager network of stations serving only the biggest cities, TGV launched and implemented a "1,000 stations for the year 2000" campaign in 1998.[11]

In a 1990 demonstration run, the TGV train *Atlantique* achieved the exhilarating speed of 320 miles per hour. It doesn't normally go that fast, of course, but travelers can always enjoy the air-suspended ride and such amenities as bar cars, a small shop, a nursery, and telephone booths.

In my brief experience on the TGV, during an epic overland trip from Marrakech, Morocco, to Rome in the early 1980s, I luxuriated in deeply padded seats akin to those in the first-class section of airplanes and watched the world whiz by through panoramic glass. It's a view seen by generations of American college kids with Eurail passes, all of whom probably come home and ask, "Why can't we have trains like that at home?" The technical answer is that we need new, electrified high-speed tracks and a huge investment in rolling stock. The nontechnical answer is that we need a different mind-set and less sprawl. Europeans take four to eight times as many public-transit trips as Americans do and rely on trains, buses, bicycling, and walking for half their travel, compared to less than 10 percent in the U.S.

In the *Atlantic Monthly,* Hans Koning contrasts European and American local train service. "One day in the Gare d'Austerlitz, in Paris," he writes, "I asked at a window when the next train to Orléans was coming, and the woman on duty looked a bit puzzled. *'Tout le temps'* was her answer. There are 40 trains a day: no need to check on the next one; another would have arrived by the time I got to the platform. Orléans is as far from Paris as New Haven is from New York, 70-odd miles, but an Orléanist can commute: his train takes 55 minutes; the New Haven train nearly two hours."[12]

Koning, a journalist, novelist, and fast-train enthusiast, sent an (unpublished) letter to the *New York Times* in early 2000, complaining about a February 3 piece on Amtrak that had claimed, "Rebuilding the American tracks to European standards would be prohibitively expensive." The story added, "Of course, no European high-speed train operates without government subsidy." In fact, countered Koning, "Within the French train system, the TGV is a profit maker." Amtrak could learn something from a moneymaking train system that offers both ultrafast schedules and state-of-the-art service.

AMTRAK'S FAST TRACK

Don't expect to see an Amtrak train traveling at 320 miles per hour anytime soon. But the service is slowly shaking off its torpor and has launched, on shaky legs, its first high-speed service, the Acela Express, from Boston to Washington.

Amtrak is making a bit of a comeback. Although it is still subsidized, 80 percent of passenger fares are now covered by ticket sales. In July 2000, it had 2 million passengers, its highest ridership month in twenty years. That same period saw revenues top $100 million for the first time. With five hundred stations, the system now extends to forty-five states (all except Alaska, Hawaii, Maine, South Dakota, and Wyoming) and covers 22,000 route miles. It employs 24,000 people, and in 1998 the intercity lines served 21 million passengers (unfortunately, still rather pathetic when compared to the 823 million carried by the French system in that same year). Another 54 million were carried on contract commuter systems operated by Amtrak in Massachusetts, Maryland, Connecticut, California, and Virginia.[13] Boston's Amtrak-run T is itself larger in terms of passenger trips than the entire Amtrak national service, with 34 million people riding in 1998.[14]

The Acela Express (the name is an amalgam of "acceleration" and "excellence") travels between Boston and Washington at 150 miles per hour. It makes the trip from Boston to New York in three hours (saving an hour over the traditional train) and the journey from New York to Washington in two and a half hours (saving only fifteen minutes because the Metroliner it replaces was already traveling at 125 miles per hour). As in an airplane, there are first, business, and coach classes, with first class offering wide seats, personal audio programming, plug-ins for laptop computers, at-seat dinner service on china plates with microbrewed beer and gourmet coffee, and even hand-delivered hot towels.

The $2 billion Acela service had a rocky start. The high-speed tilt-technology trains, designed and built by a consortium of Bombardier and ALSTOM, were originally scheduled to begin rolling on the newly electrified lines in late 1999. But as a Newhouse News Service story points out, "Only its $20 million ad campaign stayed on track."[15] Posters and signage at Amtrak stations around the country proclaimed the debut of a service that was far from ready.

In June 2000, Amtrak halted test runs of its Acela trains because cracked and missing bolts were discovered in their wheelsets, or "trucks." The trucks are part of the powercars, which contain electric propulsion equipment and engineers' compartments and are situated at the front and rear of each train. In tests, the trucks oscillated in a potentially hazardous phenomenon known as "truck hunting"; then, after a quick fix, they experienced extreme wear.[16] Part of the problem stems from the antiquated freight rails on most of the route, which give the new cars a bumpy ride.

The service also went considerably over budget. The same month that the wheelset problems were discovered, federal agents raided the Old Saybrook, Connecticut, offices of two of Acela's contractors, Balfour Beatty and Massachusetts Electric Construction, in an investigation of reported multimillion-dollar cost overruns.[17]

Acela Express started carrying paying passengers on December 11, 2000, after a VIP inaugural run the month before that included a champagne send-off and an a cappella group, Vocal Tonic, performing in the aisles. Initial one-way business-class fares of $143 from Washington to New York compared favorably with one-way air-shuttle rates of about $200. That bodes well, because, even without high-speed service, the Northeast corridor has been one of the few profitable parts of Amtrak's operations. If Amtrak meets its goal of siphoning 2.5 million passengers annually from the airlines, it will increase its yearly revenues by $180 million.

Amtrak is now in make-or-break mode, heavily dependent on the success of Acela. Bill Schulz, an Amtrak vice president, told me that the national railway service is on a congressionally mandated "glide path" to financial independence that should end in a total separation by the 2003 fiscal year. In 1999, he said, the operating subsidy was $484 million; in 2000, $362 million; and in 2001, it was projected as $242 million.

But, as Schulz puts it, "Capital costs are not part of the self-sufficiency test." If they were, Amtrak could never hope to be profitable. In *Edge City,* Joel Garreau sums up the inherent problems of making money from passenger trains. The economics, he writes, "are maddening. There is not thought to be a single commuter rail system in the United States that manages even to meet its expenses out of the farebox. They need subsidies just to move, no less to lay track. A new rail car costs a million dollars. If you could attract a hundred passengers into it each rush hour, it would still cost $10,000 per person for the rolling stock—the price of a decent automobile. And that's before you go to General Electric or General Motors and pay up to $4 million for a locomotive."[18] And then there's the track, and the land under it, ad infinitum. In 1997, when Governor John Rowland of Connecticut proposed ending the Amtrak-run, state-subsidized Shoreline East train because of declining ridership, he offered, only a little tongue-in-cheek, to provide each rider with a minivan instead. The resulting hue and cry from disgruntled passengers forced the governor to back down.

Schultz pointed out that the federal government subsidizes $33 billion in highway-related capital costs every year and $12 billion for airports, but it grants Amtrak only operating money. A recent exception was a tax credit, provided as part of the 1997 reforms, that provided the line with $2.2 billion for rail improvements, money it has spent on the Northeast corridor.

Amtrak funding would make a great leap forward under the provisions of a bill promoted by former U.S. senator Frank Lautenberg of New Jersey, the High-Speed Rail Investment Act. The bill would enable Amtrak to float capital-investment bonds with state partners and raise $10 billion over ten years.

There is as yet no electrified track or improved signal capacity outside the Northeast, so a national high-speed rail system is still a long way off. But no less than ten high-speed corridors have already been established nationwide, and congressional funding could make them all operational. Steven Taubenkibel, an Amtrak spokesman, points out, however, that the Midwest Regional Rail Initiative, with nine states as members, is seeking to establish a series of high-speed routes emanating from Chicago. "There's a general feeling, especially in the Midwest, that the states want this to happen," Taubenkibel said. Former Wisconsin governor Tommy Thompson, now the Bush administration's secretary of Health and Human Services, is a strong Amtrak supporter and served as its chairman of the board. During his tenure as governor, he pushed for 110-mile-per-hour trains to be running from Milwaukee to Madison by 2003. Madison, for one, hasn't had any Amtrak service at all since the line was founded in 1971. Thompson is one Republican who doesn't look at Amtrak as a waste of money; he talks about a "new love affair" between Americans and trains.[19]

Amtrak's Schultz thinks that rail investment has to be looked at as a quality-of-life issue. Hans Koning would certainly agree with him, and so does Joel Garreau. "Maybe they should be subsidized because they bring civilization," Garreau wrote. "A train station invariably results in a knot of dense development. . . . By building the train station you *have* [Garreau's emphasis] convinced people to build unusually high and walkable densities."[20] Former senator Lautenberg estimates that the existence of Amtrak service between Philadelphia and New York takes 18,000 cars off the road each day, and that certainly results in a better quality of life.

AMTRAK'S FRIENDS AND ENEMIES

Amtrak has some well-placed friends. The Washington-based National Association of Railroad Passengers, the parent of state groups like the Train Riders Association of California, has a $12 million annual budget gathered from five hundred transit agencies around the country, and a staff of seventy. Its longtime executive director, Ross B. Capon, is an impassioned defender of trains. "It's not a shrinking rail network anymore," he told me. "There are a lot of success stories." He pointed to the Pacific Northwest, where Amtrak ridership rose from 226,000 in 1993 to 570,000 in 1999. "The competition is weakening," Capon said. "There's a worsening situation on the highways and in the air, and it's reducing the threshold at which business travelers will accept rail. It's a hopeful period for trains, and the public is way ahead of the politicians on this one."

Especially in Florida. Capon decried the machinations of Governor Jeb Bush in pulling the plug on what looked like a done deal, the high-speed Florida Overland Express (FOX). "Bush snatched defeat from the jaws of victory," Capon said. "I think it was killed so that the earmarked funding could go to local transit agencies, which made the politicians like Jeb Bush look like sugar daddies." The governor identified several likely recipients of the freed-up funds, including mass-transit options for the Tampa Bay area's bid for the Olympic Games.

Bush did more than just cancel funding for the Tampa-Orlando-Miami train. Without consulting state transportation officials or the state's private-sector partners, he also dismantled the state's high-speed rail office and called for repeal of its enabling statute. But, in an extraordinary development, voters in Florida approved a constitutional amendment on the 2000 ballot that directed Bush to reconsider: under the provision of the amendment, the governor and legislature are to begin construction of a high-speed rail system to serve five of the largest Florida cities by 2003. A major sticking point is that the train could cost up to $20 billion, and the amendment is basically an unfunded mandate that doesn't identify any funding source. Highway forces, which value new roads far more than fast trains, vowed to kill the high-speed line once and for all.

If it is eventually built, FOX will be an incredible train, with 200-mile-per-hour Thalys equipment identical to that used on the TGV line between Paris and Brussels. It could make the Tampa-to-Orlando run, a distance of 85 miles, in 55 minutes, and Orlando to Miami (228 miles) in 86 minutes. Under the original 1996 plan, whose future is now unclear, a network of 320 miles of electrified track would have been built, connecting such far-flung cities as Saint Petersburg on the west coast and West Palm Beach on the east by 2004. The service would have reached 45 percent of the state's 15.5 million people.

FOX was targeted as a boondoggle in libertarian circles. Wendell Cox, an antitransit gadfly and consultant, pops up whenever rail funding comes up for public discussion. Cox prepares detailed, scholarly reports that plug in the negative information he's gathered nationally about train expense and ridership. "The proposed high-speed rail system is likely to be a financial disaster for Florida," he warned in a report that claimed the line would need $3.5 billion in subsidies. "High-speed rail is likely to cost much more, carry fewer passengers, and expose the state to greater financial risk than is presently anticipated."[21]

"Mention my name and it strikes terror in the veins of proponents of high-speed and light rail," Cox told me. "They call me names: right-winger, antitransit, but I think one has to be a realist. My basic position is that whatever the public wants it deserves to get for the lowest cost." Cox, who in a Cato Institute study also called for an end to Amtrak subsidies, claims that "transit is captive to special interests. It's twice as expensive as what we want. Anything you can do with light rail, for instance, can be done with buses for half the price." The Florida plan, he added, "will require all sorts of public money and then go bankrupt. It won't matter a hill of beans in terms of traffic congestion anyway." Cox has a point about the high cost of rail lines, but I think he's wrong to claim that they don't reduce highway travel.

Projects like FOX will always be easily baited on financial terms. Examined in a cold, hard, bottom-line way, rail projects usually look like losers. But as one rail defender put it to me, "Sure, they're not instant moneymakers and may never be. And the ridership numbers aren't usually high enough to justify the investment. But why don't the critics ever factor in the hundreds of thousands of commuters who are taken off the roads, which makes life easier for everyone?" Those are basically intangibles, of course, the quality-of-life issues those rail enthusiasts talk about.

The demise and rebirth of FOX was an emotional roller-coaster for Anthony Rizos, the owner and Webmaster of Amtrak Unlimited. The existence of a well-designed Amtrak fan site, complete with detailed schedules and specifics about the Superliner's bedroom amenities, is hardly news. But the fact that Anthony was only thirteen and a southern California ninth grader when he set up the site might make an interesting item for *People*.

Rizos told me that his parents took him aboard Amtrak's *Coast Starlight* to Seattle in 1996, when he was only nine, and it was an inspiring trip. "Riding the train is an experience like no other," he said. "It causes you to have no perception of time, reality, or when the trip is going to end. It is definitely one of my favorite hobbies, and before I even board the train, I start thinking about when the next trip will be!"

I found Rizos accidentally by entering Amtrak Unlimited's domain name, www.amtraktrains.com. Maybe one day he'll be able to sell that much-trafficked domain to a revitalized national passenger-rail system. For now, though, he's trying to remain upbeat. "More people every day are discovering that rail travel is the way to go," he said. "In the days of cramped, stuffy airplanes, Amtrak travel can be thought of as a refuge to those that dread flying."

I don't dread flying, at least most of the time, but I have had wonderful experiences on Amtrak. In 1992, I took an Amtrak train from my home in Connecticut to Columbia, South Carolina. The mission, I'll admit, was to buy a car, but the train provided a handy way to get down there. I've ridden on trains all over the world—in Japan, Europe, North Africa, Australia, India, Brazil—and while my Amtrak ride didn't compare with the best of those, it was nonetheless a cozy experience.

I say it was cozy because I had a tiny compartment all to myself, with its own fold-up bed and miniature bathroom. It was like traveling in a little womb. I could lie in bed and watch the South flash by, see cars waiting at crossings, farmers plowing their fields, and people on their way to church. On planes I never sit in window seats because I find there's nothing to see (and you can't get up easily). But on trains, the whole world opens up.

I made it safely to South Carolina, bought the car, and drove it back home. Days after I got back, the same train, Amtrak's *Sunset Limited,* derailed and plunged into the Connor Creek Bayou in Alabama, killing forty-four people. As I said, those were Amtrak's dark days.[22]

But do accidents and cost overruns mean we should abandon national rail service altogether? The American people don't think so. A Gallup Poll conducted in 1997 found that continued Amtrak funding is supported by 69 percent of the people who don't even believe the end of the service would affect them. Among people who *do* think they'd be affected, support ran at 81 percent.[23]

Eliminating Amtrak entirely is exactly the goal of the Reason Public Policy Institute, a libertarian group. Amtrak, the group said in 1997, "is a failed national experiment." The group wants the federal government out of the railroad business. "There's no justification for a national railroad passenger operation," the Reason report said. "America needs passenger trains in selected areas, but doesn't need Amtrak's antiquated route system, poor service, unreasonable operating deficits, and capital investment programs with low rates of return. Amtrak's failures result in part because it is a public monopoly—the very type of organization least able to innovate."[24]

I would say to the report's author, Joseph Vranich, that the highly popular and very successful European and Japanese train systems are public monopolies, too. While the enormous national rail network that existed in America before World War II was built by private interests, it was hardly a model of efficiency and probity. The phrase *robber baron* is rooted in railroad greed and rapacity; the excesses of the period were a prime motivator for antitrust legislation. And can he show me an efficient rail system anywhere in the world today that is *not* state run?

In 1997, when the Reason report was written, Amtrak really was flirting with bankruptcy. But the service is making a slow climb out of that hole. In 1998 testimony before the House Appropriations Subcommittee on Transportation, Amtrak's president, George Warrington, sounded much like a corporate CEO when he told the assembled congressmen, "I feel confident that we are in a more stable position—commercially, financially and operationally—than we have been in a very long time. In the past three years, we have significantly improved our bottom line through aggressive revenue development and cost-cutting actions."[25]

RAILS TO TRAILS

There's also another way of looking at the bottom line. The United States had a fully developed trolley network in place in the 1930s, but the trolleys themselves were losing ridership rapidly to cars. The

economic interests of the time no doubt considered it financially pru-
dent to scrap the trolleys and rip up the tracks. But consider the cost
of replacing that infrastructure today!

Luckily, somebody did think about the precious heritage of our
heavy-rail corridors, a huge number of which have sat unused since
the trains that ran on them were decommissioned. At its peak in
1916, there were 300,000 miles of track (350,000 if you count privately run rail lines), a network six times as big as the current interstate highway system. Only half of that original mileage still exists,
and railroads continue to abandon 2,000 miles of track every year. If
the corridors are sold for development, they're gone forever, and re-
creating them is so costly as to be prohibitive. It's another reason for
critics to say, "See? Trains are too expensive."

Dave Burwell, who founded the Rails to Trails Conservancy
(RTC), is an environmental lawyer by trade. His employer in the
1970s was the National Wildlife Federation, which is concerned
mainly with preserving wildlife habitats for hunting. Unused rail corridors are precisely that kind of habitat, but as railroads deregulated
in the 1970s, they began selling the corridors for development. And
hunters began to lose access to them.

Burwell began researching the corridors' history. "I found that
even though they were under railroad control, they had originated in
federal and state land grants," he said. "And so there was considerable
public investment and interest in them. The problem was that there
was no legal preservation mechanism that would be activated when
the railroads divested. The 10 to 20 percent not actually owned by
the railroads had been acquired by easements, so when they were not
used for railroad purposes anymore, they reverted to somebody, but
whom? Title problems almost guaranteed they wouldn't be saved."

In 1983, Congress enacted a powerful amendment to the National
Trails System Act that allowed soon-to-be abandoned rail lines to be
"rail-banked" for possible reactivation. And while the world waited
for railroads to be needed again, the corridors could be used as trails.
It was a brilliant idea, since rail lines go through some mighty pictur-

esque countryside, and most of the work of trail creation has already been done by the railroad.

Burwell had a hand in drafting that legislation. "After that, I basically went to work tracking railroad abandonment," he said. "I taught people how to use the law and defended it in court, because trail creation was frequently challenged by adjacent landowners as a property 'taking.' In 1990, these legal challenges reached the U.S. Supreme Court, which voted nine to zero that trail building was a legitimate purpose and the law was constitutional." The legal situation is not completely clear, however, because a federal appeals court recently ruled in favor of a Vermont couple who claimed that their property values had been damaged by a rail trail.

The rails-to-trails program has been a fantastic success. In 2000, there were 1,012 rail trails in the United States, with a total trail mileage of more than 11,000. Another 1,200 projects are currently under way, involving all fifty states and 18,000 more miles. There's unlimited potential, given the fact that more than 160,000 miles of rail corridor have been abandoned. "But some of it has been converted to roads, some plowed up for farmland," said Burwell. "We'd be happy with a third of the total, 50,000 miles of trails opened up to public use." An as yet unexplored option is the conversion of 5,000 miles of Erie and C&O Canal corridors, once a vitally important transportation route for American industry.

RTC has researched a possible rail trail across the continent, starting from either Massachusetts or Maryland and ending up in Seattle or San Francisco. Some 30 percent of the route already exists, another 35 percent is in public ownership, and the remaining 35 percent, now private, would take massive amounts of work to put together. It's a splendid ambition. If the whole network is connected, there will be off-road trails and greenways from coast to coast.

I walked and biked a rail trail before I knew it was one. My brother, an agronomy professor at the University of Missouri in Columbia, lives a quarter mile from the Katy Trail, a 200-mile pathway that marks the former corridor of the Missouri-Kansas-Texas

Railroad, popularly known as the Katy. Learning this, I finally under-
stood the meaning of the old blues tune that laments, "She caught the
Katy / And left me the mule to ride."

The Katy was decommissioned in 1986 and its iron rails and
wooden ties sold for scrap. The corridor was acquired by the Missouri
Department of Natural Resources, which turned it into a state park.
The Union Pacific Railroad donated another 33 miles of disused track
in 1991. I came along in 1999, when the Katy Trail was already very
popular with strolling university students, joggers, and serious bikers.

Between us, my brother and I have three small children, so we
borrowed some charming bicycle trailers and hauled them up the
trail. Five miles from the university, traffic thinned out considerably.
Though it runs through patches of meadow, for the most part the trail
has become shaded by a canopy of mature second-growth trees, and
it's a cool haven on hot days. We traveled to a trailside picnic spot
near the Missouri River. It was very peaceful with farms all around, a
reminder of what Columbia, now rapidly developing around the university and a hospital complex, must have been like a hundred years
ago.

But creating beautiful hiking trails is only part of what RTC is
about. It's also very serious about its role as a rail bank. "Rail buffs are
suspicious of the trail users," Burwell said. "They're afraid they'll
never get their corridors back for rail use. But if we weren't preserving them with trails, they'd be gone forever."

THE PROMISE OF MAG-LEV

Reviving the rail network is an infrastructure issue. The United States
has developed a brilliant, fully formed system for designing and
building highways, involving five-year plans, state and local gas taxes,
federal funding, lobbying groups, and engineers with specialized
training. But it has lost the networks, once similarly impressive, that
built vast rail and trolley lines. (Bikers and pedestrians never had an
infrastructure, and the trips they take are not even counted as such by
federal statistics.)

Thousands of people are engaged in a huge bureaucracy, the point of which is to continue to build roads. Where's the similar network for high-speed trains, for subways—or for other means of transportation? It's clear, in fact, that technological innovation doesn't necessarily have much to do with the way we actually travel. As an example, I started this book with high hopes for the magnetic-levitation train. Here's a technology that works, a veritable magic carpet for our time!

Back in 1966, scientists James Powell and Gordon Danby of Brookhaven National Laboratory wrote an academic paper speculating that magnets, if they were powerful enough, could suspend an electrically powered train above a track. Moving along without the friction of steel wheels on steel rails, the trains could easily achieve 300 miles per hour.

The main obstacle to mag-lev trains is the cost of building them. One type of mag-lev design uses superconducting magnets to lift the train to within a fraction of an inch of the guide rail. The system is dependent on highly accurate feedback circuits and must be engineered to very high tolerances. It is, in a word, expensive. A second type uses superconducting coils whose magnetic fields run through a conductive plate to achieve liftoff. That's expensive, too, since the coils require extremely low-temperature cooling systems.

But there are extraordinary benefits. The mag-lev train, as it was called, would be noise- and pollution-free. "All you really hear is the air disturbance, kind of a big whoosh," says Fred Gurney of Maglev Inc., which in 1999 won a federal Department of Transportation grant to study the possibility of using a mag-lev train in Pittsburgh.[26]

Japan, which has a history of carrying U.S.-developed concepts to fruition, has been experimenting with mag-lev trains since 1972. In 1997, a remote-controlled Japanese mag-lev set an official world speed record of 341 miles an hour. Japan has sunk $3 billion into development of 270-mile-per-hour mag-lev prototypes, using a twenty-five-mile test track outside Tokyo, and some Japanese critics have targeted the train as a symbol of runaway spending on big government-sponsored projects. Another prototype, in Emsland, Germany, has logged more than 200,000 test miles.

In 1992, the *American Prospect* lamented that the United States was falling behind in the mag-lev race. "[T]he story of how Japan and Germany are racing to capitalize on yet another American invention has a depressingly familiar ring to it," the magazine wrote. "Mag-lev, often touted as the next generation of high-speed rail, is on the brink of commercialization in Germany and Japan."[27] It certainly looked like that then. The German government was the first in the world to try to put a mag-lev train into actual service, authorizing construction of a line between Hamburg and Berlin in 1994. The Transrapid train would make the trip between Germany's two biggest cities in an hour, less than half the time it takes on the existing trains. Completion was slated for 2005, but in early 2000 the project was canceled.

Cost overruns and low projected ridership were the cause. Harmut Mehdorn was installed as the new manager of Germany's Deutsche Bahn, the state railway system, in 1999, with a mission to reduce costs and raise productivity. "Mr. Mehdorn quickly made clear [that] running a single-track Transrapid at what was likely to be a big loss was not part of his job remit," according to the *Financial Times*.[28] Instead, the Deutsche Bahn is pushing ahead with new routes for its existing network of high-speed conventional trains, the Inter-City Express (ICE). Investment in a new and unproven infrastructure had simply become too risky.

Mag-lev has moved on since then, and it still has many partisans. The Southern California Association of Governments is studying a mag-lev system based on the German Transrapid design for possible regional use. And transportation planners are getting excited about a new and more affordable generation of trains that run on a cushion of air. Developed at Lawrence Livermore National Laboratory, the system is called Inductrack.

A simplified mag-lev, Inductrack relies on technology familiar to any high school science class—magnetic repulsion—and is therefore less expensive than the system developed in 1966. Permanent magnets on the bottom of the train repel inductive coils on the track guideway. Standard permanent magnets would not provide enough levitation for a train. The Inductrack system uses a powerful permanent-magnet design developed by physicist Klaus Halbach for particle accelerators. A major cost advantage is that the magnets don't require their own power source. A second advantage is that these Halbach arrays, as they're known, generate almost no magnetic field above them, where the passengers sit.[29]

Another variation on the mag-lev principle is represented by Seraphim (Segmented Rail Phased Induction Motor), a magnetic-repulsion technology developed as part of the Reagan administration's "Star Wars" program in the 1980s. In 2001 the Department of Energy's Sandia National Laboratories in New Mexico received $2 million in federal funding to continue testing of the Seraphim electromagnetic motor, which is designed both to push a train forward and to provide vertical levitation force. Although Seraphim is a form of mag-lev, a full-scale transit system using the technology would ride at 70 miles per hour on wheels, like the French TGV, making it something of a hybrid. Sandia estimates that a Seraphim-based train could be built for $12 to $22 million per mile, and has proposed the system for a new transit line between Denver International Airport and downtown Denver that is still in the planning stages.[30]

Inductrack and Seraphim would be cheaper to build than other forms of mag-lev, but are they more practical than conventional trains? A 1997 feasibility study by Booz-Allen & Hamilton consultants concluded that a full-scale Inductrack system would be much less expensive than the aborted German Transrapid. The cars, for instance, would cost between $3.2 million and $4.2 million, compared to $6 million for the Transrapid. But Inductrack would still be far more expensive to build than conventional trains, even high-speed ones. The Booz-Allen study estimated that, when compared with standard rails, track costs would be 80 percent higher for this new type of locomotion. And the cars, even at the bargain price of $3.2 million, cost three times more than conventional rail cars.[31] The fact that mag-lev has been pursued at all shows that the pull of superior technology can be compelling.

Which government is going to be the first to leap into the

unknown with a huge infrastructure investment in magnetic-levitation trains? Not environmentally conscious, technologically savvy, transit-friendly Germany, apparently. In car-crazed America, federal funding has underwritten some research but is unlikely to pay for a full-sized system. Only Japan has shown the resolve to put billions into mag-lev, but it's uncertain that the technology is really needed in a country that already has superfast bullet trains.

THE HYBRID APPROACH

Prototype mag-lev trains are bullet-shaped and streamlined, but they're still recognizably trains. Suppose the train was combined with a car that could take you home from the station? Would automobile-loving Americans take to a system like that? In the early 1960s, Ford experimented with a Levacar; it floated through the magic of Levapods, which forced compressed air downward. The cars moved forward with either ducted-fan or jet power. "The Ford people talk about 300 to 500 mile per hour speeds," wrote a breathless Ralph Stein in his 1961 book *The Treasury of the Automobile.*[32] Unfortunately, the Levacar would have required glass-smooth highways, so Ford engineers hit upon the idea of running bus-sized versions on monorail tracks. The car had become a train.

A variation on this is the early 1980s battery-powered Self-Transit Rail and Road Car (StaRRcar), which, as proposed, could be driven on city streets but would also hook onto the guideway of a rapid-transit system. "Someday, people who live in the suburbs may drive this vehicle to the train station, hook it onto a track and be whisked downtown in just half the time it now takes to get there," according to *The Kids' Whole Future Catalog.* "The traveler doesn't have to worry about getting to the station at a certain time. He can set his own schedule."[33] The two-seat StaRRcar looked like a bizarre mishmash of a Honda Civic and a bullet train. Once the driver hooked on to the guideway, he could "sit back and read the newspaper." Of course, once he arrived downtown and unhooked, he'd face the thorny problem of finding a parking space, thus eliminating a major advantage of trains.

Hope springs eternal for hybrid systems like these. The Levacar and the StaRRcar died in infancy, but Robert Cotter is convinced he's hot-wired the future with SkyTran, which adapts Inductrack to a whole new arena. It's not a mag-lev train in the conventional sense but a series of independent, individually guided two-person cars moving on a mag-lev Inductrack. While it exists only in fanciful computer images, SkyTran has captured considerable interest from cities around the country as a high-tech people mover.

Picture a monorail and you're halfway there. Like a monorail, SkyTran rolls on a track elevated twenty feet in the air; the cars, moving at 100 miles per hour, are suspended from the track but don't actually touch it. Unlike a light-rail or monorail system, there is no set schedule. The podlike cars, which look like eggs with windows, stay at the station until they're accessed with a SkyTran credit card. The passenger then programs in a destination. The pods can depart every fifteen seconds, so there shouldn't be too much waiting, and they're kept apart by an adaptive cruise-control system like the one pioneered by Delphi.

SkyTran was designed by Irvine, California, inventor Douglas Malewicki, an aerospace engineer whose composite-bodied, gas- and diesel-powered California Commuter car has two entries in the *Guinness Book of World Records* for high-mileage driving. It averaged 150 miles per gallon on road trips between Los Angeles and Las Vegas. A more dubious invention was a forty-foot-tall "car-nivorous" mechanical grinder that crushes automobiles at monster-truck shows. SkyTran, originally called the People Pod, was next.

After some unfortunate faux pas, in which the inventor reportedly soft-pedaled his own invention, Malewicki no longer talks to the press. That role has fallen to Raleigh, North Carolina, resident Cotter, who has an interesting background of his own. Cotter, who grew up as a car-loving kid on Long Island, fulfilled his fantasies with service jobs at BMW and Porsche after college. But a stint in southern California caused him to reconsider his automotive passions. "The pollution was so overwhelming out there that the love affair turned into love-hate," he said. "By this point, I was working for Porsche, and was offered the chance to head up the company's assault on Indianapolis."

Instead, he quit the car business and became vice president of the International Human-Powered Vehicle Association, which sponsors an annual race for all sorts of unusual vehicles. Cotter designed a special high-speed, lightweight tricycle that enabled a rider to reach 60 miles per hour on level ground. He also got involved in the association's successful attempts at ultralight human-powered flight, including Dr. Paul MacCready's *Gossamer Albatross,* a pedal plane that weighed only fifty-five pounds. In 1988, he directed and sponsored the first solar car race, the American Solar Cup. For him, SkyTran is the next logical step.

"We think it can take care of a lot of commuting hassles for people," Cotter notes enthusiastically. "With SkyTran, everybody wouldn't have to leave work at 5:00 P.M. to get home at 6:30. It's not like a train on a fixed schedule. You could leave at 5:10, 5:25, anytime you wanted." Still, rush hour is rush hour, no matter what the transportation system, and would SkyTran be able to handle the onrush of hundreds of commuters at the same time, all intent on their own pod?

SkyTran could perhaps most easily be put into production as a closed-loop system for shuttling employees on today's vast corporate campuses. Computer-chip manufacturer Intel has one such campus, with 13,000 employees, in Chandler, Arizona, and has shown some interest in the concept. North Carolina State University has funded a $60 million monorail between its two campuses in Raleigh. The school studied a SkyTran proposal but finally rejected the idea because the pods can hold only two students and can go faster than necessary for a short run. The small Connecticut city of New Haven has nibbled at a SkyTran system as a way of replacing shuttle buses on a run from downtown to a new mall on the outskirts of town. "There's no doubt the technology is already here to do this," said Brian McGrath, New Haven's traffic chief. "But who would pay for it?"[34] Interest has also been shown in Italy, the Philippines, and Holland. Airports are intrigued at the prospect of SkyTran as a shuttle between parking lots.

But enthusiasm is one thing, working capital another. Even

though Cotter asserts that SkyTran could be built for $1 million a mile, a fifth of the cost of comparable light rail, investment has not been forthcoming. It would cost SkyTran $5 million to build the one-eighth-of-a-mile test track that was supposed to be operational by December 31, 2000 but wasn't. And that casts doubt on the plan to have a citywide, one-hundred- to five-hundred-mile system in place by 2005. The problem, says Cotter, is that "everyone wants someone else to try it first."

The Danes have developed their own car-train hybrid, called the Rapid Urban Flexible (RUF). Like StaRRcar, it envisions an electric vehicle (EV) with a thirty-mile range that can connect to a monorail via a V-shaped channel on its undercarriage. The car, which has wheels for both road and rail, then hooks into six or seven other RUF-equipped vehicles via computer and becomes an energy-saving train. The system is reportedly capable of moving 3,600 cars per hour on each rail, nearly double the capacity of a highway lane. While on the monorail, the car's batteries are recharged by the same electric supply that powers the track. A variation, the Maxi-RUF, is a ten-passenger minibus that can run on the same rail.

In 2000, inventor Palle R. Jensen told me, RUF was still "looking for a 'real' project," which he imagined would be in Denmark, though strong interest has been shown in Holland and Mexico. "We gain more and more political goodwill here," he said, "and Danish politicians love to be seen as strong on the environment." Jensen added that RUF has also had discussions with several carmakers. "They would love to produce the vehicle," he said. "But we have to start it as a public-transport project in order to get the first rails built." And there's that chicken-and-egg infrastructure problem again. Jensen estimates the cost of the RUF track as $7 million per mile, which means a considerable investment in a working system that would do little more than prove that the technology works.

Trains captured the human imagination more than 150 years ago, and they still exert a powerful grip. After a dark period of constant retreat in the face of automotive ascendancy, trains are once more gaining public favor. Rail's incredible ability to efficiently move large groups of people from place to place, without taking up space on the crowded highway, has pushed it to the forefront again. High costs, for both track construction and operations, remain a problem, but municipalities are realizing that a rail network, once built, becomes a permanent asset.

Rail's problems contrast sharply with those of the airline industry. While Amtrak and the regional lines struggle to gain ridership, the nation's air carriers—and especially their passengers—are paying the cost of overcrowding.

9

THE FUTURE OF FLYING

I CAN'T RELAX ON PLANES. While other people fall instantly asleep and spend most of the flight gently nodding off onto their fellow passengers, I read magazines, watch the movie, work the computer. On cross-country red-eye flights, mine is often the only light left on. And so it was when I took to the friendly skies in search of material for this book. Up above Pennsylvania, I thumbed absently through the *Wall Street Journal.* "United Grapples with Summer of Widespread Discontent," I read, suddenly quite a bit more alert. "CHICAGO—The past four months haven't been kind to customers of UAL Corp.'s United Airlines," said the story, by Susan Carey.[1] "Thousands of travelers have arrived at airports only to find their flights canceled without warning for mysterious reasons. United's hub airports are beginning to look like refugee camps stuffed with cots for stranded passengers. Flights that should take four hours have become dayslong ordeals." United's midwestern hub is Chicago. And I was flying United to Chicago.

United is hardly alone. This kind of disruption is becoming almost routine for airline passengers, as an unprecedented demand for new routes and added capacity meets an overstrained airport network. I loved the softly gliding aircars in the Bruce Willis film *The Fifth Element,* which seemed to be moving in orderly but invisible traffic lanes. In the real world, things are a bit more complicated.

STACKED UP AT THE AIRPORT

How did we get into this mess? The airlines industry is choking on its own success. As a result of highly competitive, deregulated fares, more people are flying than ever before. Global demand for air travel is expected to triple from 295 million passengers in 1990 to an incredible 938 million by 2010, according to the International Air Transport Association. The U.S. aviation industry, the largest in the world (with 38 percent of all miles flown) grows at 5 percent a year, rivaling the computer industry.[2] Despite this, airport infrastructure has remained largely stagnant.

Airport congestion is developing into a major crisis. "The system is starting to show strains," admits Monte Belger, second in command at the Federal Aviation Administration (FAA). "Aircraft that can fly 600 miles an hour are forced to average only 250 miles per hour between Washington, D.C., and New York City. You might as well be flying on a DC-6."[3] An emergency airport congestion meeting called by Transportation Secretary Rodney Slater in August 2000 failed to produce many results, other than an agreement to focus on the problem.

Between 1978, when the airlines deregulated, and 1991, the number of U.S. passengers flying annually increased by more than 80 percent,[4] but the infrastructure didn't grow along with the increase. No major airport was constructed in that period. Thirty-two of the fifty busiest airports in the United States have announced plans to expand. But even if the airlines and the communities are willing, airport construction and expansion is often constrained by environmental factors and just plain NIMBY. La Guardia Airport in New York City, for example, is boxed in between a major highway and Flushing Bay, making any major expansion impossible. But traffic grew from 200,000 takeoffs and landings a year in 1964 to 350,000 in 2000.[5]

Construction of the Munich Airport Extension terminal in Germany took twenty-six years from proposal to completion because of community opposition. When London's Heathrow Airport opened in 1955, its planners thought that a capacity of 3 million passengers a year would suffice until 2000. But in 1999, the airport had 62 million passengers. Also in Europe, several air-cargo operations have had to close or relocate because German host cities Nuremberg and Cologne could not accommodate their growing business.[6]

Opposition to airport construction or expansion is often well-founded. A classic example is that of Florida's proposed Homestead Airport in Dade County, which fiercely divided the state before it was killed in the final days of the Clinton administration. The airport would have offered 230,000 flights in its first year and taken pressure off congested Miami International Airport. The new field would have been built on the site of Homestead Air Force Reserve Base, which was mothballed in the early 1990s. Homestead Airport would have been surrounded by three critically important national parks: Biscayne National Park, Everglades National Park, and the Key Largo National Marine Sanctuary, none of which are more than ten miles from the site.

According to the Sierra Club, which bitterly opposed the proposal, flights would have taken off almost every minute from the airport, bombarding park visitors with noise pollution. The airport would have damaged already threatened coral reefs in Biscayne National Park and harmed birds, mammals, and fish with airport runoff and fuel dumping. Airborne nitrates would have increased fifty-four times, the club said, and there would have been daily emission of seven tons of toxic air pollutants, including nitrogen oxides and volatile organic compounds.[7] The U.S. Air Force's own environmental-impact study showed serious effects to neighboring wildlife, but these concerns alone were not enough to stop the airport.

The airport had fiercely partisan defenders in a region hit hard by the departure of the air base. They pointed to the projected 38,000 jobs the airport would have created, and what proponents claim would have been $800 million in local earnings by 2015. "Too many residents of the Homestead area have been left out of the economic prosperity enjoyed by the rest of the nation in the 1990s," read a "fact sheet" given out by the pro-airport faction. "This includes a disproportionate share of minorities and low-income individuals."[8] Mayor

Otis Wallace of neighboring Florida City proclaimed, "I've been doing a little study of my own on environmental conditions in South Dade and . . . I quickly discovered an endangered species. It has two eyes, two arms, two legs, a brain. It has pride, it has dignity, and an overwhelming desire to support its family."[9] Many local politicians supported the Homestead airport, and that was probably a factor in Vice President Al Gore's decision to take no sides in the controversy, despite past leadership on Everglades issues.

And sometimes building an airport isn't enough. In response to overwhelming congestion at Lambert Field in Saint Louis (which processes 17 million people per year), developers opened MidAmerica Airport in Mascoutah, Illinois, in 1998. It's called the $310 million "gateway to nowhere" because major carriers have been reluctant to abandon the hub fields.[10]

Though the horrors of air travel keep some people earthbound, the fact is that flying has become relatively comfortable and affordable, which is why people fly. It wasn't like that in the early days. According to T. A. Heppenheimer's book *Turbulent Skies,* the venturesome few who took commercial airliners in the 1930s often had a "highly unpleasant" experience. With no pressurization and inadequate heating, passengers froze when planes flew at 20,000 feet. Airsickness was common. One passenger complained, "When the day was over my bones ached, and my whole nervous system was wearied from the noise, the constant droning of the propellers and exhaust in my ears."[11] In those days, no less an authority than Nevil Shute (later to write the postapocalyptic novel *On the Beach*) proclaimed in his capacity as manager of a dirigible that commercial flight faster than 130 miles per hour would never be possible.[12]

But planes did get faster and much more convenient. Because Congress deregulated air cargo in 1977 and passenger service in 1978, airline routes that had been closely held for forty years were suddenly open to competition. That meant cheaper fares (often accompanied with a sharp decrease in service) and more people flying. "We have become mass transit," said Frank Borman, then president of Eastern Airlines.[13]

Are commercial airliners public transportation? Most people don't think of them that way, but they're fulfilling that role. The *1995 American Travel Survey,* released in 1997, revealed that commercial flights account for 19 percent of all household trips. For round-trip journeys of between five hundred and one thousand miles, they account for 27 percent of household trips.[14] For an increasing number of Americans, taking a plane is no longer a major event.

Because air travel is increasing at such a rapid rate, planes are polluting more than ever. Writing in *Earth Island Journal,* Gar Smith notes that with 10,000 large commercial jets flying today and the number expected to double by 2020, "contrails (short for 'condensation trails') pose a growing environmental threat." Scientists say that those lovely jet trails in the sky are affecting the climate, especially on heavily trafficked flight corridors like the North Atlantic route between the United States and Europe. Between seven hundred and eight hundred planes traveled this route every day in 1990, and the number has undoubtedly grown since then. A 1996 National Aeronautics and Space Administration (NASA) report estimated that flights in that corridor since commercial flights began in the 1950s had increased atmospheric soot by 10 percent, sulfur oxides by nearly 10 percent, and nitrogen oxides by from 10 to 100 percent.[15]

During takeoff, Smith's article points out, a jumbo jet gulps down 526,344 gallons of air per second, and in the first five minutes consumes as much oxygen as that produced by 49,000 acres of forest in a day. A Boeing 747 flying from Washington to San Francisco burns 17,232 gallons of jet fuel and generates 190 pounds of nitrogen oxides, about what your car would do if you drove it 53,500 miles. Aviation fuel use crept up 3.9 percent between 1983 and 1989, increasing faster than overall energy consumption.

NASA predicts that aircraft fuel consumption will more than double between 2000 and 2015, and that carbon dioxide and nitrogen oxide emissions will increase 50 percent. Assuming that the horrific crash of an Air France Concorde plane in July 2000 does not seriously affect commercial supersonic flight, the new generation of faster-than-sound aircraft scheduled to debut as early as 2005 could have a serious impact on both marine life and the people in the path of their ground-shaking sonic booms.

Airports are a problem, too, reports *Environmental Health Perspectives.* "Airports are known to be major sources of noise, water and air pollution," the magazine said in 1997. "They pump carbon dioxide, volatile organic compounds and nitrogen oxides into the atmosphere, as well as dump toxic chemicals—used to de-ice airplanes during winter storms—into waterways." In addition, "Auxiliary power units, little jet engines in the planes' tails that power appliances while the planes are at the gate . . . also produce quantities of pollutants."[16]

Noise pollution is a serious problem, too, as airlines discovered when capacity problems forced them to route Newark International flights over the Catskill Mountains in the late 1980s.[17] Storms of citizen protest followed. Critics charge that the Federal Aviation Administration allows too high a noise threshold for airports. According to the Natural Resources Defense Council, federal regulations allow airports to apply for grants to buy out homeowners or pay for soundproofing if noise exceeds a day-night average sound level of 65 decibels. But, the group points out, setting the threshold at 65 reflects political expediency—what is possible without significant added expense—rather than actual levels of annoyance.

At Westchester County Airport in New York, the noise is particularly galling because some of it has occurred during new predawn flights. Widespread complaints led to a bill in Congress designed to impose a mandatory curfew from midnight to 6:30 A.M. on the airport.[18] Turf battles between Westchester County and Greenwich, Connecticut, mean that early-bird fliers—including me—have arrived to find Westchester police blocking the entrance to the parking garage. Even when the average noise level is bearable, the brief sound spikes caused by airplanes taking off can be very disruptive. A jet taking off can generate 105 decibels or more, louder than a rock concert, a shotgun firing nearby, or a thunderclap.

CLEARING THE SKIES

La Guardia Airport in New York makes an interesting test case for solving gridlock in the skies, precisely because its problems have proven so intractable. The airport can't possibly expand, yet traffic continues to increase. "There are 26,000 airline flights a day in the United States, and sometimes it seems as if every last one of them flies into La Guardia Airport," said the *New York Times*.[19] The actual number is 1,000 flights a day. This is not an abstract issue for me: I've experienced my own personal nightmares at La Guardia.

What was I thinking? In the fall of 2000, I booked an itinerary requiring tight connections both in and out of La Guardia. I rushed down to the airport amid lightly falling snow and made it in plenty of time for my 5:55 P.M. flight to Montreal. But weather events disrupt La Guardia's fragile balance, and the snow resulted in a growing ripple of delayed and canceled flights. My flight was pushed back several times, then finally canceled at 8:15 P.M.

I was stuck in New York with no way of getting to Montreal, where I was scheduled to speak at an 8:00 A.M. conference. I frantically waved my ticket and tried to get the blasé counter personnel interested in my plight. They pointed me to a supervisor who, as it turned out, was checking people onto a flight to Burlington, Vermont. "Burlington's only seventy-five miles from Montreal," she told me. "If you take this flight we'll provide surface transportation from there." No other solution offered itself, so I flew through the snow to the Burlington airport, which was absolutely deserted when we arrived at 11:00 P.M. The promised surface transportation was nowhere in sight.

The only thing that saved me from having to sleep on the floor in an empty airport was a chance encounter with a fellow passenger who was driving to Montreal that night. We scooped up two other stranded travelers and headed into the night. I arrived at my hotel at 1:00 A.M. and delivered my speech bleary-eyed. Unfortunately, my flight to Detroit the next day was also routed through La Guardia, and I experienced a whole new round of hellish delays.

In 1999 and 2000, La Guardia added approximately 200 new

flights a day to its already packed schedules. The expansion in service was a response to a new federal law designed to increase flights between New York City and smaller cities. The law opened up takeoff and landing slots for small regional carriers and added to the airport's burden. In August 2000, the FAA reports, delays doubled at La Guardia when compared with the same month a year before.[20] A few months later, on November 1, the airport hosted a record 1,344 take-offs and landings.

In the face of a barrage of complaints, airport officials are responding with some measures that should, over time, reduce congestion. And they mirror efforts at other crowded American airports. In the first place, New York's Port Authority, which controls the airport, showed some restraint. Although the federal law could have allowed even more new flights, the Port Authority responded to the new delay data by at least temporarily banning any additional traffic during the morning and evening rush hours.

The FAA also stepped in with a lottery system that gave retroactive preference to small carriers in reallocating new flights. For some of the big airlines, like Delta and US Airways, which lost more than sixty flights each, that meant cancellation of expansion plans.

The imposition of rationing systems at airports like La Guardia sets off a debate about how much airlines should be paying to use the airport. The traditional system at La Guardia is based simply on weight—$5 for every thousand pounds of plane. But as the Port Authority points out, it's the small planes that actually use up more landing time because they fly slower and have to stay out of turbulence from large jets. An alternative is to charge all planes the same fee, or even to charge small planes more—an idea that makes it difficult to meet the demand for expanded regional service.[21] Congestion could also be cut down by imposing fees in a structure similar to variable toll pricing on highways, with significantly higher fees for flights at peak travel times.

Conservatives think the whole congestion problem can be solved with "market forces." Airports operated as private businesses, instead of government entities, would be freed from any constraint except maximizing profit. They would impose what's called "market-clearing pricing," with far higher fees at the more desirable travel times. Small carriers would obviously lose out in any such scenario, but traffic would be reduced.

Examining gridlock at Chicago-O'Hare International Airport, the FAA offered air-traffic solutions that might also apply elsewhere. In one, called "piggybacking," arriving planes are closely stacked within one thousand vertical feet of each other, easing landing procedures. Another efficiency maneuver, called "land and hold short," has aircrafts crisscrossing each other's runways. Each solution presents problems: piggybacking was suspended at O'Hare because of computer problems, and "land and hold short" was reduced in scope after some near collisions.[22] This is not a minor problem: Los Angeles International Airport was forced to create a Runway Incursion Action Team after experiencing a sharp increase in such incidents.

Changes in taxiing could also lower emissions. Delta Airlines, for instance, uses a single engine to taxi its planes, and at its hub in Atlanta alone the measure saved the company $5.9 million in fuel costs in 1995. Not all airplanes are able to taxi with just one engine, and in wet conditions the practice can cause the plane to slide to one side. Emissions reductions can also be achieved by powering ground-service equipment with electricity or alternative fuels and having aircraft sitting at gates plug directly into the terminal for electricity instead of running polluting auxiliary engines. Jet engines with dramatically lower emissions of carbon dioxide and nitrogen oxide could be in commercial use by 2008.[23]

Taxes raised from airline tickets, air cargo, and fuel sales are deposited in the federal Aviation Trust Fund (ATF), which raises $10 billion a year. Only $4 billion of that money is used to improve airport infrastructure, and there have been some calls for all ATF money to be used for that purpose. But even an extra $6 billion a year is unlikely to buy free-flowing air traffic.

Another approach holds that passenger frustration would be reduced with a better flow of information. Passengers waiting for delayed flights often have no more clue to what's happening than a bare-bones message board. In late 2000, the federal Transportation Department proposed using the ubiquitous TV monitors in airport waiting rooms to display detailed information about the cause of delays and the likely prognosis. Other information-based schemes include mobile-phone paging of passengers with flight-delay information and accelerated electronic check-in.

Regional airports could help catch some of the overflow from congested fields like La Guardia, though the expansion of nearby Westchester County Airport has not had a notable effect on traffic there. "While this solution would meet with public resistance from local residents surrounding such airports, it is perhaps the most expedient and practical solution to airport congestion at the moment," writes Kenneth A. Cubbin.[24] For instance, a study at the University of Western Sydney concluded that diversion of small aircraft of up to thirty-six seats from Sydney Airport to nearby Bankstown Airport "seems to offer a phenomenal tradeoff in terms of improving the capacity of Australia's major aviation gateway," according to Australia's *Business Review Weekly.*[25] But regional airports are major developments, often creating environmental problems of their own. That would obviously be the case if Florida's Homestead Airport were built.

Small airports are the hub for Richard Nobel's plan to offer a national air-taxi service for business travelers, using an Internet-based reservation system. The Scotland-born Nobel, who in an earlier incarnation set a land-speed record in a jet-powered car, says that harried frequent fliers could summon his high-speed planes to the nearest small airport, just as they would call a ground taxi. According to *Business Week,* Nobel bases his business plan on the fact that there are 5,736 airfields in the United States, only 3 percent of which are served by large commercial jets. Nobel claims that larger planes and bigger airports are "precisely what passengers don't want. We're coming the other way, offering point-to-point service that you schedule at your convenience."[26]

Nobel's approach is interesting, but it would be limited to expense-account business travelers. To really make a difference at our congested airports, more drastic changes are needed. Suppose we made airports obsolete?

DECENTRALIZING FLIGHT

There has to be a better way. Anyone who's taken a flight from a congested metropolis in recent years knows that the elapsed time in getting to the airport, parking, and finding your gate is often longer (and certainly more aggravating) than the flight itself. Such annoyances are a factor in record increases in train travel, especially when railroad stations are well located. I was once stuck in immovable traffic on the way to Kennedy Airport and watched my plane to the Netherlands Antilles island of Bonaire take off without me. The next flight was in a week, so I went elsewhere for my vacation.

In March 2001, the *New York Times* had three of its reporters race from Washington to New York City via train (the new Acela Express), plane (the US Airways shuttle), and automobile (a 1973 Checker Marathon). As it happened, the plane beat the train to first place, but only by a relatively insignificant 25 minutes.[27]

Suppose the airport was the vacant lot across the street? Suppose you could make your own schedule and take off whenever you felt like it? "Science-fiction writers have often projected a world in which ordinary people have their own airplanes, flying them as casually as we drive our cars on freeways," says the book *Turbulent Skies*.[28] That situation did indeed exist in the early days of aviation, especially after World War I, when surplus planes were very cheap and neither licensing nor regulation was widespread.

But let's take it further than that, to aircraft that can actually land in your driveway. Igor Sikorsky, one of the pioneers of the helicopter, dreamed of just that. I've always had a soft spot for the Russian-born Sikorsky, since the helicopter factory that bears his name is just up the road from me. When he was working for what was then United Aircraft, Sikorsky's Rube Goldberg–style helicopter, little more than a frame with a rotor, first flew over Connecticut in 1939.

During World War II, Sikorsky produced experimental helicopters for the army, but he was already thinking of a postwar use for his invention. In a fascinating 1943 film hosted by the Russian-accented Sikorsky himself, an announcer asks, "Let's see what might happen after the war is won." An American dad leaves work and is seen buying bread and milk at the supermarket, then loading it into a ludicrous little basket on the nose of his curbside Sikorsky helicopter. He takes off for home.

The announcer continues, apparently unaware that his commentary is totally sexist: "The missus calls the children, Betsy, Tony, and Curry the pooch. She tosses off a little light laundry, just like any American housewife. It's about time for the man of the house to be coming home with the groceries for supper. Here he is now, coming in through the trees to land in his own backyard, way out in the suburbs, miles from the office."

A crisis develops. The guy forgot the butter, so the missus, "womanlike and wifelike," sends him back to the store in his enormous helicopter. "A fanciful scene that can't happen tomorrow," the announcer concludes, adding that the home-based helicopter may take a few years. Indeed, almost sixty years later it hasn't happened. "We don't think the personal helicopter will ever be reality," says a current Sikorsky spokesman, Bill Tuttle. "We never say never, but we're not working on it as a mass consumer item."

Why not? It seems easy enough when you first think about it. Many of us were reared on the 1960s TV cartoon *The Jetsons,* whose breadwinner husband, George, drove a twenty-first-century flying car that could hit five hundred miles per hour and fold up into a suitcase. (The show was rather inconsistent, in that some episodes featured those same folding cars sitting in parking lots.)

Flying cars founder on the unimaginably difficult air-traffic-control nightmare they present, not to mention high insurance costs and the training necessary to turn every ordinary driver into a pilot. The dream of personal flight does not die easily, however. Though nobody's ever been able to make the concept work commercially, there have been some fascinating might-have-beens. In the course of my research, I came upon the legend of the postwar flying cars and found the story irresistible. Why can't your airplane also be your automobile? To answer that question, I sought out a pioneer who just happens to live near me.

Robert Edison Fulton Jr. lives in a converted barn on fifty acres of rolling hills in Newtown, Connecticut. Fulton, who's ninety-two and has the full head of white hair expected of the slightly eccentric inventor, would have a secure place in history if he'd stopped after developing one of the world's first flight simulators. And his Skyhook system for rescuing downed pilots has also proven itself in the field. But Fulton's most fanciful invention is the one that brought me to Newtown: in the 1940s, just after World War II, he designed and built a flying car, the Airphibian, and proved that it could be safely manufactured.

Young Fulton grew up in an era when both internal combustion and aviation were new fields. He was immersed in both. During World War II, Fulton flew around the country demonstrating his flight simulator. Since fuel was rationed, he occasionally got stranded at local airports, and that started him thinking: why couldn't his plane, which after all had wheels, controls, and an engine, simply drive him to town? Why couldn't it be both a car and an airplane?

"I got started on it right after the war," he remembers with undiminished enthusiasm. "I figured that an airplane can't drive down the road because of the wings, so why not leave the wings behind?" On the Airphibian, which indeed looks like half a car meshed with half an airplane, the wing assembly can be disconnected from the cockpit section with a system of push rods and rolled away. Then the propeller is removed, the rear-wheel drive engaged, and the "pilot" drives off. A safety interlock prevents the plane from being started unless the wings are properly reattached. A working Airphibian was first shown to the press at the Danbury Municipal Airport in 1946. Not surprisingly, the public was crazy about it. A "gag" photo of the period shows a cop giving Fulton a ticket for "flying too low," attended by a large, grinning crowd.

From here on the story takes a sad turn. The Civil Aeronautics Administration granted Fulton an aircraft certificate for his Airphibian in 1950, but not before it had crash-tested eight complete planes and blown up a pile of engines. The prolonged testing put Fulton into a financial hole, and he had to find investors (usually flying out to meet them in the Airphibian, then giving them rides). Fulton's major investor bought control of the company with his money and eventually decided to shut the operation down—just after it won the coveted certification. "I was disgusted and discouraged," said Fulton. "I was sure there was a market. Lots of people wanted to buy an Airphibian." The car-plane would have cost about $7,500—not cheap then, but not bad either when you consider that it was both a car *and* a plane.

"One friend told me that the problem is you can't have a vehicle that's both a good car and a good airplane; it has to be a compromise," Fulton says. "I told him he had it the wrong way around. The cars and planes we build today are compromises because they can do only one thing." Today, one of Fulton's Airphibians is in the Smithsonian.

Fulton is certainly not the only person to dream of a flying car in every garage. The Curtiss company built an experimental Autoplane as early as 1917. *Air and Space* magazine said in 1995 that more than seventy-six patents for automobiles with wings had been filed in the United States since 1918.[29] Moulton Taylor was inspired by Fulton to build his own Aerocar, five of which were produced (and one of which was purchased and used by actor Bob Cummings). Singer Chuck Berry sang about an "airmobile" in his 1956 song "You Can't Catch Me"; it had "a powerful motor and some hideaway wings."

A company called Consolidated Vultee built a working model of a flying car in 1947. Consolidated thought it had hit upon a sure thing. "The market for this flying automobile will be far greater than a conventional light plane," the company promised. "The purchasers can obtain daily use from the car to get more out of the investment."[30] The actual appeal of the car-plane is hard to judge. It certainly looked good; it weighed only 725 pounds because of its fiberglass body; and it could achieve forty-five miles per gallon on the ground. The ConvAIRCAR looked like a typical sedan of the period, with the airplane wings, motor, and tail in one removable structure mounted on the roof.

Unfortunately, before the public got a chance to buy a ConvAIRCAR, the one prototype crash-landed in the California desert. While no flying cars have ever made it to market, a car that *swims* did. It was the Amphicar, built from 1961 to 1968 by IWK in West Germany. Some 3,700 were sold, and most of them were imported to the States. A 1960s road test described the Amphicar, whose light weight and high center of gravity made it prone to crosswinds, as "not a very good car, and not a very good boat either."[31] The Amphicar was not a huge marketing success, but it has its fierce partisans today and is eminently collectible.

It would be fifty years before the dream of flying cars was revived. Their main advocates today are not backyard inventors with big dreams but respected aerospace engineers and even a NASA scientist.

Branko Sarh, a senior engineer at McDonnell Douglas Aerospace, promotes an ultramodern four-passenger airplane with folding wings called the Advanced Flying Automobile, which he believes would cost $200,000 on the retail market. Ken Wernicke, who was lead engineer on the experimental XV-15 tilt-rotor aircraft and director of the troubled V-22 Osprey while at Bell Helicopter Textron, has his own concept, the Aircar, that saves money by using short, stubby wings that don't fold in. On the road, the Aircar is the width of a city bus.[32]

My favorite of the new designs is the four-seater M400 Skycar, a decidedly modern flying car, powered by eight rotary engines, that can take off and land vertically like a British Harrier jet—and, it must be said, like a helicopter. If you're going to land it in your backyard, such vertical capability would seem to be essential.

Dr. Paul Moller, the Davis, California, designer of the Skycar, certainly has the credentials. Though he grew up on a rural chicken ranch in British Columbia, it was plain from an early age that Moller would never be a farmer. He built a two-story model house when he was nine, and his own Ferris wheel when he was eleven. A sports car followed at age fifteen. But flight had taken hold of him, and he designed his first helicopter later that same year.

Unlike Igor Sikorsky, however, Moller knew that the helicopter—with its dangerous rotor and inherently high costs—would never be an appropriate commuter vehicle. Though he was not a college graduate, Moller so impressed McGill University's aeronautics department that he was invited into its doctoral program, which he completed in three years. From there, he moved to the University of California at Davis, where he taught aeronautics for eleven years and further developed his ideas of personal aircraft.

Moller's ideas centered on vertical takeoff and landing, known as VTOL in the trade. He built and tested his first prototype, the XM-2, with UC-Davis graduate students in 1964. A succession of VTOL prototypes followed, incorporating Wankel rotary engines after 1969. By 1990, the inventor had two dozen patents, but still no production-ready aircraft.

With the Skycar, Moller is getting close. It's actually far wilder looking than George Jetson's commuter car, resembling a canopied rocket pod with huge engines mounted on either side. The four-seat Skycar, something of a flying Batmobile, has a range of 900 miles and a maximum speed of 350 miles per hour, gets fifteen miles per gallon, and can run on almost any fuel, including diesel, propane, or French fry oil. On the road, using a built-in electric motor, it can cruise at thirty miles per hour, though getting such an odd-looking contraption certified for the road will be a tall order. It's loud and wide and may have to be licensed as a motorcycle.

If marketed today, Skycars would cost $1 million each, though Moller thinks the cost could be brought down to $60,000 with the economies of scale inherent in mass production. Alas, I myself have not seen the Skycar, but *Marketplace* reporter Wendy Nelson, who did, compared it to a "noisy weed whacker."[33]

When I spoke to Moller, he seemed preoccupied with funding questions, wondering out loud why all the federal aeronautical research money was going to space flight instead of the admittedly more mundane problem of moving people around on our own planet. "There's no vision about how we can build airports to accommodate the phenomenal growth of aviation," he said. "There are more and more delays every year. The infrastructure has gotten close to saturation. It's a terminal state of affairs."

I'm not sure that Moller intended the pun there, because he's a very serious guy. At the time we talked, he was fresh from congressional testimony in which he urged renewed funding for aeronautical research. Engineers today, he said, go into mechanical engineering because there's no money to be made designing airplanes anymore.

Skycar makes practical sense, Moller said, because 85 percent of all travel mileage is clocked in round-trips of one hundred miles or more. The Skycar would probably not be a commuter vehicle, but it could be used, particularly by people who live in low-density neighborhoods, for longer trips from home to "vertiport."

Can the average American be expected to pilot something as fast and fearsome as the Skycar? Not even Moller thinks so. "It would be better if they never piloted anything in their life," he said. "In most aircraft today, the human being is the only weakness in the system." Skycar flights would be totally automated, programmed like the SkyTran pods. There is a precedent for this, since, between landing and takeoff, commercial jets are largely operated on autopilot. Moller pointed out that the F-16 fighter jet, as one example, is inherently so unstable that no person could actually fly it. Like the F-16, the Skycar would have quadruple backup systems to take over if the autopilot failed.

Moller's first customer could be the military, for which a $1 million price tag is not a big obstacle. The Skycar could be a kind of flying jeep. The cost per passenger mile is about a fifth of that of a B-52 bomber, so there may be future uses for counterterrorism and other fast intervention. Border interdiction and search-and-rescue operations are other possibilities that might take precedence over civilian sales. Moller estimates that personal aircraft like the Skycar will be "fully deployed and part of everyone's life" within twenty-five years. Don't believe it? Keep in mind that, in 1907, a prominent Detroit businessman described cars as a "mindless menace of no use but scaring horses and small children." It's very hard to predict with any accuracy if Moller's vision will be realized, but it certainly demands suspension of current realities.

One of Moller's biggest champions is Dennis Bushnell, chief scientist at the NASA Langley Research Center in Virginia. He's been at NASA for more than thirty-five years, beginning with work on the Apollo and Gemini space programs. In more than three decades, he's worked on the Space Shuttle, submarines, mag-lev trains, and even America's Cup racers. NASA has funded the $70 million Small Aircraft Transportation System (SATS) program, with the aim of getting frequent fliers out of big hub airports and into some of the 14,000 regional alternatives around the country. Instead of large jumbo jets, the commuter of tomorrow might fly in something like the six-seat Eclipse 500, an affordable $775,000 jet limousine promoted by former Ford chairman Red Poling.[34]

"Every ten years or so the personal aircraft idea is revived, and it makes the cover of *Popular Mechanics*," says the fast-talking Bushnell. "It's never gone anywhere because of the absolute requirement that the operator be a pilot. But now we have the computer technology to make that unnecessary." Bushnell offered details of very sophisticated satellite-based GPS systems that would make short work of flying a plane like the Skycar. "Where we end up is the possibility of totally automatic flight available to the very young, the infirm, and the inebriated alike," he said.

Bushnell cites statistics blaming 80 percent of all air accidents on human factors. "And we kill 40,000 a year with human-operated ground vehicles," he said. "Half of all car accidents are caused by road rage, and computers are not prone to that." But, of course, computers do crash.

The Skycar, says Bushnell, leapfrogs the congested airport infrastructure. Instead of driving to an airport, flying to a hub city, then taking a regional aircraft to your actual destination, the Skycar could deliver passengers right where they want to go at 350 miles per hour. "The total market for machines like this is $1 trillion," he asserts, though high initial prices would obviously deter all but the wealthy.

But if prices do come down and the air is filled with Skycars, there could be serious air-traffic questions. Such obstacles are not necessarily insurmountable. Bushnell describes Moller as "one of the most creative engineers in the country" and asserts that he will offer ingenious solutions to these problems. The Skycar, he adds, is "like the initial entrepreneur's approach to what may turn out to be General Motors."

But the concept of personal aircraft has its influential critics, among them Dr. Paul MacCready of AeroVironment, an aviation pioneer himself, in ultralight aircraft. I asked MacCready if people would ever routinely fly to work. "Nothing is impossible," he said. "Moller's been at it thirty-five years. They used to say that personal aircraft were twenty years in the future, now it's thirty. It's technologically feasible. There are GPS navigation systems that can take off and land by themselves without a pilot on board, though I personally wouldn't want to ride in something like that. But the American public is not enthused, for good reason, about losing control of their vehicles. Drivers want to be in charge, though they love things like adaptive cruise control, which will warn them if the car ahead is braking. It's a far different culture to turn over control of the car to something automatic, then sit back and read a paper. And that's on the ground. In an airplane, it gets much more complicated."

MacCready doesn't expect to see widespread adoption of personal aircraft for at least the next thirty years. But he remains enamored of the possibilities. He looks at nature and compares the mouse, which can spend all night wandering around a quarter acre, to the bat, which can roam over a million acres in a single evening. Who wouldn't rather be the bat? MacCready has some intriguing ideas for the future of decentralized flight. How about a remote-operated unmanned aircraft that could deliver pizza, for instance? "The highway in the sky is very attractive, but we have to figure out how to actually use it," he said.

I forgot to ask MacCready about the SoloTrek, but I have a pretty good idea what he would have said about it. If you think the Skycar is too confining and too complicated, this personalized flight pack is for you. For much longer than people have dreamed of flying cars, they've imagined having their own wings. Icarus tried out a pair and flew too close to the sun, which resulted in a fatal crash. Many's the nineteenth-century inventor who took the plunge with a homemade construction of wood, canvas, and feathers.

Buck Rogers moved around with a rocket pack, and a latter-day rocket pack actually flew over Houston for twenty-eight seconds in 1995, the *Salt Lake Tribune* reported.[35] A second flight wasn't possible for the RB-2000 belt, which used hydrogen peroxide and nitrogen as fuel, because the partners had a serious falling out—one ended up dead, and a second one was accused of the murder.

Michael Moshier has his own vision. Moshier doesn't have the aerospace experience of Paul Moller, though he was a jet fighter pilot during the Vietnam War. His SoloTrek, which has also received NASA funding, looks like an upended Jet Ski. The pilot is strapped to it in a standing position, then takes off with 120 horsepower on tap, operating through horizontally mounted twin fans. The craft is steered with handheld controls.

Theoretically, SoloTrek can run on regular gas, hover for three hours, reach speeds of up to 70 knots, and travel 150 nautical miles. The prototype features a two-cycle gasoline engine, but nonpolluting electric power is also envisioned. Its performance is theoretical because, at the time of this writing, it had not yet been tested in actual flight. If it ends up on the ash heap of history, personal flight division, it will have considerable company.

I don't mean to be flip about some of these inventions: I love the fact that entrepreneurs are willing to toil away, raising their own money and risking their reputations on our intractable transportation problems. Anything that addresses the challenge of airport congestion and the pollution associated with large airliners is worth pursuing seriously.

10

THE WATER ROUTE:
A DREAM OF FAST FERRIES

I HAD A VISION of how waterborne transit could work when I visited Sydney, Australia, and saw the graceful ferryboats come in past the famous Opera House and deposit hundreds of commuters on the dock right downtown. Sydney's ferry services are so extensive that a color-coded route map looks like a guide to London's Underground. There are no less than eleven routes radiating from five wharves in the main hub at picturesque Circular Quay, each connected by bus services to inland points.

More than any other place I've seen, Sydney has turned its ferryboats into an integral part of daily commuting. As in Washington, D.C.'s subway system, passengers move through automatic ticket gates, inserting stubs bought at vending machines.

Sydney has modern ferries—it added two low-wash Harbor Cats, the *Anne Sargeant* and the *Pam Burridge,* in 1998. But it also has a thing about continuity. *Kangara,* for instance, entered service as a nine-hundred-passenger coal-fired steamer ferry in 1912. The boat was still going strong carrying commuters in 1959, when it was fitted with a diesel engine. *Kangara* was finally retired in the 1980s and is now a museum exhibit.

Not all cities have been able to make conventional ferry service work, even when traffic congestion, inclinations toward mass transit, and ideal harbor conditions would seem to argue for it. San Francisco, for instance, has a majestic natural harbor and bay, and plenty of reason to want to get its harried commuters off the road and onto the water. The city did have a major ferry system that thrived until the great era of bridge building in the 1930s. But as the Bay Area Council reported in 1998, "Since that time, the use of the Bay for water transit has declined, and it has become a significantly under-utilized resource."[1] The Bay Area is slowly reviving its historical use of water routes, as I discovered when taking an excellent high-speed ferry from Larkspur in Marin County straight into the heart of the city.

The council is an advocate for San Francisco ferries, and to that end it took a close look at how other cities—Seattle, Sydney, Vancouver, and Hong Kong—make it work. The results are fascinating. What the water-transit systems had in common, the report said, were a comprehensive network of routes, frequent and convenient departure times, travel times competitive with other means of travel, guaran-teed on-time service and reliability, a high quality of service, efficient dockside facilities, reasonable fares, a good assurance of safety, and an intermodel interface with other travel, including both surface trans-portation and pedestrian walkways.

Bringing all these crucial elements together, on time and on budget, has proven elusive for many municipal transit agencies. And that's one reason ferry service remains a minuscule part of today's public-transit picture, at least in the United States. According to the American Public Transportation Association, ferryboats provided 0.6 percent of all transit trips in 1998. A possible explanation is that the ferries in active service are an average of twenty-six years old and travel, on average, at the crawling speed of 8.3 miles per hour. Most are powered by dirty diesels, and virtually none are air-conditioned.[2]

Things are better in Europe, where ferries are generally more modern and faster and perform a vital role in international travel. According to *Market Intelligence Report,* an industry newsletter, "Conventional ferries have become more sophisticated in design, tech-nology and comfort in a market that could be likened to a roller-coaster ride." Some ferry routes have been hit hard by a loss of duty-free shopping as Europe moves to a single currency and breaks down border barriers. Escalating fuel prices have also had an impact, as they have on all forms of travel in Europe. The Channel Tunnel from England to France, opened in 1994, was also a major blow to ferry travel, since the sleek Eurostar trains that pass through it can make the trip from London to Paris in just two hours and forty-nine minutes.

Some American cities treasure their ferryboats, especially Seattle. The Puget Sound Regional Council reports that passenger service on the sound increased by a whopping 600,000 trips from 1997 to 1998. Regional ferry services, with eighty-one miles of routes, carried 23.4 million riders in 1998. An added benefit of the Seattle-bound car ferries (traveling from Bremerton, Bainbridge Island, and Vashon) is that they carry a significant number of walk-on passengers, 60 percent on the Seattle-Bremerton run. All but one of Puget Sound's ferry docks, operated by Washington State Ferries, connect to public transit, making it easy for those walkers. And many downtown Seattle jobs are within walking distance of the terminals.

One reason Seattle-Bremerton enjoyed one of the highest ridership increases in 1998 was the addition of a new and faster passenger boat, the *Chinook,* which cut travel time from fifty minutes to thirty-five. But the *Chinook* was forced to slow down after developing major wake problems. Auto gridlock, terrible and getting worse in Seattle, was probably another factor in sharp ridership increases.

Will Seattle be able to sustain its incredible ferry growth? There are some serious danger signs, including heavy pressure to raise fares substantially in the wake of the 1999 Initiative 695, which cut automobile license taxes that had funded 30 percent of ferry operations.[3]

But Seattle needs its ferries desperately. I talked to Laura Hitchcock, a legislative analyst for the Seattle City Council and a veteran of the fight for alternative transportation there. I had assumed that Seattle had a public-transportation system comparable to Portland's, but I was shocked to discover that it's not so at all. "Traffic is just terrible in Seattle," Hitchcock told me. "It's the third or fourth worst city for congestion in the country, and the vehicle miles traveled are growing disproportionately to the population increase." The water on two sides of Seattle pushes traffic onto narrow corridors, she explained, creating near-total gridlock, particularly on the bridges to Redmond, home of Microsoft. "It would make a considerable difference if Microsoft allowed more telecommuting, but they're fanatical about wanting everyone on the campus," Hitchcock sighed.

Seattle is only now building its first single-line light-rail system, a process fraught with the usual legal challenges. A plan to build a station in a low-income neighborhood aboveground, instead of below the surface like the other stations, has brought charges of racism. A referendum approved plans to extend Seattle's venerable monorail system, built in 1961 for the World's Fair, but the extension is unfunded. As in Portland, transit has its critics in Seattle: one sponsored a voter initiative that would have reserved all transportation funds for highways only.

"Transportation ranks consistently at the top of what people in Seattle want their government to do," Hitchcock said. But in Seattle, as elsewhere, development and transportation priorities sometimes clash. Nordstrom's recently agreed to retain its downtown department store as a redevelopment anchor only if the city would help it build a $70 million parking garage. The city agreed.

Sydney, with a population slightly larger than Seattle's, carries about half as many passengers (13 million a year) in a watery network that is nearly as large (sixty-seven miles of routes). As the Bay Area Council report notes, "Today's modern [ferry] fleet provides a myriad of inner harbor and river ferry services, as well as services across the outer harbor to the seaside resort of Manly." State Transit's main emphasis is on commuter service, and several ferry routes offer multiple stops to enhance ridership. Harbor cruises are popular, too, including a "Nightzoo" run to see the animals after dark. Patronage on the Sydney services increased 18 percent between 1994 and 1997.

Sydney's ferry services are fully intermodal, connecting to buses, trains, and the city's monorail. Passengers can purchase seven-day Sydney Pass tickets that allow unlimited use of all transit modes.

Hong Kong is one of the most crowded cities in the world, and more than 90 percent of its 6.5 million residents depend on some form of transit. I've experienced Hong Kong's legendary gridlock firsthand, and the hilly geography makes it almost impossible to add any new roads. It's not surprising, then, that some one hundred miles of ferry routes carry an amazing 30 million passengers per year. Regional ferries move more passengers than Hong Kong's international airport. The ferries, most of them on short runs of less than two miles, are the essential link to Hong Kong's outer islands. Terminals offer intermodal connections, which in Hong Kong means trains, trams, minibuses, and taxis.

Hong Kong ferries are experiencing both rising operating costs and declining patronage, according to the Bay Area Council report. The result has been the cancellation of some nonessential routes. Private companies have taken up some of the slack. In the short term, Hong Kong will probably experience some loss of ferry riders, though the long-term health of the system seems assured.

Vancouver, British Columbia's system is small compared to the others in the Bay Area Council report, but it is very important to the region. Some 1.8 million residents make 5 million ferry passenger trips per year. And that's all on a single 1.75-mile route between North Vancouver and the downtown area across Burrard Inlet. The two SeaBus ferries, on schedule 99 percent of the time, are fully integrated with Vancouver's excellent and automated light-rail system, SkyTrain. Sixty percent of all ferry rides are transfers from other forms of transit. Service is uniformly high: the ferries can unload one group of four hundred passengers and board another in a thrilling ninety seconds.

So there are stresses and strains in these ferry systems, but an overall efficiency and integration into daily life ensures their continued survival. A worrisome element, however, are those naggingly slow average speeds. When a crossing is measured in hours, not minutes, it becomes a cruise rather than a commute. Some of the biggest ridership increases are on ferry routes that have added faster ships. Fortunately, high-speed technology is allowing the modern ferryboat to take a giant step forward in moving passengers in comfort and at speeds commensurate with other forms of travel.

FAST FERRIES

The bridge of the catamaran ferry *Tatobam,* which carries gamblers across Long Island Sound between New London, Connecticut, and Glen Cove, on Long Island, looks like a jetliner's cockpit. Captain Grant Parker, who doubles as Fox Navigation's director of marine operations, allowed me into this lofty perch to see a fast ferry in action.

A catamaran ferry looks like a monohull craft with a giant tunnel punched down the middle. It achieves speed by keeping most of its weight out of the water. When its 13,000-horsepower twin gas-turbine engines are throttled up, the *Tatobam,* like its sister ship the *Sassacus* (both named after Pequot Indian chiefs), can reach forty-seven knots (fifty-four miles per hour), making it the fastest ferry in the world on a regular run. *Tatobam,* which can carry 290 passengers, offers computerized steering via its twin water jets and state-of-the-art global-positioning and radar equipment to keep it out of harm's way (which on the sound mainly means lobster pots and small pleasure crafts).

Parker's crew shouted observations as we moved slowly down the Thames River through a busy commercial harbor lined with freighters, warehouses, and cranes that caught the early morning light.

"Doors secure!"

"Nozzles and buckets [the ship's version of a rudder and propeller] are responding. Port is reset, starboard is reset, going for lock-in. All clear on the stern."

"All clear to start."

Like a pilot requesting clearance, Parker kept in close contact with the harbormaster. "We're heading southbound for the ledge," he said into his radio. The ship's horn sounded. The *Tatobam* was moving forward at eleven knots, which felt like idling speed.

"There's a small motorboat on the starboard side," warned the navigator.

"Acknowledged," Parker said.

As we passed the harbor lighthouse, the traffic eased up, and

Parker told me about his ship, one of five built only a mile away from the ferry dock at the Pequot River Shipworks. One of the others is working in the Bahamas; another makes regular runs from Long Beach, California, to Catalina Island. A third is heading for Argentina. Like Fox Navigation, the shipyard is a wholly owned subsidiary of Connecticut's very wealthy Mashantucket Pequot Tribe, owners of Foxwoods, the world's most profitable casino. These fast ferries aren't some transportation agency's answer to traffic congestion; they're a speedy and ultraefficient way to deliver "gamers" to the casino's door.

"We have a lot of redundancy on board this ship," Parker told me. "Three global-positioning units, two radars. We also have a night vision camera system that can magnify ambient light 300,000 times. We're not designed to any national code, but to an international one, which has much higher standards." Safety is part of that code: the *Tatobam* carries four one-hundred-person Inflatable Buoyant Apparatuses (better known as rubber rafts) and can be fully evacuated in twelve minutes. Because of its speed, it can also be used as a rescue vessel in the sound.

The *Tatobam* is far more maneuverable than a conventional ferry, which can move only in a straight line and needs considerable open water to turn around. Catamaran ferries like it not only have very shallow drafts but can move laterally, making them ideal for changeable tide conditions and busy ports of call. "We can service previously unreachable routes," Parker said.

The captain told me that catamaran ferries are environmentally friendly. "Our gas turbines produce .03 grams per kilowatt hour of nitrogen oxides, compared to 1.77 grams in a conventional diesel," he said. He also claimed that the ship's water jets help oxygenate the pollution-challenged sound, making it better able to support marine organisms. The considerable wake produced by catamaran ferries is a problem, but on the whole they're considerably more environmentally friendly than large oceangoing diesels. The Bluewater Network reports that some commercial ships pollute as much as two thousand diesel trucks, partly because they burn what's called "bunker fuel," a low-grade fuel that contains five thousand times the sulfur of standard diesel.[4] Large catamarans have the potential to handle some of the freight now carried on dirty ocean diesels, and even to be competitive with air freight on delivery times.

Richard "Skip" Hayward, chairman of the Mashantucket Pequot Tribal Council, was the driving force behind creating the tribe's fast-ferry business. "Hayward wants to build the marine superhighway of the future," Parker said. "Ferries like this can relieve the impact of building traffic on our highways, cut down on carbon dioxide emissions, and help end road rage."

By this point, with open water ahead, the *Tatobam* was cruising at forty-five knots, close to its top speed. There was no great sensation of movement, though the engines produced a muted roar. The ride was comparable to that on an Amtrak train.

If there's a significant difference between this ferry and those slow boats that cruise to the islands in the summer, it's the absence of any passenger decks. Because of the speed at which they travel, fast-ferry riders have to stay indoors, and the effect is a little claustrophobic.

The captain sent me below and I headed down into the Clipper cabin, otherwise known as second class. Even in "coach," there was thick carpeting on the floor, gold basins in the bathrooms, and free bagels, coffee, and juice at the snack bar. Upstairs in Admiral Class ($30 more for a round-trip) there were bigger seats and windows, free pastries, and even liquor. After all, these are casino boats.

Trish, one of five stewards, was responsible for the Van Morrison CD playing softly in the cabin. "They're usually pretty quiet on the way back to Long Island," she told me. "They've spent their money, so they mostly just sleep." But Walter Cienkowski, a heavyset man with a crew cut from Oyster Bay, was awake after gambling most of the night. "It's a very comfortable trip," he said, "and much better than the bus to Atlantic City." Cienkowski had one gripe, however. "We only have five and a half hours to gamble," he says. "It's not enough."

Tatobam was now entering Glen Cove's pretty natural harbor, which is dotted with moored sailboats. The ferry dock is, in fact, part of a harbor-revitalization program for Glen Cove that has seen the launch of a Superfund cleanup, including the removal of a polluting incinerator and two smokestacks.[5] The city was cited as a federal showcase "brownfield," or abandoned and contaminated industrial site, in 1998.

Only eighteen passengers disembarked on Long Island, but hundreds got on, filling the boat to near capacity for the two-hour 9:00 A.M. run. Almost all were Foxwoods gamblers like Hilda Ciaccio, a Uniondale secretary, and her friend Viola Ryan, who is retired from a career at the Long Island Lighting Company. "It's a great way to travel," Ciaccio told me. "You get met by a very clean bus, and in ten minutes you're at the casino. The bus to Atlantic City takes three hours and it's terrible." Ciaccio and Ryan paid $59 for their round-trip tickets, which includes the bus ride, a meal voucher, and—a big plus for them—$10 in blackjack coupons.

A big line formed for the free breakfast, though everyone studiously avoided the New York Council on Problem Gambling flyers on the counter. The gamblers, many of them elderly, were dressed in a variety of leisure wear. When the *Tatobam* recrossed the sound and reached the New London dock, its passengers filed out and straight onto a fleet of five Arrow coaches. Although the dock is a five-minute walk to New London's charming and as yet ungentrified downtown, most fast-ferry passengers never see it.

As the passengers transferred from ferry to bus, a process that takes about ten minutes, I wandered up the street to another intermodal connection, New London's venerable Union Station. Now attached to a Greyhound Bus terminal (which offers nine buses to Foxwoods daily) and exclusively serving Amtrak passengers, the brownstone station was built in 1887 by the noted nineteenth-century architect Henry Hobson Richardson in an understated Romanesque style that's said to prefigure twentieth-century designs. In a typical period gesture, the forces of urban renewal nearly tore down the terminal in 1961.

Union Station boasted a large poster for Amtrak Acela service, which it proclaimed, erroneously, was "arriving in late 1999." I sat down and watched a New Yorker inquire about the next coach to Manhattan, while a waiting passenger talked into a cell phone in Russian. The place has a cosmopolitan aura, somewhat marred by the hideous circa 1976 interior renovation, which damages the building's inherent grace.

Just up the hill from Union Station is Bank Street, the heart of downtown and once home to a thriving whaling community. There are the inevitable eighteenth-century homes turned into pubs and coffee bars, but Bank Street has a lively, unpretentious feel. It's a very walkable street. A centerpiece is the Hygienic Restaurant, not an eatery at all but an art gallery (though retaining the former restaurant's stools and Formica tabletop, complete with spots worn smooth by coffee drinkers' elbows).

The Hygienic's storefront (like Union Station, it is listed on the National Register of Historic Places) was built in 1844 as a whaling office and crew quarters; it became a restaurant in 1919 and was locally famous for remaining open all night (explaining the worn spots). The Hygienic, which closed as a restaurant in the 1980s but remained as a showcase for local artists, also almost disappeared under the wrecking ball but was saved at the last minute by a massive community outpouring and some state grants.

After a $700,000 restoration, the Hygienic was fully transformed into a gallery space with artists' cooperatively owned lofts above. It is, in short, a prime example of a smart city project. Unfortunately, I was the only visitor to the Hygienic's show of female nudes on a recent Saturday. Sherry Stidfole, who was looking after the space, noted that Operation Sail had, like the ferryboats, recently brought thousands of tourists to downtown New London. "But even when that was going on, you wouldn't have found it crowded down here," she said.

Part of the problem is physical. At the time of my visit, the ferry dock was cut off from the railroad station and downtown by a high barbed-wire fence and the tracks themselves. Even a visitor not being herded onto a bus would have little sense that a thriving downtown lay across that barren stretch of waste ground. A planned passenger walkway should improve matters, but the situation illustrates a common urban problem: showcase revitalization projects, from football stadiums to casinos, are so entirely self-contained that they don't create "spillover" traffic for nearby restaurants and other businesses. And that can be true even when they're served by a model intermodal transportation hub like the one in New London.

GROWING PAINS

One would think that ferry services would be relatively uncontroversial: they're not airports, highways, or railroad tracks, and people seldom get displaced or inconvenienced by them. But the road to a national network of fast ferries has been fraught indeed.

The Pequots have had their own problems. Plans to use the *Sassacus* on gambling runs between New London and Manhattan fell through in 1998, after the state Department of Transportation disapproved its lease with Chelsea Piers.[6] After the *Sassacus* began docking at Martha's Vineyard that same year, an upset Tisbury Board of Health imposed a $100-a-day fine, citing the pier's lack of a proper septic system and handicapped-access bathrooms. The dispute was resolved, and the service continues.[7] In Glen Cove, antiferry contingents opposed to gambling on moral grounds staged pickets, and city councilmen objected to the terms of the deal that established the dock.[8]

Those are fairly normal development hassles. But some of the problems relate to the specific nature of fast ferries. In 1999, the showplace fast-ferry operation from Bremerton to Seattle, Washington, a factor in a sharp increase in ridership there, was forced to slow down after shoreline residents along the route in Kitsap County complained that their beach was being "battered to bits" by the *Chinook*'s wake. "When the waves hit the bulkhead, it sounds like someone's hitting it with a baseball bat," said shoreline homeowner Jackie Rossworn, who added that her beach has lost most of its sand since the fast ferry began.

A superior court judge ordered the *Chinook* to slow down from

thirty miles per hour to a mere fourteen in its traverse through the
Rich Passage. The irony of a fast ferry becoming a slow ferry, and of
environmental objections to an environmentally motivated transit
project, was not lost on the participants. Washington State Ferries
says that its own engineering studies showed that beach damage was
probably due to natural erosion, but an emergency request for a stay
of the judge's ruling was turned down.

The ferry was forced to cut back from seventeen one-way trips a
day to a mere eleven, and passengers complained of lost productivity.
"I have to get up earlier and I have to shift my own schedule,"
groused ferry rider Bill Thaete, who works at Intel in Seattle.[9]

Wake problems also doomed a fast-ferryboat service in British
Columbia. After investing six years and $462 million in a projected
service between the city of Vancouver, on the mainland, and Nanaimo,
on Vancouver Island, B.C. Ferries and the state government gave up
in March 2000 and put two of its three 403-foot car ferries up for sale.
"The fast-ferry project was a failed experiment, and now we need to
move on," said Joy MacPhail, the British Columbia provincial minister in charge of the ferry service. The problem, as in Seattle, was out-
cry about high-energy waves damaging beaches and docks. Speed was
cut from forty-two to twenty-six miles per hour, making the ferries
slower than conventional boats, despite their appetite for more fuel.[10]

Plans to run fast ferries in my own Fairfield County, Connecticut,
commuter corridor have been similarly affected by delays and problems. In 1997, it looked like it was about to happen, motivated by
the sheer difficulty of getting to New York City's busy airports,
which, incredibly, have no direct train or subway service. The city of
Stamford, home to many Fortune 500 companies, had applied for two
federal grants, totaling as much as $7 million, to build a ferry termi-
nal at a twenty-eight-acre brownfield site, home to a former power
plant, in the city's economically challenged South End. John Byrne,
Stamford's director of public safety, health, and welfare, told me that
Stamford would build the terminal, a parking lot, waiting area, and
rest rooms, and private operators would run ferries to La Guardia
Airport and midtown Manhattan.

"It's clear that the private sector can't finance a facility like this," said Byrne, who during a stint as a city official in neighboring Bridgeport lined up the financing for construction of that city's ferry terminal, completed in 1996. "It's a marginal business at best, and it's hard to make a profit." Stamford businesses send 200,000 executives to La Guardia a year, so such a route should be "a home run for any operator," Byrne said.

There were then projected to be multiple operators at the Stamford dock. Dale Strand, a Stamford publisher who doubled as chairman of U.S. Multi-Hull, wanted to run a 112-foot, thirty-five-knot, 350-passenger ShuttleCat catamaran with service to La Guardia and midtown Manhattan. Strand had already been shut out of a deal at another marina, in Norwalk, because of concerns over parking and docking.

New Haven–based SeaConn Flying Boats wanted to build a $100 million high-speed ferry link that would, beginning in the fall of 1999, take passengers from Bridgeport's existing facility and the to-be-built Stamford dock to Manhattan and La Guardia Airport in Queens. "We think we'll be the first in the world to do something like this," said entrepreneur Doren Voeth, who has previously worked as a marketing executive with ferryboat services. "These will be, at seventy-five miles per hour, the fastest catamaran ferries anywhere." He predicted that his ferries could make the Stamford–to–La Guardia run, which can take up to two hours on trains and buses, in thirty-three minutes. In a year, said Voeth, a ferry commuter could save sixty eight-hour days.

None of this happened. A frustrated Dale Strand told me in 2000 that he'd found that "people just don't want to change things." Strand had given up his idea of service to La Guardia and instead promoted a more limited commuter service from Rye in Westchester County to New Haven, with the potential of providing 2 million rides a year. Strand claimed major support from commuters, who were "howling mad about traffic choking us to death."

By this point, Strand no longer had the thirty-five-knot ShuttleCat he'd showed to interested transit officials in 1997, but he pronounced his willingness to buy eight of them if he could just get a route approved. Unfortunately, Strand has track-record problems. While pursuing the Fairfield County plans, he also launched successful efforts to win a contract from the Rhode Island Public Transit Authority (RIPTA) to run a fast catamaran from Providence to Newport.

"He never came through," said Lee Beliveau, a RIPTA spokesman. "He was given a notice of award and was supposed to come back with specifications. It was never done. There was no boat in the water." The award was redirected to Boston Harbor Cruises, which runs conventional ferries. Passengers can now take a leisurely trip of eighty minutes from Providence to Newport, which Strand—whose catamarans could have made the trip in half the time—claims destroys the route for commuting. He blames RIPTA for not completing promised ferry terminals, and he is suing.

Despite a clear need, by 2000 SeaConn, U.S. Multi-Hull, and a third company, Lighthouse Landings, had all failed to initiate fast-ferry service between Connecticut and New York. The companies, wrote the *New York Times,* "have encountered numerous obstacles, from difficulty in raising capital to regulatory bureaucracy to local concerns about parking."[11]

The Metro-North Railroad did get into the ferry business late in 2000 when it began offering $3 one-way service across the Hudson River, connecting Rockland and Westchester Counties and giving harried commuters a chance to avoid the gridlocked Tappan Zee Bridge. Early indications were that it would take some convincing to get acculturated drivers out of their cars, despite the regular indignities visited on them. Meanwhile, New York–bound commuters continue to suffer, as traffic on the highways builds at 1.5 percent a year.

EVEN FASTER FERRIES

Because the wakes from thirty-five-knot ferries have caused substantial problems, especially in the congested areas most likely to want commuter boats, the successful launching of a boat that goes *one hundred* knots seems remote, but that's exactly what Ken Cook is planning.

Cook, who runs the Florida-based Hydrofoils Incorporated, is no transit person. Instead, from a very early age, he's been interested in skimming the water as fast as he possibly can. "I started when I was thirteen and have built sixty boats, mostly for racing," he told me. His first effort, built in 1955, was a 13.5-foot racing hydrofoil that ran at ninety miles per hour. It was designed to overcome the tendency these boats, which race in the unlimited class, have to flip over when making turns. He's still working on that, and he has "sunk a lot of boats" in the pursuit. Cook has designed hovercrafts for the U.S. Coast Guard, a radio-controlled hydrofoil for toymaker Tyco, a remote-controlled rocket boat that could exceed Mach 1 on water, a minesweeper, and a thirty-foot dive boat. "People kept asking me to build a ferry, but I said I'd only do that when I grew up," he joked.

Now he's grown up. Cook's twin gas-turbine-powered ferry design looks like a jet (or a mag-lev train, for that matter), with a completely enclosed cabin and thin "legs" that are the only part of the ferry that actually sits in the water. These are 8,000-horsepower "supercavitating" boats, meaning they travel faster than sixty knots. And why not, he asks? Cars go that fast on the highway, and boats have "thousands of feet of clearance." Cook claims that his designs are actually more stable in rough water, which can be a problem for conventional catamarans.

Supercavitating boats are environmentally sound, Cook said, because they displace only two and a half feet of water while in operation. That fact also means they create a very small wake, he added, canceling that particular objection to one-hundred-knot speeds.

No small transit agency or entrepreneur is going to be buying boats from Hydrofoils Incorporated, since the larger of his two designs, a 150-foot ferry that can carry 250 passengers, costs $23 million. Such a large capital investment raises questions about how any ferry line running a supercavitating boat could be profitable, even with municipal subsidies. Even on slower catamaran ferries, fares are often higher than surface transportation. SeaConn proposed a $637 monthly commutation ticket between Stamford and lower Manhattan, which compares rather unfavorably to the $218 Metro-North fare for the same trip. And ferry terminals are expensive to build. But Cook is undaunted. Unless ferries can keep up with road travel, he says, they will never truly be intermodal. "Why let the other forms of transportation claim most of the funding when most of the earth is water?" he asked. "In ten years, most industrial ferry companies will be using our boats."

Cook is probably being overly optimistic, but high-speed ferries *are* moving beyond the experimental stage. Fast catamarans ply Victoria Harbor in Hong Kong and many other Far East ports. There are many fast ferries in the Mediterranean, where in 1956 the very first fast people carrier started work between southern Italy and Sicily. Surface-effect, or hovercraft, ferries came into wide use in the 1960s. In the early 1980s I had a memorable ride in one from Tangier, Morocco, to Algeciras, in southern Spain. Catamarans appeared a little later, and the inherent superiority of their design quickly doubled fast-ferry production.[12]

The history is there, but the ferryboat has not yet begun to meet its potential. While I was out on the *Tatobam,* I marveled at all the empty water around us. On the whole crossing, we saw only a few distant pleasure boats.

Fast ferries are mostly powered by gas-turbine engines, which have large environmental advantages over diesel power. Cook's 150-foot fast ferry would produce emissions comparable to that of about thirty cars, while removing 250 cars from the road. Not too bad. Many hurdles remain in place before these super-fast boats routinely race around the world's waterways, but they can certainly play a vital role in the construction of a sustainable, intermodal transportation grid for the twenty-first century.

11

MOVING FORWARD

MY DAUGHTERS' favorite cartoon show is *The Wild Thornberrys,* which offers some useful nature lessons but also features a family traveling the world in a gigantic recreational vehicle (RV). When we told our seven-year-old that the family was considering going to the Belize jungle for a vacation, she replied solemnly, "We can't. We don't have an RV."

A version of the American dream is offered by the Winnebago Adventurer, designed to provide "the most homelike environment possible" as it follows the sun from campground to campground. Powered by Ford with a 6.8-liter Triton V-10 attached to a seventy-five-gallon gas tank, the Adventurer can boast of a satellite-ready Mobile Theater Sound System, a side-by-side refrigerator-freezer, and most likely, as Albert Brooks memorably described it in his film *Lost in America,* "a microwave that browns."

RVs like this take the American penchant for being king of the road to its ultimate extreme. The RV is a self-contained world, asking only for an electrical hookup and sewer connection. The RV's view is inward, not outward, and it's a good way *not* to see the U.S.A. But these castles on wheels are increasingly popular at the nation's national parks, which are suffering from terrible air pollution problems. A 2000 study by Abt Associates reported that poor visibility and haze are causing parks and nearby businesses to lose millions of dollars in revenue.

The parks' solution is mass transit. In the summer of 2000, Zion National Park in Utah initiated a mandatory shuttle-bus system, greatly reducing auto access to the most scenic vistas. At the Grand Canyon, a voluntary-use light-rail train is planned for the South Rim area, connecting visitors to trailheads and shuttles. At Acadia, a voluntary shuttle system was initiated on Mount Desert Island in 1999. An open-air tram will be used for special events and tours at Golden Gate Bridge. And Yosemite, considered by many to be the crown jewel of America's park system, is experimenting with voluntary shuttles to move visitors into and around the scenic valley.[1]

EMBRACING TRANSIT

For the parks, mass transit offers the only refuge from the RV onslaught. It's a good model for the nation to follow. While it's highly unlikely that America will become a nation of bus and light-rail passengers, public transportation offers the only possible solution to relieving an untenable traffic congestion and pollution problem. As painful as it may be for auto-dependent America, we will eventually have to get out of our cars.

We know we can't build out of the mess we've created. It's really pretty elementary, though it took a paper by Lewis M. Fulton, a researcher at the International Energy Agency in Paris, to really bring the point home. "At some level of congestion, any given driver will choose to avoid dealing with the congestion, either in favor of an alternative route, an alternative mode, changing the departure time of the trip, a shorter trip to a similar activity, or avoiding the trip altogether," Fulton wrote.[2] And the reverse is true, too. If the congestion eases because a new road is built or an old one enlarged, the cost of travel is reduced and the number of trips, even spontaneous ones, will increase.

Mass transit use is definitely up. In 1998, according to statistics provided by the American Public Transportation Association (APTA), there were 8.7 billion transit trips taken in the country, a 4.6 percent increase since 1997 and a 16 percent increase since 1995.[3] That's encouraging, even if auto use continues to overwhelm everything else. Donna Aggazio, an APTA spokesperson, attributes the rise to "a strong economy, which has increased investment by federal and local governments and enabled transit services to expand and modernize. It's also meant more customer-oriented service." If you don't like your ride on Amtrak, the company has said it will give your money back.

As Aggazio suggests, government investment has made a difference. The importance of the Transportation Equity Act for the Twenty-first Century (TEA-21), cannot be overemphasized. From 1998 to 2004, TEA-21 will spend $217 billion on 1,850 local projects. The federal transportation package was once nothing more than a highway bill, but transit advocates are at least cautiously pleased with what they got in 1998, which continues the pattern of the 1991 Intermodal Surface Transportation Efficiency Act, or ISTEA. The money's there for federal assistance to light-rail lines, bicycle corridors, subway planning, and pedestrian trails, if municipalities understand and undertake the process of asking for it. "Overall, TEA-21 provides an excellent tool to create a diverse and environmentally sustainable transportation system for the twenty-first century," says the Natural Resources Defense Council, "*if* it is properly implemented by federal, state and local governments and metropolitan planning organizations, and properly guided by citizen input."[4]

The 1998 bill represented a 40 percent funding increase over ISTEA. It provides a respectable $8.1 billion over the six years to help state and local governments meet national clean-air regulations. Under TEA-21, funds can now be used for off-road safety improvements to bicycle and pedestrian trails; there's money for congestion-pricing projects and for all-important regional planning; and a new grant program will help welfare recipients get to work. Tax breaks for van pools and transit use are also increased, from $65 to $100 a month.

Of course, there's still plenty of "pork" in TEA-21, and lots and lots of highway funding. "Changing Directions," a report on federal spending in the 1990s by the Surface Transportation Policy Project, reveals the chilling fact that between 1998 and 2000, federal spending on new and wider roads grew by 21 percent, but funding on alternatives fell by 19 percent.[5] One of the problems is that when municipalities were given the option of "flexible" funding as part of the ISTEA and TEA-21 process, only 7 percent of them took advantage of the opportunity and put money into something other than roads. Overall, though, it's a mildly encouraging picture. TEA-21 works, and that's why it has so many opponents on the libertarian right, which opposes it as government meddling with free-market transportation options. The Cato Institute—which generally opposes federal aid for transit—called TEA-21 and its ilk a "poisonous brew for American cities."[6]

Mass transit needs nurturing; it will never make it on the bottom line alone. And that's where the critics miss the point. Not all of these transit opponents are on the right. One I spoke with, Jonathan Richmond, has taught at MIT and Harvard. He lives in Cambridge without a car and calls himself "left-leaning." But he's an implacable opponent of light rail. "Environmentalists have been misled about what causes environmental benefits and what doesn't," he said to me. "Rail projects bring in money for a large number of contractors and other special interests, but they actually encourage driving by building park-and-ride lots. They just don't work in low-density regions. Cities like Houston could do more by expanding their busways."

The possibilities of dedicated busways are demonstrated by the experience of Curitiba, Brazil, but why is it an either-or question? My experience in Portland was that the transit system works because it's multifaceted and intermodal. The buses connect to light rail, which connect to Amtrak, the airport, and the new trolley lines. Car sharing and heavy bicycle use help, too.

What I loved about Portland is that you can live there without a car, even in the suburbs. And both for practical reasons and as a conscious lifestyle choice, people in Portland are actually divesting themselves of automobile ownership. They tell me it's a liberating feeling, one that makes them aware of just what a burden a car can be.

Portland isn't alone, of course. For most of the Third World, obviously, an automobile isn't an option, though that's slowly changing. Half of all households in New York City are carless, a breathtaking achievement that New Yorkers take in stride. What's new is that people who grew up with cars are choosing to abandon them. There are strong pockets of voluntary car-free living in Ottawa, Philadelphia, and many other urban centers. And Europe, of course, offers many models for escaping the automobile's clutches. As the twenty-first century begins, the car-free movement has spawned a very lively subculture that's forcing us to reexamine the way we live.

LIVING CAR-FREE

In the fall of 1997, anticar activists from fifty groups in twenty-one countries converged on Lyons, France, for a conference that was far more than the usual round of speeches. Although there were workshops on everything from bicycle repair and green city planning to creatively blocking traffic and "car walking" (basically, climbing right over a pedestrian-blocking vehicle and leaving a note about it), the real action at "Toward Car-Free Cites" was in the streets.

Randy Ghent, a conference organizer who also edits the online magazine *Car Busters,* calls what happened next "the ultimate in experiential workshops." Four groups of protesters fanned out across Lyons, each with a different strategy. One hung a banner reading ENOUGH CARS across a busy highway during the morning commute.

A second group, led by celebrated German car walker Michael Hartmann, clambered atop cars parked on the sidewalk, leaving signs that read, "I walked over your car because I didn't want to slide under it!" The same group also wrapped cars in fake police ribbons and plastered them with official-looking letters explaining the environmental consequences of car ownership. Drivers were confronted with the option of having their car crushed (in exchange for a free bike) or paying a "car tax" of 100,000 francs. The activists even took matters into their own hands by physically lifting cars off the sidewalks and depositing them in the streets, where they blocked traffic and attracted tickets.

Other groups, some wearing tutus and walking on stilts, held forth at major intersections, passing out leaflets asking motorists to tear up their driver's licenses and abandon their cars. The street theater concluded two days later with a massive Reclaim the Streets rally in which hundreds of protesters dragged an old car through the center of the city, chanting, "The car it stinks, it kills, and it pollutes!" Then they planted the car in the middle of a busy intersection, further blocking the road. Ketchup-smeared "accident victims" collapsed in the street, musicians played, and impromptu bicycle lanes sprang up. For a brief time, cars were second-class citizens in the heart of a busy French city.[7]

Ghent, an American now based in the Czech Republic, says that anticar sentiment is far more common in Europe than it is in the United States. He volunteered to post an item about my interest in car-free living on his *Car Busters* Web site, and the result was that my e-mail box filled up with accounts from all over the world. "I am fifty, live in Montreal, and am vice president of a cycling organization. I travel by bicycle, by foot, taxi and subway," wrote Robert Boivin. "My wife, two children, and I live in Brussels, Belgium, with no car at all," recounted Bernard Delloye. "In Amsterdam, people who *do* have a car are inconvenienced, since parking fees are very high and the city is (relatively) car-unfriendly," said Frank van Schaik, who bikes everywhere. "I am an enthusiastic Austrian who has so far lived in half a dozen countries without a car. My group, Iniziativa da las Alps, recently painted a mural on a wall at the Mont Blanc tunnel to remember the drivers who died there," wrote Renate Zauner from Switzerland, referring to a spectacular 1999 crash and fire that killed forty-three people. "My wife and I have completed five years without a car," wrote Chris Bradshaw, a former municipal planner who is now an enthusiastic member of Canada's blossoming Auto-Free Ottawa.

I find it interesting that so many Canadians choose to live car-free, since the cold up there would seem to be a deterrent. Ottawa is the second-coldest world capital, and temperatures can reach twenty degrees below zero, but Auto-Free Ottawa is quite successful, and the city also hosts Citizens for Safe Cycling. Ottawa-based journalist Sharon Boddy wrote about her country's hardy activists in an article for *E* magazine. She quoted enthusiastic biker Heather Mullen as proclaiming, "I'm not a wimp!"[8]

The movement to "liberate" drivers from their cars can be seen, perhaps, as a close relative of road rage. It's an activism in reaction to not only an increasing international obsession with the private car but also the dire environmental impact of all those automobiles. "You can't call yourself an environmentalist unless you do something to curb the automobile," said Donna Merlina in a letter to *E*.[9]

CREATING CAR-FREE CITIES

Though it's not noticed much in America, a quiet movement to rid city centers of cars is growing. "The cutting edge of city planners in Europe has realized that the surest way to cut down on traffic is to reduce the amount of public space devoted to the car," says Randy Ghent. "David Engwicht [a former window cleaner who evolved into an anticar activist and the author of *Reclaiming Our Cities and Towns: Better Living with Less Traffic*] is trying to get across the idea that street space should be primarily for interpersonal exchange, rather than entirely devoted to moving people somewhere else."

European Car-Free Day, first held in 1998, has many enthusiastic participants. In Eurobarometer opinion polls, 51 percent of respondents mention "density of traffic" as their greatest concern.[10] In 1998, 75 percent of the British public said they supported Car-Free Day. More than 150 towns and cities across Europe took part in the September 22, 2000, event, which involved 65 million people. In Italy, with the highest per capita auto ownership in Europe, Car-Free Sunday was a hit. "Look around, people are happier," said Fabio Matarazzo, a government manager in Rome.[11]

In 2000, European environmentalists attempted to contrast the benefits of car-free living with the agonies endured by motorists because of high fuel prices and the popularly supported oil terminal blockades associated with them. As the British Broadcasting Corporation reported, "The green lobby used [Car-Free Day] to stress that there is a line between cheaper fuel, traffic congestion and pollution."[12]

Car-free days are not limited to Europe, either. Bogotá, Colombia, where a thousand people are killed in traffic accidents every year, held one in the winter of 2000—and it was mandatory. Even though buses and taxis were still allowed out, an estimated 665,600 cars were left in their garages.[13] Also in 2000, Bogotá's city government adopted an ordinance stating that, by 2015, private cars would no longer be permitted on city streets during peak travel times. Santiago, Chile, whose diesel-fueled commuting is daily shrouded in thick, brown smog, is the scene of an increasingly militant protest movement called Movimiento Furiosos Ciclistas, demanding both car-free days and bike paths. Hong Kong, where air-quality advisories are frequent, closed parts of its central commercial district to cars in 2001.

The only completely car-free city in Europe is Venice, of course, and that's nothing new. Sixty European cities, from Barcelona to Birmingham, have signed on as members of the Car-Free Cities Network and are trying to reduce traffic in their city centers. An irony is that as Europe and (to a much lesser extent) the United States try to reclaim territory from the car, other countries that are traditionally bike-friendly are eagerly surrendering turf. Both India and China, which together house a third of the world's population, are sharply increasing auto production. As the magazine *Sustainable Transport* noted, "Until 1990, China was one country environmentalists working on transport issues didn't have to worry about." In 1990, it had one car per every one thousand people. Since then, however, car ownership has increased at a rate of 15 percent a year in China, and the number of bicycles has plunged.[14] The *San Francisco Chronicle* reported in a story about Shanghai, "On the outskirts of this booming metropolis, where skyscrapers and industrial parks and freeways march toward the horizon, there is a grand vision of China's future, and it looks a lot like Los Angeles."[15]

BLOCKING THE HIGHWAY

In Europe, the organized protest against the automobile has some roots in the English antiroads movement, a phenomenon that has yet to travel across the Atlantic. In 1991, a direct-action group called Reclaim the Streets was formed in London. The group was campaigning, it said, "FOR walking, cycling and cheap, or free, public transport, and AGAINST cars, roads and the system that pushes them."[16]

Do-it-yourself bicycle lanes appeared on London streets, and the 1993 Earls Court Motor Show was disrupted. Protesters gathered against the proposed M11 Link Road, but the battle became more intense after the passage in late 1994 of the Criminal Justice and Public Order Act, which increased the penalties for highway squatting and blockades. In what was known as the Battle of Claremont Road, police knocked down barriers and scaffolding the demonstrators had erected across the site of the proposed road.

In early 1996, activists took on the would-be Twyford Down bypass, which would have bulldozed through three areas designated by the government as sites of special scientific interest, containing ancient bogs, wildflower meadows, and archaeological artifacts. Also in 1996, Reclaim the Streets persuaded eight thousand people to take temporary control of the M41 motorway in West London. The protesters "partied and enjoyed themselves, whilst some dug up the tarmac with jack hammers and in place planted trees that had been rescued from the construction path of the M11."[17]

The overall campaign was eminently successful. Though authorities were loath to attribute the change to the protesters, road-building schemes were dramatically cut from 467 new roads to 7 in a 1996 budget cut.[18] The antiroads movement took a hiatus, though small skirmishes continued. In 1999, traffic was brought to a standstill in the Norwich city center by two hundred Reclaim the Streets activists. What a local newspaper called a "street party" continued for two and a half hours, without the police taking action. According to Julia Guest, who wrote on the subject for *E* magazine, the antiroads protest was reenergized in 2000 by a plan announced by Deputy Prime Minister John Prescott to build eighty new bypass roads. Prescott announced that £4 billion would be spent on road construction through 2005, enough to build forty equivalents of the proposed Newbury bypass, the scene of memorable battles during the antiroads campaign.

There are parallels between the British barricades and U.S.-based global trade activism. "The struggle for car-free space must not be separated from the struggle against global capitalism," read a Reclaim the Streets leaflet handed out at the Norwich event. Evidence that some of that thinking had made it across the Atlantic became apparent when activists with connections to earlier Seattle street protests revealed plans to organize a "Day of Outrage Against the Auto," complete with what they called "Multiple Simultaneous On-Ramp Lockdowns," in Detroit as part of Earth Day 2001. Other links could be drawn to the U.S. movement against clear-cut logging, which has frequently used road-blocking tactics to protect old-growth trees. But in the center of auto addiction, the United States, very few large-scale protests have targeted the car.

DEPAVING AMERICA

In the United States, activists take some comfort from Federal Highway Administration statistics that show that bicycling and walking displace between 7 and 28 billion passenger vehicle miles annually, as well as up to 1,590 million gallons of gasoline and 15 million tons of carbon dioxide emissions. Cost does deter some driving. Jane Holtz Kay, in her book *Asphalt Nation,* tallies the average annual cost of maintaining a car in the United States as $6,000 for such internal expenditures as gas, parking, tires, depreciation, and maintenance, plus $3,000 to $5,000 for such external social factors as land consumed in sprawl, police protection, environmental damage, and uncompensated accidents. She adds that "hidden costs" for cars add a burden of $750 billion to the American economy.[19]

The most visible American anticar group is the Alliance for a Paving Moratorium, headed by a dedicated Arcata, California, activist named Jan Lundberg. He would appear to be a rather unlikely anticar agitator, since he started out "wearing suits and ties, reporting gas prices for his family's petroleum trade magazine, the *Lundberg Letter,*" according to *Audubon* magazine, which added that "he had servants and a yacht."[20]

Lundberg disputes this account, which he calls "exaggerated." He was only reluctantly part of the family business, but it's certainly true he's come a long way from his roots. When he still owned a home,

Lundberg dug up the driveway that came with it. The alliance publishes a quarterly magazine with a circulation of 15,000. Called the *Auto-Free Times,* it features articles like "How We Pay Oil Companies to Pollute," "The Joys of Carlessness," and "Turn Your Ignition, Melt a Glacier." But Lundberg is hardly a deskbound editor. He travels quite a bit by bicycle and last owned a car in 1989. He has been arrested and jailed for blocking highways. He has a band called the Depavers.

"I don't *think* the auto will be replaced," Lundberg told me. "I *know* it will be." He is not in favor of reforming the automobile, in the form of hybrid and fuel-cell cars, which he says contribute to urban sprawl and pavement as much as conventional automobiles. "The techno-fix is too little and too late," he said, "and does nothing to address the carnage on the roads." I asked Lundberg why there isn't an antiroads movement in the United States to compare with that in Europe. "The British movement happened because the situation was absurd and out of control, with off-the-charts road-building plans," he said. "There is an antiroads movement here, but it's still small."

Few Americans, even environmental activists, would be able to sign the Pledge for Climate Stabilization petition distributed by Fossil Fuels Policy Action, another arm of the alliance. A signature would commit the activist to taking some or all of these actions: cut down on driving, cut down on working just for money, depave the driveway, unplug or retire the television and try to get off the electricity grid, publicly oppose new road construction, take vacations without jet air travel, plant trees, buy as little plastic as possible, and not have children or limit offspring to one.

Randy Ghent, who worked as the alliance office manager from 1993 to 1997, doesn't see a mass movement against the car developing in America. "The U.S. was thoroughly designed for and around the automobile," he told me. "There are greater distances between destinations and lower density, which makes it harder. A U.S. movement has only been able to form in big cities and college towns. It has been a movement to a strange extent centered around the bicycle."

BRAVO FOR BICYCLES

Fighting for bicycles is a guerrilla action in car-crazy America. While the United States has the highest per capita bicycle ownership in the world, according to the League of American Bicyclists, automobiles are used for more than 95 percent of our trips. Only 3 million Americans say they ride their bikes "frequently," meaning more than 14 or 15 times a year. According to Alex Campbell, a spokesperson for leading electric bicycle maker Zap, as many as 120 million bikes sit forlornly on flat tires, waiting for riders. In America, bicycles are overwhelmingly used for recreation and exercise, not for commuting.

Bicycles got a boost from the federal Intermodal Surface Transportation Efficiency Act (ISTEA), which in 1991 increased federal funding for bikes by a factor of one hundred. According to the Environmental Working Group, in the eighteen years before ISTEA was passed, only $40 million was committed. Since 1991, $1 billion has been spent.

The San Francisco Bicycle Coalition is another tough campaigner, fighting for urban pathways, encouraging traffic-calming policies, and lobbying for bike-friendly legislation. "Providing safe streets for bicyclists is like making a grant of $420 (a year's worth of bus passes) to thousands of people with limited incomes," the group proclaimed. "That would improve the quality of life for the one-third of San Francisco households who do not have access to a car."[21]

San Francisco is also home to a monthly event called Critical Mass, in which thousands of bicycle riders take to the streets, many of them in colorful costumes. "We wanted to celebrate the bike and dominate the streets for a change," said one spokesman for the loosely organized group. Police broke up a five-thousand-strong Critical Mass ride in 1997 and arrested one hundred people for blocking traffic, but there were ultimately no convictions.[22] In 1999, state judge Sue Kaplan ruled that the arrests were illegal, and Critical Mass has operated without harassment since then.

People are finding innovative uses for bicycles. Joan Stein and Jim

Gregory own and operate the pedal-power Fresh Aire Delivery Service in the small town of Ames, Iowa. Fresh Aire has transported furniture, lumber, and even a children's playhouse. There are *two* bicycle delivery services in Berkeley, California, run by Pedal Express and Berkeley Youth Alternatives. Both, in a national first, will deliver organic produce to a customer's door."[23] I'm fascinated that groups like these would, in the name of the environment, return us to the kinds of hard manual work that the entire postwar "labor-saving" movement in the United States was designed to make obsolete forever. Lundberg advocates clearing fields with a scythe.

The Colorado-based Bicycle Transportation Systems has an idea that makes a crazy kind of sense, combining pedal power with an innovation in mass transit. It's a kind of two-way tunnel in which bike riders are pushed along by a constantly moving column of air, reducing air resistance and allowing speeds of up to twenty-five miles per hour. The company claims its system is 90 percent more efficient than normal cycling, and bikers can travel six miles with the energy it would otherwise take to travel one. The system can reportedly be used to move freight as well as bike riders, but it would require an expensive and fully enclosed dedicated bikeway. Only a city intensely dedicated to bicycle transportation would even think of building such a corridor.

Bike racks are sprouting up all over. According to the International Bicycle Fund, 3,000 have recently been installed in Santa Cruz, California, and 1,600 in Seattle. In Portland, I saw some ingenious bike lockers that make the enclosed bicycle nearly impossible to steal. Another hurdle for many metropolitan areas is allowing bicycles on rush-hour trains.

Perhaps it says something about America that our anticar campaigns are couched in the positive rhetoric of encouraging the open-air sport of bicycling. Like motherhood, bicycling is very hard to oppose, even though our traffic regulations discriminate regularly. The rock band bicycle (with a small "b"), led by bike activist Kurt Liebert, toured from Portland, Maine, to Washington, D.C., in the summer of 2000 entirely by bike. That struck me as a laudable thing to do, and indicative of the extraordinary dedication of some cyclists.

LESSONS LEARNED: FINDING A WAY FORWARD

If I began recounting all the interesting things I saw from the windows of buses, subway cars, light-rail trains, and catamaran ferries, they would fill another whole book. But as I rode around I saw patterns emerge, and I began to form some conclusions about what works and what doesn't. It's plain that we've taken just about every wrong turn in building a transportation network in America. The die for those mistakes was cast by the 1950s, when we built the interstate road network, and a healthy highway lobby has maintained the status quo. What can we do about it now? Here are some lessons.

Don't try to build out of congestion. It's never worked. If it did, Los Angeles traffic would flow smoothly. New highway construction should be a last resort in America. I talked to many civic planners in the course of writing this book, and none of them expressed regret about the highways left on the drawing boards. But they had plenty of pride in the mass-transit projects that replaced the roads. In addition to their role as purveyors of pollution, highways are enemies of social interaction. I see a prime example in my own community, where the path of I-95 cut straight through a vibrant Hungarian neighborhood, scattering its residents to the suburbs.

Refuse to accept bottom-line thinking. On paper, transit will never make sense. Given the huge capital investment necessary to launch any light-rail system, it will always look like a loser. Even bus lines, with their higher ridership and lower infrastructure investment, can't meet their costs on the fare box alone. The best way for municipal planners to think of mass transit is as a safety valve. Look at any subway system. See all the people? They'd be blocking the highways with their cars if they weren't on board. Consider the cost of all that extra gridlock. If the city, state, and federal governments have to subsidize mass-transit fares, it's usually worth the investment in the long run. Hank Dittmar, who founded the Surface Transportation Policy Project and now runs the Great American Station Foundation, simply looks for bodies in seats. "The libertarian academics look at San Francisco and say that the Bay Area Rapid Transit trains, which carry 250,000 people a day, haven't stopped automotive growth," he said. "But, gosh, if the trains are full every day, aren't they succeeding in their mission?"

Don't underestimate the infrastructure barriers. My shelves are full of books that point the way to a green transportation future. Much of it works perfectly well: automated highways, suburban light-rail lines, electric-car rentals at airports and train stations, high-speed trains, magnetic levitation. But most of these solutions, particularly the rail-based systems, have infrastructure costs of many millions per mile, without anything comparable to the highway lobby pushing for funding. Mass-transit advocates have to organize much more effectively than they have in the past, and they have to make clear the quality-of-life improvements that transit can bring. I saw those improvements clearly in Los Angeles, whose brand-new subway system is already packed with riders from all strata of society. At Union Station, I saw school outings, families headed for the beach, and commuters on their way to distant suburbs, all of them freed from car dependence. The L.A. subway loses a great deal of money, and every one of those riders is heavily subsidized. But if they were on the highway, they'd be fueling an already untenable gridlock, and we'd be subsidizing them, too. Los Angeles had to make a giant leap of faith that its huge financial commitment would be justified. That justification may not be at hand right now, but it will be soon.

Consider the hidden costs of cars. Environmental Defense calculates the annual health cost of car-related smog and particulate emissions in southern California as $3.7 billion. Do L.A.'s subway critics factor that in when they measure rail's high cost against its value to the city? Author Jane Holtz Kay asks, "Since the carbon dioxide from the fossil fuels used in the world's cars cause 50 percent of global warming, and America's automobiles cause half of that, the question is unavoidable and agonizing: is it worth a planet to buy that bar of soap?"[24] But most calculations of automotive impact consider only the more obvious, observable factors. The cost of rebuilding a single suburban interchange in the San Francisco Bay Area, between Interstate 680 and Route 24, is estimated by municipal planners at more than $300 million. Isn't that a hidden cost of cars? And what kind of alternative transportation would that money buy?

Learn from Europe. This is useful only to a certain point. Europeans' much greater reliance on mass transit, bicycling, and walking is admirable and instructive, and the planning process that produced those numbers can be modeled. U.S. cities can also discourage downtown parking, narrow and calm roads, and subsidize efficient light-rail and bus lines. But European development is high-density, without America's endless suburban sprawl. Portland's Orenco Station and Seaside, Florida, are attempts to model European development patterns, but we'd need tens of thousands of Orenco Stations to make a significant difference in America. Ultimately, the solution to transportation problems in the United States must be made in the U.S.A. We may never be as transit-friendly as Europe, but mass-transit projects in key areas of gridlock and a nationwide fast-rail link with one thousand stations or more will help us from driving off a cliff.

Take timely action. There are cusps in history, moments when societies take decisive action. Leverage at that point, even small leverage, can have huge consequences. A classic example is the purchase by General Motors and other companies of America's failing trolley lines between the 1920s and the 1950s. GM's front company, National City Lines, controlled streetcar operations in eighty cities by 1946. Whether GM was purposely attempting to derail trolleys is a matter that can be debated, but the fact remains that for a small investment, the company cleared the way for diesel-powered bus hegemony on city streets. At the cost of a $5,000 conspiracy conviction, it permanently disconnected a rail network that would cost us many billions, if not trillions, to replace today.

There's a similar opportunity in the Third World today. In China, for instance, auto use is growing, but so is interest in hydrogen power. Fuel cells could be used not only for clean transit but to provide a decentralized, wireless electricity grid for the country. With some of the world's worst air pollution, China has an incentive to make an historic switch. In Africa, I'm encouraged by the grassroots groups that distribute solar cookers, helping to protect forests and encourage the spread of labor-saving sustainable technology at the same time.

Give transit a try. Many people I talked with, even environmentalists, have never been on the public-transportation systems that quite often run right past their doors. The bus stops are out there: you probably drive by a dozen on your way to work every day. In Connecticut, where I live, the morning slog on I-95 is an ingrained part of the culture. Most people think of Metro-North's commuter trains, even though they stop in every city on the coastal corridor, as New York City–bound transportation only. Despite my many visits to Detroit, I never met a soul who'd ever ridden on the city's monorail. My own cousin, Charlie, who draws environmental cartoons, had never been on the Los Angeles subway until I took him down there.

Drive smart. I'm flabbergasted by how few people take advantage of the high-occupancy vehicle-lanes in American cities, despite the clear advantage of doing so. Couldn't a lot of those people carpool, saving energy, time, and aggravation? Despite frequent civic reminders that carpooling is good for you, the once prevalent practice is being abandoned. I'm familiar with the arguments Robert D. Putnam makes in his book *Bowling Alone,* which depicts America as a nation of loners, but traveling together has clear rewards. One clear alternative is telecommuting, which is slowly capturing the attention of American workers who find they get more done if their desk is down the hall instead of down the road. Finally, it's also a good idea to ask, "Is this trip necessary?" Try to combine shopping trips if you can. Better yet, get your bicycle out of storage and combine chores with exercise. Rediscover the joys of walking, and get a close-up look at the neighborhood you usually see through a windshield.

Plan for transit. Portland is a good example of a city that incorporates transit into an overall plan for sustainable development. Nothing happens in Portland without detailed studies and an inclusive public-hearing process. Tri-Met, the city's transit agency, spells out its goals in a strategic plan that runs until 2003. "How we get there matters" is its slogan. According to the plan, "Without an effective, comprehensive transit system coupled with thoughtful land development, the metropolitan area risks losing its treasured livability and will invite the type of problems we associate with urban growth throughout the country: air pollution, frequent long drives to reach jobs and services, burdensome costs for road and utility construction to serve suburban fringe development, and a seemingly endless demand for new highways."[25]

Portland is one of several U.S. and Canadian cities (including Atlanta, Vancouver, and San Francisco) to have what are known as transportation-management associations (TMAs), which get business, government, and nonprofit groups together to work on transit issues and foster trip reduction. TMAs, many of which were formed in response to the 1990 Clean Air Act provisions, have put together ride-sharing databases, telework and guaranteed-ride-home programs, and shuttle-bus services. In San Francisco, the Countywide Transportation Plan looks thirty years ahead to the demands made by increasing population, envisioning the need for two new subway lines and transit-only lanes on busy streets.

Don't be passive. Perhaps we're being too mild in our reaction to destructive transportation planning. New highways are not a given, and commitments can be fluid. By refusing to play by the rules, the British antiroads movement got the attention of the media and captured hearts and minds across England. In the United States, the highly confrontational Rainforest Action Network—which directly targets corporate retailers participating in forest destruction—has produced spectacular results, bringing three major players, Mitsubishi, Home Depot, and Lowe's, to the bargaining table. Greenpeace gets the most done when it engages in nonviolent direct action. Activists should by all means participate in the civic process, but adding a little street theater can be helpful as well.

Don't trust technological fixes. When modestly applied, communications technology can dispatch paratransit vans, help ensure on-time bus and rail travel, provide real-time information to travelers, and even enhance the driving experience. If we're going to be hung up on the way home because of gridlock, a car phone at least allows us to call home and announce the bad news. But I find it hard to believe that adaptive cruise control, centralized traffic control, and automated highways are the key to our commuting future. At best, they offer a temporary fix that can quickly be erased by the steady buildup of vehicle miles traveled and new cars on the road. And the cost per mile of automated highway systems is enormous.

Encourage new ideas. One of the best aspects of researching this book was the encounters it afforded me with transit entrepreneurs, who offer some truly innovative—and fun—approaches to the dilemma of getting from here to there. Even if it turns out to be impractical, who doesn't applaud the concept of SkyTran, with its one-hundred-mile-per-hour pods and individualized destination planning? We need to be thinking out of the box on transportation issues. Ferries may never travel at one hundred knots on America's waterways, but Ken Cook is right when he argues that we have to imagine doing so. It's amusing to note the historical record of popular opposition to everything from the automobile to train travel and airplane flight, but we need to be similarly wary of dismissing today's bright ideas. There's no guarantee that we *won't* be strapping on personalized flight packs in the twenty-first century. I'm certainly willing to try one on.

At the end of the last trip for this book, I got home at midnight and dropped my bags in the hall. "I'm home," I said, but everyone had gone to bed. I was due at work the next day, so I sat down at the kitchen table and asked myself an important question: How was I going to get there?

People Interviewed

I INTERVIEWED the following people specifically for this book; quotes from those interviews are found throughout the text.

Dennis Aldridge, collision-warning-systems manager, Delphi Automotive Systems
Katie Alvord, author, *Divorce Your Car*
G. B. Arrington, consultant, Parsons Brinckerhoff
Linda Baker, freelance journalist
Janine Bauer, executive director, Tri-State Transportation Campaign
Rachel Bauer, civil engineering student
Milton Beach, spokesman, Delphi Automotive Systems
Dan Becker, transportation campaigner, Sierra Club
Lee Beliveau, spokesman, Rhode Island Public Transit Authority
Moshe E. Ben-Akiva, professor of civil and environmental engineering, MIT
Robert J. Bienenfeld, environmental spokesman, Honda
Earl Blumenaur, congressman, Portland, Oregon
Sharon Boddy, freelance writer
George Boucher, director, Shore Line Trolley Museum
David Brook, president, CarSharing Portland
Rodney Brunlinger, Arcata transportation activist
Dave Burwell, founder, Rails to Trails Conservancy
Dennis Bushnell, chief scientist, Small Air Transportation System, NASA
Reeves Callaway, car designer
James Cannon, president, Energy Futures

Ross Capon, executive director, National Association of Railroad
   Passengers
John A. Charles, environmental policy director, Cascade Policy Institute
Don Chen, executive director, Smart Growth America
Doby Class, deputy public works director, Arcata
Kenneth E. Cook, president, Hydrofoils Incorporated
Rob Cotter, vice president, SkyTran
Joseph Coughlin, director, MIT Center for Transportation Studies
Wendell Cox, antitransit consultant
Hank Dittmar, director, Great American Station Foundation
Robert Engelman, vice president, Population Action International
William Clay Ford Jr., chairman, Ford Motor Company
Robert Edison Fulton Jr., inventor, Airphibian
Randy Ghent, director, *Car Busters* magazine and Resource Center
Jonathan Gifford, public management professor, George Mason University
Tonya Goodier, safety engineer, Delphi Automotive Systems
Deborah Gordon, transportation consultant
Julia Guest, freelance writer
Greg Hanssen, Production Electric Vehicle Drivers Coalition
Carl Haub, demographer, Population Reference Bureau
Kevin Hoover, editor, *Arcata Eye*
Joe Jacuzzi, communications manager, General Motors Truck Group
Palle R. Jensen, inventor, Maxi-RUF
John Kaehny, executive director, Transportation Alternatives
Seth Kaplan, attorney, Conservation Law Foundation
Jane Holtz Kay, author, *Asphalt Nation*
Reid Kells, commuter and CarSharing Portland user
Ronald S. Killian, manager, environmental permits, Massachusetts
   Turnpike Authority
Charles Komanoff, transit activist, Right of Way
Hans Koning, author and fast-train enthusiast
Fred Krupp, founder and president, Environmental Defense
Ty Lasky, engineering professor, University of California
Robert Liberty, executive director, One Thousand Friends of Oregon
Jan Lundberg, Alliance for a Paving Moratorium
Paul MacCready, chairman, AeroVironment
Charles Mark-Walker, Los Angeles commuter
Jerry Martin, director of communications, California Air Resources Board

Denise McCluggage, syndicated automotive columnist

Dr. Byron McCormick, fuel-cell developer, General Motors

Tasios Melis, biologist, University of California

Paul Moller, developer, Skycar

Bill Moore, editor, *EV World*

Jerry Nichols, Fairfield County commuter

Jack Nilles, telecommuter and founder, JALA International

Craig O'Connell, Friends of Amtrak

Sean O'Neill, spokesman, Massachusetts Turnpike Authority

Randall O'Toole, executive director, Thoreau Institute

Grant Parker, captain, *Tatobam* ferry

Rod Parlee, Connecticut bus driver

Christine Parra, research engineer, Shatz Energy Lab

Srinivas Peeta, engineering professor, Purdue University

Mark Petersen, car-free transit operator

Lynn Ann Peterson, Tri-Met

John Pucher, urban planning professor, Rutgers University

Jonathan Richmond, transit critic

Anthony Rizos, Webmaster, Amtrak Unlimited

Clarence Rogers, driver, People to Places

John Rountree, solar architect

Fred Salvucci, lecturer, Civil and Environmental Engineering, MIT

Bill Schulz, vice president, Amtrak

Robert W. Shaw Jr., president, Arete Incorporated

Richard Silver, executive director, Train Riders Association of California

Gar Smith, editor, *Earth Island Journal*

Michael Smith, transit activist, Right of Way

Maren Souders, manager, CarSharing Portland

Daniel Sperling, professor, University of California

Robert Stempel, chairman, Energy Conversion Devices

Dale Strand, chairman, U.S. Multi-Hull

Gregory Lee Thompson, author, *The American Passenger Train and the Motor Age*

Bill Tuttle, spokesman, Sikorsky Helicopter

Rich Varenchik, spokesman, California Air Resources Board

Watts Wacker, CEO, FirstMatter

Earl Weston, Portland cyclist

Resources:
Getting Involved with Transit

TRANSIT GROUPS take many forms, from mainstream advocates for greater rail and bike use to radical anticar activism. Some organizations excel at compiling statistics, others at direct action. All the groups listed here have done useful work.

Alliance for a Paving Moratorium, P.O. Box 4347, Arcata, Calif. 95518; (707) 826-7775; www.culturechange.org. The alliance advocates a car-free, depaved America and publishes *Auto-Free Times* magazine.

American Public Transportation Association, 1201 New York Avenue, N.W., Washington, D.C. 20005; (202) 898-4084; www.apta.com. APTA pushes for increased public-transportation subsidies and publishes an annual guide to U.S. transit habits.

Amtrak Unlimited is a Web resource about the national rail service: www.amtraktrains.com.

Car Busters is an on-line magazine based in the Czech Republic. It offers information about the anticar movement in Europe at www.carbusters.com.ecn.cz/MAGINDEX.htm.

Car-Free Times is an elegantly produced on-line magazine dedicated to building car-free cities: www.carfree.com.

Friends of Amtrak is an on-line resource for passenger rail information: http://www.trainweb.com.

Great American Station Foundation, 615 East Lincoln Avenue, Las Vegas, N.M. 87701; (505) 426-8055; www.stationfoundation.org. Headed by Hank Dittmar, the founder of the Surface Transportation Policy Project, this philanthropic organization works to preserve historic railroad stations and return them to productive use.

National Association of Rail Passengers, 900 Second Street, N.E., Suite 308, Washington, D.C. 20002; (202) 408-8362; www.narprail.org. This group works for a better deal for the transit consumer.

Smart Growth America, 1100 Seventeenth Street, N.W., Tenth Floor, Washington, D.C. 20036; (202) 974–5132; www.smartgrowthamerica. net. Smart Growth America is a nationwide advocacy coalition devoted to promoting a better way to grow—one that protects open space and farmland, revitalizes neighborhoods, keeps housing affordable, and makes communities more livable.

Surface Transportation Policy Project, 1100 Seventeenth Street, N.W., Tenth Floor, Washington, D.C. 20036; (202) 466-2636; www. transact.org. STPP is a very effective informational resource and lobbying force for transit and against increased highway construction.

Tri-State Transportation Campaign, 240 West Thirty-fifth Street, #801, New York, N.Y. 10001; (212) 268-7474; www.tstc.org. Although its focus is the New York, New Jersey, and Connecticut region, this well-organized nonprofit group produces a huge amount of material that's transferable to any metropolitan area wanting to build a transit base.

Notes

Introduction

1. *Bridgeport Post,* January 7, 1938. The local papers were muckrakers in those days. The *Bridgeport Sunday Herald* lambasted the "mysterious realty companies" that profiteered on land sales for the new highway, for which an exorbitant $3,000 an acre was paid.
2. Thomas J. McFeeley, "Some Lack Faith in Traffic Proposals," *Greenwich Time,* March 20, 2000. As McFeeley put it, "Many commuters say state officials' track records leave them less than confident that a plan to take 5 percent of rush-hour vehicles off local highways and Route 1 can be achieved."
3. Ken Dixon, "Traffic Cure to Cost $6 Billion," *Connecticut Post,* September 29, 2000, p. A1. "We are being crippled by our transportation problems," Governor John Rowland admitted at the summit. Prominent state businessman James C. Smith, chairman of Webster Bank, added, "We're on the verge of a transportation crisis, putting in jeopardy economic development and public safety."
4. "Report: 98 Percent of U.S. Commuters Favor Public Transportation for Others," *Onion* on-line magazine, November 29, 2000, posted at www.theonion.com.

1. Looking Forward from the Past

1. Arthur C. Clarke, *Voices from the Sky: Previews of the Coming Space Age* (New York: Harper & Row, 1965), p. 211.
2. Quoted in Jules Verne, *From the Earth to the Moon* (London: P. F. Collier & Son, 1905; memorial edition).
3. Quoted in Arthur B. Evans and Ron Miller, "Jules Verne, Misunderstood Visionary," *Scientific American,* April 1997.

4. Jules Verne, *Paris in the Twentieth Century* (New York: Random House, 1996), p. xxv.

5. Ibid., p. 26.

6. Clarke, *Voices from the Sky,* p. 212.

7. H. G. Wells, *The Short Stories of H. G. Wells* (London: Ernest Benn Limited, 1927).

8. These wonderful cartoons are reproduced, albeit in murky black and white, in John Durant, *Predictions* (New York: A. S. Barnes and Company, 1956). The *New Yorker* recently described the sad process by which original color newspaper illustrations and cartoons are being lost as libraries convert their bulky inventories to microfilm.

9. Edward Bellamy, *Looking Backward: 2000–1887* (Chicago: Packard and Company, 1962), pp. 24–25.

10. Phil Porter, "Automobile Led Revolution of Transport," *Columbus Dispatch,* July 25, 1999. "Nobody spotted the automobile," says Amos Loveday, an Ohio state historic preservation officer. "They saw the plane coming." He added, "It was the internal-combustion engine, not the vehicle type, that changed transportation."

11. Sidney C. Schaer, "A Robot for Every Chore," posted in 1999 at http://future.newsday.com as part of Long Island *Newsday*'s "Countdown to 2000" series.

12. Ray Kurzweil, *The Age of Spiritual Machines* (New York: Viking, 1999), p. 195. "Once your car's computer guidance system locks onto the control sensors on one of these highways, you can sit back and relax," the author writes. The technology for that kind of travel has indeed arrived, but implementation is unlikely before 2010, if ever.

13. Seymour Dunbar, *History of Travel in America* (Indianapolis: Bobbs-Merrill, 1915), pp. 232–67. Dunbar's account will make you weep, so great was John Fitch's determination to share the news of his wonderful steamboat, and so indifferent the public.

14. P. J. Mark, "Book Proposal Adds to 'IT' Mystery," posted at www.inside.com, January 9, 2001. Apple founder Steve Jobs proclaimed, "If enough people see the machine [IT], you won't have to convince them to architect cities around it. It'll just happen."

2. We Can't Go On Like This

1. Corey Kilgannon, "Technology Puts Gridlock to Business Use: Fancy Cars and Gadgets Help Keep Road Rage at Bay," *New York Times,* August 15, 2000, p. B1.

2. Patricia Leigh Brown, "In 'the Other California,' a Land Rush Continues,"

New York Times, December 27, 2000, p. A14. The new residents of Tracy are called BATs, for Bay Area Transplants.

3. "Electronic Devices Pose Traffic Threat," *New York Times,* July 19, 2000, p. A20.

4. "In Atlanta, More Births on the Road," *New York Times,* August 14, 2000, p. A11.

5. The statistics in this paragraph come from a perceptive and engagingly written book by James Howard Kunstler, *Home from Nowhere: Remaking Our Everyday World for the Twenty-first Century* (New York: Simon & Schuster, 1996), pp. 68–69.

6. Paul Hawken, Amory Lovins, and L. Hunter Lovins, *Natural Capitalism: Creating the Next Industrial Revolution* (New York: Little, Brown and Company, 1999), p. 40.

7. The cartoon, by Kevin Kallaugher (KAL) of the *Baltimore Sun,* was reproduced in the *New York Times* "Week in Review" section on March 26, 2000.

8. 1995 Nationwide Personal Transportation Survey, U.S. Department of Transportation, 1999, p. 9.

9. Kunstler, *Home from Nowhere,* p. 58.

10. The information cited in this paragraph is from "Transportation Statistics Annual Report, 1999," Bureau of Transportation Statistics, U.S. Department of Transportation, 1999.

11. Robert D. Putnam, *Bowling Alone: The Collapse and Revival of American Community* (New York: Simon & Schuster, 2000), pp. 212–13.

12. Daniel B. Klein and Gordon J. Fielding, "Private Toll Roads: Learning from the Nineteenth Century," *Transportation Quarterly,* July 1992.

13. "Turnpike Roads," *Albany Register,* June 13, 1796.

14. Matthew Purdy, "Inching Along in a Slow Lane to Frustration," *New York Times,* July 19, 2000, p. B1.

15. Rocco Parascandola, "Drivers Pay Twice for Trip in E-ZPass Rip-Off," *New York Post,* August 7, 2000, p. 6. Apparently, 4,634 drivers who drove through temporary cash-only lanes on some New York bridges paid the $3.50 fare twice.

16. "Dark Side of SunPass," editorial in the *Orlando Sentinel,* June 13, 2000.

17. "Curbing Gridlock: Peak-Period Fees to Relieve Traffic Congestion," Vols. 1 and 2, National Research Council, 1993.

18. "Public Funds Should Not Be Used to Build Toll Roads," *Los Angeles Times,* March 19, 1991.

19. Robert W. Poole Jr. and C. Kenneth Orski, "Building a Case for Hot Lanes," Reason Public Policy Institute, Study No. 257, April 1999.

20. Dr. John Holtzclaw, "New Emissions Assay: Freeway Growth Pollutes; Traffic Calming Cleans," posted on the Sierra Club Web site at www.sierraclub.org/sprawl/transportation/hwyemis.asp.

21. Poole and Orski, "Building a Case."

22. Daniel Sperling, *Future Drive: Electric Vehicles and Sustainable Transportation* (Washington, D.C.: Island Press, 1995), p. 24.

23. Tom Lewis, *Divided Highways: Building the Interstate Highways, Transforming American Life* (New York: Viking, 1997), p. 43.

3. SPRAWLING OUT: HIGHWAYS TO NOWHERE

1. Sim Van der Ryn and Peter Calthorpe, *Sustainable Communities* (San Francisco: Sierra Club Books, 1986), p. 43. I visited Sim Van der Ryn once, and his home, near Point Reyes, California, is certainly the antithesis of a suburban ranch. Banisters are made of driftwood and sinks carved from tree stumps. Among his many works is *The Toilet Papers,* a highly informative short history of the commode.

2. Phillip Langdon, *A Better Place to Live: Reshaping the American Suburb* (Amherst: University of Massachusetts Press, 1994), p. 1.

3. Rosalyn Baxandall and Elizabeth Ewen, *Picture Windows: How the Suburbs Happened* (New York: Basic Books, 2000), p. 111.

4. Ibid., p. 56.

5. Robert A. Caro, *The Power Broker* (New York: Random House, 1974), p. 919.

6. Baxandall and Ewen, *Picture Windows,* p. 26.

7. Tom Lewis, *Divided Highways: Building the Interstate Highways, Transforming American Life* (New York: Viking, 1997), p. 7.

8. Ibid., page 122.

9. Peter Samuel, "The Transportation Lobby: The Politics of Highways and Transit," a report prepared for the Capital Research Center, p. 6.

10. "Unclogging America's Arteries: Prescriptions for Healthier Highways," a report prepared for the American Highway Users Alliance by Cambridge Systematics, November 1999.

11. James Howard Kunstler, *Home from Nowhere: Remaking Our Everyday World for the Twenty-first Century* (New York: Simon & Schuster, 1996), p. 67.

12. Tom Horton, "Rethinking Growth," *Land & People,* Fall 2000, p. 20.

13. The July 2000 poll was conducted by Mason-Dixon Polling and Research on behalf of the group Negative Population Growth. The poll showed that negative attitudes about population growth, sprawl, and traffic increased exponentially the closer voters were to the Washington, D.C., commuter corridor. Traffic was the number one problem cited by northern Virginians, but those in the southern part of the state rated education and crime as more serious.

14. The three-paragraph section on Loudon County is adapted with permission from Linda Baker, "Growing Pains: The Fast-Moving Fight to Stop Urban Sprawl," *E* magazine, May–June 2000.

15. Haya El Nasser, "Survey Favors Controlling Sprawl," *USA Today,* October 17, 2000, p. 3A. Don Chen, director of the coalition that sponsored the survey, described the results repudiating sprawl as "stunning." He added, "What that tells me is that the public really wants government to do something about sprawl. If I were a public official, I'd start paying attention."

16. Horton, "Rethinking Growth," pp. 20–21.

17. Mike Sunnucks, "Maryland's Smart-Growth Policies Garner Accolades," *Washington Business Journal,* October 20, 2000. Sunnucks notes that Maryland's program won it a $100,000 award through the Innovations in American Government Program administered by Harvard University and the Ford Foundation.

18. The interview with Peter Calthorpe was conducted by Scott London for the radio series *Insight and Outlook* in 1996.

19. Robert Cervero, *The Transit Metropolis: A Global Inquiry* (Washington, D.C.: Island Press, 1998), p. 72.

20. Dr. Joseph Coughlin, "New Forms of Travel in the New Century," ABC News live "chat" transcript, June 24, 2000. The full chat session is on the Web at www.abcnews.go.com/sections/tech/DailyNews/chat_future-transport062499.html.

21. Cervero, *Transit Metropolis,* pp. 265–96.

22. Kunstler, *Home from Nowhere,* p. 67.

23. Joel Kugelmass, *Telecommuting: A Manager's Guide to Flexible Work Arrangements* (New York: Lexington Books, 1995), p. 65.

24. Jan Paschal, "This Friday, Just Commute Down the Hall," Reuters News Service, July 19, 2000.

25. The results of the Telework America 2000 survey are posted on the Internet site of the International Telework Association and Council at www.telecommute.org.

26. Jeff Westover, "Telecommuting: Added Perk or Added Work," www.myjobsearch.com, April 2000. The Arthur D. Little study also says that if 10 to 20 percent of car-driving commuters switched to telecommuting, it would eliminate 1.8 million tons of pollutants, save 3.5 billion gallons of gas, and free up 3.1 billion hours of personal time.

27. "Transportation Implications of Telecommuting," Department of Transportation in consultation with the Department of Energy and the Environmental Protection Agency, posted at www.bts.gov/ntl/DOCS/telecommute.html. With federal understatement, the program notes that

"estimates of the future level and impacts of telecommuting are highly uncertain."

28. "Saying Adios to the Office," a *Business Week* special report, October 12, 1998. The information on specific companies was compiled by *Business Week* as part of a companion story entitled "Telecommuting-Friendly Employers."

29. "State Statutes Citing Telecommuting," posted on the Web at www. nctr.usf.edu.

30. Neil Strother, "Is Your Job Goin' Mobile?" ZDNet, June 14, 2000, posted on-line at www.zdnet.com. By 2004, the survey forecasts, 90 percent of the employees of large companies will be connected to the corporation's electronic network, a factor that makes telecommuting much easier.

31. Alice Bredin, *The Virtual Office Survival Handbook* (New York: John Wiley & Sons, 1996), p. 8.

32. Lisa Shaw, *Telecommute! Go to Work Without Leaving Home* (New York: John Wiley & Sons, 1996), p. 7.

33. Christine Chen, "Will Amazon(.com) Save the Amazon?" *eCompany Now,* March 2000. Joseph Romm is a former Assistant Secretary of Energy and author of the book *Cool Companies,* which outlines how corporations are reducing greenhouse gas emissions.

4. Transit Cities

Boston

1. For most of this section on the early transit history of Boston, I am indebted to Lawrence W. Kennedy and his book *Planning the City on the Hill* (Amherst: University of Massachusetts Press, 1992).

2. "First Car off the Earth," *Boston Daily Globe,* September 1, 1897, p. 1. The *Globe* account is amazingly florid, in the typical language of the day. Here's a sample: "The trolley hissed along like a brood of vipers, and the car shed where was housed the coach destined to be the first regular to get off the earth was reached just as the gray of morning smiled sleepily over the high piles and lofty spires."

3. Jane Holtz Kay, *Asphalt Nation: How the Automobile Took Over America and How We Can Take It Back* (New York: Crown Publishers, 1997), p. 62.

4. Katie Alvord, *Divorce Your Car!* (Gabriola Island, B.C.: New Society Publishers, 2000), p. 230.

5. Kennedy, *Planning the City,* p. 167. Proposals to run the Central Artery underground were floated in the 1970s and 1980s but were delayed.

6. The project's own Web site, www.bigdig.com, is a wealth of statistical information.

7. "Big Dig Wins Second Porker," press release from Wisconsin Congressman

Tom Petri, September 19, 1997. The Porker Award was given for spending "big money on Big Dig expenses that had little or nothing to do with the legitimate purposes of Boston's Central Artery Project."

8. Thomas C. Palmer Jr., "Review Cites Flaws at Big Dig," *Boston Globe,* January 8, 2001.

9. Petri, "Big Dig Wins Second Porker."

10. Guy Rosmarin, "Missing Link: Connecting North and South Stations Would Close a Crucial Gap," from "Turning Point," a *Boston Globe* special section on transit, October 30, 1994, p. 17.

11. Steven Wilmsen, "Obstacle Cited in Harbor Project," *Boston Globe,* July 19, 2000.

Portland

12. "Beyond the Field of Dreams: Light Rail and Growth Management in Portland," a Tri-Met report dated February 2, 1997.

13. Alan Ehrenhalt, "Suburbs with a Healthy Dose of Fantasy," *New York Times,* July 9, 2000, p. 15.

14. Ibid.

15. Gordon Oliver, "Harvard Transit Study Gives Black Mark to Light Rail," *Oregonian,* July 8, 1998. Like many critics of light rail, Richmond favors dedicated busways as well as van pools.

16. Linda Baker, "High-Mileage Moms," *Oregonian,* May 7, 2000.

17. I found an account of the Federal Office of Road Safety report on the Internet site www.drivers.com.

18. "U.S. Women as Consumers," a Ford fact sheet, updated January 31, 2000. I thank Ford's Kathleen Hamilton for providing it to me as "helpful research."

New York City

19. Department of City Planning, City of New York, "Land Use Facts," posted at www.ci.nyc.us/html.

20. Robert Geddes, ed., *Cities in Our Future* (Washington, D.C.: Island Press, 1997), p. 130.

21. New York Metropolitan Transportation Council, "Regional Transportation Statistical Report," 1998.

22. Diane Cardwell, "Survey Finds Subway Riders' Biggest Gripe Is Crowding," *New York Times,* November 30, 2000, p. B3. Rick Anderson, an art dealer, said of the Fifty-first Street station, "It is absolutely the worst. It's crowded, and the platform is jammed. Sometimes if I'm standing at the edge of the platform it feels unsafe."

23. The letter is quoted in the December 2000 issue of "Mobilizing the Region," a weekly fax bulletin from the Tri-State Transportation Campaign.

24. Gene Russianoff, "New York's Butterfly," *New York Times,* December 7, 2000, p. A39. Voting on the proposition, says Russianoff, "was like playing 'Where's Waldo?'"

25. Charles Komanoff, "Bikes Are Safe, It's Cars That Kill," *New York Daily News,* December 10, 1997.

26. Charles Komanoff, "For Rachel Fruchter," posted on the Right of Way Web site at www.panix.com.

27. The history of this critical roadway is detailed in "West Side Highway," a lengthy treatise posted at www.nycroads.com.

28. New York's colorful ferry history is celebrated in Brian J. Cudahy, *Over and Back: The History of Ferryboats in New York Harbor* (New York: Fordham University Press, 1988), pp. 7–19.

29. Gene Russianoff, "Fare's Frozen but Subways Still Suffer," *New York Daily News,* December 5, 2000.

30. Jane Holtz Kay, *Asphalt Nation,* pp. 256–57.

31. Randy Kennedy, "Bearing Stunned Commuters, the Subway of the Future Begins a 30-Day Test Run," *New York Times,* July 11, 2000, p. B3.

32. Iver Peterson, "E-ZPass System Faces $65 Million Deficit, and Its Success Is Partly to Blame," *New York Times,* December 9, 2000, p. B5. Another problem for revenue collection is that fewer drivers than expected tried to dodge the tolls. Fines have not yielded the anticipated windfall.

33. "Comments on the NYC Transportation Coordination Committee draft 2000–2004 Transportation Improvement Program," Tri-State Transportation Campaign, June 25, 1999.

34. John Pucher and Lewis Dijkstra, "Making Walking and Cycling Safer: Lessons from Europe," *Transportation Quarterly,* Summer 2000, p. 2.

35. Ibid., p. 19.

36. Thomas J. Lueck, "Public Transit Is Essential for Stadium, Mayor Says," *New York Times,* December 9, 2000, p. B2. Football executives said their own studies showed that fans could get to the stadium on existing public transit or could find parking spaces in existing lots, a dubious proposition.

Los Angeles

37. The statistics in this paragraph are from Hugo Martin, "Watch for Slowing Traffic," *Los Angeles Times,* June 24, 1999. With some pessimism, Martin notes that "commuters are slow to try ride-sharing. Subway tunneling is too expensive, and monorail trains running down the middle of our freeways are too controversial."

38. Annette Kondo and Edgar Sandoval, "Parking Spot-Check," *Los Angeles Times,* August 16, 2000.

39. The statistic is from the East-West Transit Coalition, based in Santa

Monica, a rail-supporting coalition encompassing the Transportation Committee of the Los Angeles chapter of the Sierra Club, the Latino Urban Forum, and Southern California Transit Advocates.

40. The statistics are from *Public Transportation Fact Book* 2000, published by the American Public Transportation Association.

41. President George W. Bush's remark was reported on the Web site www.newscom.com on February 28, 2000. It's uncertain how a marked insensitivity to people dependent on mass transit played out among California's Hispanic voters, who make up more than 13 percent of the electorate statewide.

42. The details of the settlement are described in Robert Garcia, "Transportation Equity in Los Angeles: The MTA and Beyond," posted on the Environmental Defense Web site at www.edf.org/programs/Transportation/Equity/b_justice.html. Garcia, as an attorney for the NAACP Legal Defense and Educational Fund, was a lead counsel for the plaintiffs in the case. He has since taken a job with Environmental Defense, which is advising the Bus Riders Union.

43. Mike Davis, *City of Quartz: Excavating the Future in Los Angeles* (New York: Vintage Books, 1992), pp. 110–13.

44. Kevin Starr, *Inventing the Dream: California Through the Progressive Era* (New York: Oxford University Press, 1985), p. 41.

45. Stephen Longstreet, *All-Star Cast: An Anecdotal History of Los Angeles* (New York: Thomas Y. Crowell, 1977), p. 212.

46. Robert Dawson and Grey Brechin, *Farewell, Promised Land* (Berkeley: University of California Press, 1999), p. 99.

47. Robert P. Sechler, "The Seven Eras of Rapid Transit Planning in Los Angeles," a report posted on the Web site of the Electric Railway Historical Association of Southern California at www.erha.org/seveneras.htm.

48. Davis, *City of Quartz,* pp. 122 and 205–06.

Arcata

49. Walter C. Schafran, *The Northwest Coast of California and Humboldt Bay: Seen by Few, Missed by Many* (Arcata: Center for Community Development, Humboldt State University, 1983), p. 14.

50. Lewis Keysor Wood, *The Discovery of Humboldt Bay* (San Francisco: Society of the California Pioneers, 1932), p. 10.

51. Wallace W. Elliot, *History of Humboldt County* (San Francisco: Wallace W. Elliot and Company, 1881), p. 131.

52. A very useful early history of transportation in the Humboldt region is contained in an essay by Ben Kessler of Arcata High School, "Why the Lost Coast Is Lost," posted at www.northcoast.com.

53. Lawrence Williams, "Route Concepts," *Arcata Eye,* June 20, 2000.

54. Daniel Pierce, "Existing Rails Could Become Arcata's Trolley System," *Arcata Eye,* June 13, 2000.

55. "Arcata Nation: Just Another Week in the Life, Such as It Is, of Our Tofu-Powered Town," unsigned editorial, *Arcata Eye,* July 3, 2000.

56. Arno Holschuh, "Workin' on the Railroad," *North Coast Journal Weekly,* April 13, 2000, p. 1. Arcatans have only to visit the Eel River Canyon to see how the train carries off their natural heritage: several lumber-laden freight cars were marooned by the landslides.

57. Jim Shields, "$60 Million Down the NCRA Sinkhole," *Arcata Eye,* July 11, 2000. When Caltrans assessed NCRA's performance, Shields writes, it "gloomily diagnosed the carrier's financial lifestyle as 'high risk.'"

58. Pierce, "Existing Rails."

59. Mark Tide, "Rails to Trails from Arcata to Blue Lake," *Arcata Journal,* October 1, 1999.

5. EUROPE AND AMERICA: DIFFERENT ROADS TAKEN

1. Timothy Beatley; *Green Urbanism: Learning from European Cities* (Washington, D.C.: Island Press, 2000), pp. 109–10.

2. Robert Cervero, *The Transit Metropolis: A Global Inquiry* (Washington, D.C.: Island Press, 1998), pp. 300–302.

3. Ibid., p. 307.

4. Beatley, *Green Urbanism,* p. 128.

5. Ibid., p. 140.

6. Ibid., p. 140.

7. Peter Newman and Jeffrey Kenworthy, *Sustainability and Cities: Overcoming Automobile Dependence* (Washington, D.C.: Island Press, 1999), p. 150.

8. Bryan Cartledge, ed., *Transport and the Environment* (New York: Oxford University Press, 1996), p. 39. The statistics about Copenhagen's transport priorities are drawn from an article in the British *Independent,* dated March 25, 1994.

9. Ibid., p. 25. The figures on miles traveled by car versus rail, bus, and cycle in Great Britain are drawn from 1993 Department of Transport statistics.

10. "Manufacturers Strive to Communicate Benefits of Telematics to Consumers," Frost & Sullivan press release, June 14, 1999. A full report on the company's strategic research is on the Internet at www.frost.com.

11. "Cars Gear Up to Cruise the Info-Bahn," MSNBC report, June 16, 2000.

12. Ibid.

13. Information on these programs in the United States, Europe, and Japan is from James B. Reed, Janet B. Goehring, and Chris Pattarozzi,

"Intelligent Transportation in America: Prospects and Perils," a report prepared for the National Conference of State Legislatures, January 1996.

14. James H. Rillings, "Automated Highways," *Scientific American,* October 1997. This article was written by the program manager of the National Automated Highway System Consortium before the federal government pulled the plug on that enterprise.

15. The current use of automation technology in vehicles is described in a Department of Transportation report entitled "Current AVCS Deployment," available on the Internet at http://ahs.volpe.dot.gov/avcsdoc/inuse.html.

16. A summary of how real people react to automated highways is contained in the federal report "Human Factors Design of Automated Highway Systems: Progress to Date," May 1996, posted on the Internet at http://ahs.volpe.dot.gov/human/human.html.

17. "National Automated Highway System Research Program: A Review," Transportation Research Board, Special Report No. 253.

6. RETHINKING THE CAR: A FUTURE FOR FUEL CELLS

1. Ariane Sains, "Battle of the Pumps," *Tomorrow,* July–August 2000, p. 12.

2. John Tagliabue, "Translating S.U.V. into European," *New York Times,* December 14, 1999, p. C1.

3. Keith Bradsher, "Was Freud a Minivan or S.U.V. Kind of Guy?" *New York Times,* July 17, 2000, p. A1.

4. James Cannon, *Harnessing Hydrogen* (New York: Inform Inc., 1995), p. 57.

5. The quotes are taken from a summary of the June 25, 2000, London *Sunday Telegraph* story that appeared in the German newsletter *Hydrogen-Gazette,* which is available via e-mail and on-line at www.hydrogen.org/News/gazette.html.

6. Schrempp talked about the coming oil crisis during a speech celebrating World Engineers Day in Hanover, Germany, June 19, 2000.

7. Katharine Q. Seelye, "Price of Gasoline Emerges as Issue in Bush-Gore Race," *New York Times,* June 22, 2000.

8. Wayne Madsen, "Cheney at the Helm," *Progressive,* September 2000, p. 21.

9. Cheney was quoted in Mike Allen and Michael D. Shear, "Democratic Ads Lambaste Bush Record," *Washington Post,* October 10, 2000, p. A7.

10. Elaine Sciolino, "Washington Insider and Family Loyalist Poised for Job of Bush Chief of Staff," *New York Times,* November 28, 2000, p. A23.

11. Bill Moore, "Shell Hydrogen's Name Says It All," a synopsis of Alastair Livesey's keynote speech delivered at the 1999 Environmental Vehicle Conference, Ypsilanti, Michigan, July 24, 1999. The synopsis is posted

on the invaluable *EV World* Web site at www.evworld.com. *EV World* is a key source for up-to-date information on just about every aspect of the hydrogen economy.

12. Eric Johnson, "Big Step Toward Hydrogen Fuel Stations," United Press International, July 15, 1999.

13. Sains, "Battle of the Pumps," p. 12.

14. Paul Hawken, Amory Lovins, L. Hunter Lovins, *Natural Capitalism: Creating the Next Industrial Revolution* (New York: Little, Brown and Company, 1999), pp. 35–36.

15. Ibid., pp. 34–37.

16. Glen Martin, "Enzyme Lets Algae Produce Hydrogen to Use as Clean Fuel," *San Francisco Chronicle,* January 31, 2000. The fact that algae give off small amounts of hydrogen has long been known. The professors' breakthrough was dramatically increasing production of the gas by a "nutrient stress" to the algae.

17. "DaimlerChrysler Joins California Fuel Cell Partnership with Goal of Bringing Fuel Cell Technology to Production," PRNewswire press release, April 20, 1999.

18. Ian Wylie, "Whoosh! Iceland's Got a Hot Idea," *Fast Company,* October 2000, p. 50. Iceland could also become a major international producer of hydrogen.

19. Jeffrey Ball, "Will California Pull the Plug on Push for Electric Cars?" *Wall Street Journal,* March 28, 2000.

20. Bill Moore, "CARB Staff Report: Reading Between the Lines," *EVWorld,* August 21, 2000.

21. Toyota News Wire e-mailed the study to me in a press release dated May 31, 2000.

22. Bill Moore, "Do 10 Million Californians Want EVs?" *EVWorld,* October 9, 2000. The study was conducted over the Internet by Dohring Research and surveyed nine hundred California drivers who said they planned to buy a new car within two years.

23. "Fuel Economy Standards Called Deadly," Environmental News Network, July 15, 2000.

24. John DeCicco, Roland Hwang, Jim Kliesch, and Candace Morey, "Pollution Lineup: An Environmental Ranking of Automakers," Union of Concerned Scientists report, March 2000, p. vi.

25. Ibid.

26. Jerry M. Flint, "G.M. Develops Emission Curbs Expected to Pass Federal Test," *New York Times,* September 25, 1972, p. 1. Among the howlers in the story was this: "G.M. now believes that, with its developments, emissions can be virtually eliminated from car exhaust."

27. Keith Bradsher, "General Motors Raises Stakes in Fuel Economy War with Ford," *New York Times,* August 3, 2000, p. C1. If Ford and GM do improve sport-utility fuel economy as promised by 2005, it could have a major effect, since each automaker builds more than a million of them every year.

28. "Selling Fuel Cells," *Economist,* July 1, 2000, p. 83. "It looks increasingly likely that the eventual replacement for the internal-combustion engine in motor vehicles will be the fuel cell," the magazine wrote.

29. John Lippert, "GM Plans High-Volume Production of Fuel-Cell Vehicles," Bloomberg News, June 30, 2000.

30. Keith Bradsher, "Can Motor City Come Up with a Clean Machine?" *New York Times,* May 19, 1999, G1.

31. A copy of the letter, dated June 19, 2000, was sent to the journalist and author Lesley Hazleton, who passed it on to me.

32. DeCicco, Hwang, Kliesch, and Morey, "Pollution Lineup," pp. v–vi. Honda's performance might be worse if it produced more light trucks.

7. Greening the Bus: Next Stop, Sustainability

1. Angie Farleigh and Leah Kaplan, "Dangers of Diesel," a report from the U.S. PIRG Education Fund, Washington, D.C., 2000, p. 2.

2. Jason Mark and Candace Morey, "Rolling Smokestacks: Cleaning Up America's Trucks and Buses," a report from the Union of Concerned Scientists, Cambridge, Mass., 2000.

3. Michael McCarthy, "Hidden Cost of the Freight Trade," *Independent,* November 11, 2000.

4. "Cancer Risk from Diesel Particulate: National and Metropolitan Area Estimates for the United States," press release, State and Territorial Air Pollution Program Administrators and Local Air Pollution Control Officials, March 12, 2000. According to the release, "Diesel exhaust contains over 40 chemicals that are listed by EPA and California as toxic air contaminants, known human carcinogens, probable human carcinogens, reproductive toxicants or endocrine disrupters."

5. Gary Polakovic, "13 States Join California's Bid to Curb Diesel Emissions," *Los Angeles Times,* November 20, 2000.

6. H. Josef Hebert, "Engine Makers Accused on Pollution," Associated Press, August 1, 2000.

7. Matthew L. Wald, "13 States to Unite to Cut Truck Emissions," *New York Times,* November 19, 2000, p. A20.

8. "NRDC Applauds 13-State Action to Clean Up Dirty Diesels," NRDC press release, November 20, 2000.

9. Stephen B. Goddard, *Getting There: The Epic Struggle Between Road and Rail in the American Century* (New York: Basic Books, 1994), p. 122.

10. Deborah Gordon, *Steering a New Course: Transportation, Energy and the Environment* (Washington, D.C.: Island Press, 1991), p. 20.

11. Edwin Slipek, Jr., "The Road to Nowhere," *Style Weekly,* February 7, 1997.

12. Amanda Caracci, "University, Bus Riders Resist City Rail Line," *Daily Trojan,* October 3, 2000.

13. John I. Gilderbloom, "Creating the Accessible City," a report posted on the University of Louisville Web site at www.louisville.edu/org/sun/housing/cd_v2/Bookarticles/Ch1.htm.

14. Robert D. Bullard, Glenn S. Johnson, and Angel O. Torres, eds., *Sprawl City: Race, Politics and Planning in Atlanta* (Washington, D.C.: Island Press, 2000), pp. 50–51.

15. Diane Cardwell, "Environmental Group Files Complaint Against M.T.A.," *New York Times,* November 16, 2000, p. B3.

16. Gordon, *Steering a New Course,* p. 134.

17. "Benefits of Electric and Hybrid-Electric Buses for Public Transit Systems," Electric Transit Vehicle Institute Web page posted at www.etvi.org.

18. The story of the Chattanooga electric shuttle is told on the Chattanooga Area Regional Transportation Authority Web site at www.carta-bus.org.

19. Paul Griffith, "The Electric Bus: Expectations and Realizations," posted on the Santa Barbara Electric Transportation Institute Web site at www.sbeti.com.

20. Leon Drouin, "California Strives to Cut Pollution Emitted by State's School Buses," *Detroit News,* September 20, 2000.

21. "Air Quality Management District, General Motors Announce Community Clean Air Partnership," General Motors press release, August 20, 2000.

22. Robert Cervero, *The Transit Metropolis: A Global Inquiry* (Washington, D.C.: Island Press, 1998), p. 243.

23. Ibid.

24. The dedicated busway is described in "SpeedLink Fact Sheet," a handout distributed by Detroit's Metropolitan Affairs Coalition.

25. Information on Los Angeles's Metro Rapid signal-priority system is posted at http://brt.volpe.dot.gov/projects/losangeles.html.

26. Diana Sahagun, "North Las Vegas Chosen to Test New Electric Bus," *Las Vegas Sun,* August 4, 2000. The buses are large enough to carry 140 passengers, double the capacity of Las Vegas's standard transit buses.

8. On Track with High-Speed Trains

1. Wolfgang Schivelbusch, *Histoire des Voyages en Train* (The History of Train Travel) (Paris: La Promeneur, 1977). The book was published in German

and French, and Hans Koning was kind enough to translate from the French edition.

2. Clifton Hood, *722 Miles: The Building of the Subways and How They Transformed New York* (New York: Simon & Schuster, 1993).

3. Stephen B. Goddard, *Getting There: The Epic Struggle Between Road and Rail in the American Century* (New York: Basic Books, 1994), p. 14.

4. Ibid., pp. 43 and 56.

5. Ibid., p. 174.

6. Bob Johnston, "Amtrak's *City of New Orleans* Alive and Kicking," *Trains,* February 1998.

7. John F. Stover, *The Life and Decline of the American Railroad* (New York: Oxford University Press, 1970), p. 216. The railroads enjoyed a brief renaissance in the 1950s when they added domed observation cars called vista-domes, astra-domes, and strata-domes. The style was so popular that it was copied in the late 1960s by General Motors on a station wagon, the Oldsmobile Vista Cruiser.

8. Goddard, *Getting There,* p. 227.

9. "Japanese Bullet Train Technology," *New Technology Japan,* December 1994.

10. The information about the bullet trains is contained in a "Frequently Asked Questions" posting sponsored by the Japanese railroads at www2.neweb.ne.jp.

11. Copious amounts of information about the TGV is available on the railroad's Web site at www.railway-technology.com/projects/frenchtgv. It's in English. Interestingly enough, when my friend Hans Koning wrote and asked for information on my behalf, the TGV sent a beautiful press kit— in French.

12. Hans Koning, "A French Mirror," *Atlantic Monthly,* December 1995.

13. "Amtrak Fact Sheet," posted at www.amtrak.com.

14. The information is from a letter to the editor sent by E. S. Bagley, president of Amtrak Northeast Corridor, to the *Boston Business Journal* on March 26, 1999. "During the 1990s alone," the letter said, "the number of T trains we operate daily has grown 43 percent."

15. Kevin Coughlin, "U.S. Will Have to Wait Still Longer for High-Speed Rail," Newhouse News Service, June 28, 2000.

16. Don Phillips, "Amtrak Halts Tests of New Fast Trains," *Washington Post,* June 20, 2000, p. A14.

17. Coughlin, "U.S. Will Have to Wait."

18. Joel Garreau, *Edge City: Life on the New Frontier* (New York: Doubleday, 1991), p. 130. Garreau estimates that because of interminable stops, commuter rail has an average speed lower than that of cars stuck in rush-hour traffic.

19. Larry Sandler and Frank A. Aukofer, "Amtrak Bets on the Need for Speed," *Milwaukee Journal Sentinel,* February 13, 2000.

20. Garreau, *Edge City,* pp. 131–32.

21. Wendell Cox, "Evaluation of the FDOT-FOX Miami-Orlando-Tampa High-Speed Rail Proposal," prepared by the Wendell Cox Consultancy and listed as James Madison Institute Policy Report No. 21, April 1997. The full text is on the Internet at www.jamesmadison.org/high-speedrailonline.html.

22. "Deadliest Train Crash in Amtrak History Kills 44," an EmergencyNet News press release dated September 23, 1992 and posted on the Internet at www.emergency.com.

23. "Public Strongly Supports Continuing Government Subsidies for Amtrak," Gallup Poll press release, 1997.

24. Joseph Vranich, "Replacing Amtrak: A Blueprint for Sustainable Passenger Rail Service," Reason Public Policy Institute, Study No. 235, October 1997.

25. Testimony of George Warrington, acting president and chief executive officer of the National Railroad Passenger Corporation before the House Appropriations Subcommittee on Transportation and Related Agencies, March 11, 1998, 1:00 P.M. Warrington pointed out to Congress that Amtrak had achieved its gains in a period when federal operating support had declined by nearly 50 percent.

26. Michael Martinez, "Marvelous Maglev," ABC News report, posted at www.abcnews.go.com, June 24, 1999.

27. Peter H. Stone, "The Faster Track: Should We Build a High-Speed Rail System?" *American Prospect,* Fall 1992.

28. "Germany: Mag-lev Dropped for Fast Trains," *Financial Times,* February 11, 2000.

29. The description of the various types of mag-lev technology is adapted from an understandable summary in Scott R. Gourley, "Track to the Future," *Popular Mechanics,* May 1998.

30. "Sandia's Magnetically Powered Train Development Project Funded by Congress, Approved by President," press release, Sandia National Laboratories, October 31, 2000. Sandia would also like to use Seraphim to build a transit system between Santa Fe and Albuquerque, New Mexico, along the route of the congested I-25 highway.

31. Dr. Richard F. Post, "Maglev: A New Approach," *Scientific American,* January 2000. Dr. Post invented Inductrack at Lawrence Livermore National Laboratory.

32. Ralph Stein, *The Treasury of the Automobile* (New York: Golden Press, 1961), p. 243.

33. Paula Taylor, *The Kids' Whole Future Catalog* (New York: Random House, 1982), p. 144.
34. Paul Bass, "Meet George Jetson," *New Haven Advocate*, June 29, 2000. Bass, one of the country's most civic-minded columnists, reports that he "ran the idea [of SkyTran] by some transportation honchos. Guess what? None of them dismissed the idea as crazy."

9. THE FUTURE OF FLYING

1. Susan Carey, "United Grapples with Summer of Widespread Discontent," *Wall Street Journal*, August 8, 2000, p. A2.
2. Statistics from Dr. Ian Humphreys, "Air Transport: An Overview," posted on the Internet at www.farnborough-aircraft.com/Crisis_Watch/Air_Transport_Overview.asp. Dr. Humphreys is air transport management coordinator at Loughborough University in England.
3. Jon Hilkevitch, "FAA Says Some of the Flak It Takes Is Right on Target," *Chicago Tribune*, July 18, 1999.
4. William G. Laffer III, "How to Improve Air Travel in America," Heritage Foundation, *Backgrounder* No. 806, January 25, 1991. It's not surprising that the conservative Heritage Foundation proposes the privatization of airports as a way out of congestion problems.
5. Randy Kennedy, "Doing the Math of Air Delays," *New York Times*, August 25, 2000, p. B1.
6. Humphreys, "Air Transport: An Overview."
7. "The Homestead Air Base Deal," Sierra Club fact sheet, on the Internet at www.sierraclub.org.
8. "Fact Sheet," posted on the Internet site www.homsteadairport.com.
9. Ibid.
10. Jo Thomas, "An Airport Hopes to Build Traffic, Even Just One Flight at a Time," *New York Times*, August 19, 2000, p. A8.
11. T. A. Heppenheimer, *Turbulent Skies: The History of Commercial Aviation* (New York: John Wiley & Sons, 1995), p. 25.
12. Ibid., p. 17.
13. Ibid., p. 314.
14. "1995 American Travel Survey," Bureau of Transportation Statistics, U.S. Department of Transportation, October 1997.
15. Gar Smith, "Oil Spills in the Sky," *Earth Island Journal*, Winter 1997, p. 34.
16. David Holzman, "Plane Pollution," *Environmental Health Perspectives*, December 1997.
17. Ibid.
18. David W. Chen, "Westchester Officials Join Forces to Oppose County Airport's Predawn Flights," *New York Times*, September 30, 2000.

19. Matthew L. Wald, "Can Capitalism Reduce Flights and Delays at La Guardia?" *New York Times,* December 26, 2000, p. B1.

20. Randy Kennedy, "Delays Double at La Guardia Within a Year," *New York Times,* September 30, 2000, p. B1. Kennedy reports that most of the delays were caused "not by weather or mechanical problems but because the airport simply has too much traffic."

21. Wald, "Can Capitalism Reduce?"

22. Hilkevitch, "FAA Says Some of the Flak."

23. Holzman, "Plane Pollution."

24. Kenneth A. Cubbin, "Delays Malaise: Time for Change?" a "guest commentary" posted on AVWeb at www.avweb.com. Cubbin is a flight engineer at an unnamed "major international airline."

25. Ben Sandilands, "A Plane and Simple Answer," *Business Review Weekly,* posted on the Internet at www.brw.com.au.

26. Otis Port, "Taxi! Get Me to Nebraska," *Business Week Online,* November 20, 2000, posted at www.businessweek.com.

27. Randy Kennedy, "Planes, Trains, and a Vintage Cab," *New York Times,* March 13, 2001, p. B1.

28. Heppenheimer, *Turbulent Skies,* p. 5.

29. Gregory Freiherr, "Auto Pilots," *Air and Space,* December 1995.

30. The saga of the ConvAIRCAR is told on the Retrofuture Web site, www.retrofuture.com, in Eric Lefcowitz, "The Only Car That Flies: The ConvAIRCAR."

31. Keith Martin, "Ahoy! Cars That Move on Surf or Turf," *New York Times,* July 21, 2000, p. F1.

32. Freiherr, "Auto Pilots," *Air and Space.*

33. Wendy Nelson, "The Moller Skycar," *Marketplace,* July 10, 2000.

34. Simon Hirschfeld, "Technology Executive Sees Limousines for the Air," Reuters, March 6, 2000.

35. "Rocket Pack Partnership Turns Tragic," *Salt Lake Tribune,* July 27, 1999.

10. The Water Route: A Dream of Fast Ferries

1. Bay Area Council Action Plan, Appendix B: "Summary and Analysis of Major Water Transit Systems," 1998.

2. *Public Transportation Fact Book* 2000 (Washington, D.C.: American Public Transportation Association, 2000), p. 135.

3. Hunter T. George, "Ferry Riders Might Face Biggest Fare Increase Ever Due to I-695," *Seattle Times,* January 20, 2000.

4. "Big Ships Pollute as Much as 2,000 Diesel Trucks," Environmental News Network, July 26, 2000.

5. The cleanup is described in Zefy Christopoulos, "Ferry Tale Comes True in Glen Cove," *Record Pilot*, May 15, 1998.
6. "New York Blocks Mashantucket Pequot Ferry Service," *Danbury News-Times*, March 14, 1998.
7. Paula Peters, "Out of State Service Questioned," *Cape Cod Times*, July 13, 1999.
8. Christopoulos, "Ferry Tale Comes True."
9. Karen Gaudette, "Seattle's High-Speed Ferry Told to Stop Making Waves," *Seattle Times*, August 27, 1999.
10. Larry Lange, "High Wakes Doom B.C.'s High-Speed Ferry Project," *Seattle Post-Intelligencer*, March 15, 2000.
11. David M. Herszenhorn, "For Ferry Plans, One Nautical Mile Forward, Two Back," *New York Times*, August 17, 2000.
12. The history of fast ferryboats is told on the Internet site www.fastferry.co.uk.

11. MOVING FORWARD

1. The two paragraphs on the national parks are derived from Leslie Pardue, "Park and Ride to the Park," *E* magazine, September-October 2000.
2. Matthew L. Wald, "Do Additional Roads Increase Congestion?" *New York Times*, January 28, 2000, p. F1.
3. *Public Transportation Fact Book* 2000 (Washington, D.C.: American Public Transportation Association, 2000), p. 11.
4. Matt Raimi and Kaid Benfield, "Is It a Better Cup of TEA?" Natural Resources Defense Council, 1998.
5. "Changing Directions: Federal Transportation Spending in the 1990s," a report from the Surface Transportation Policy Project, March 20, 2000.
6. Randall O'Toole, "ISTEA: A Poisonous Brew for American Cities," Cato Institute Policy Analysis No. 287, November 5, 1997. O'Toole is executive director of the Thoreau Institute. He called ISTEA the "Urban Immobility and Pork-Barrel Act."
7. The description of the French conference-demonstration is derived from a lively account, "La Death in Lyon," posted on-line in *Car Busters* magazine at www.antenna.nl/eyfa/trafrep.htm.
8. Sharon Boddy, "Car Free and Carefree," *E* magazine, March-April 2000.
9. The letter appeared in the May-June 2000 issue. "When will environmentalists band together and just say NO to auto addiction?" asked the author, Donna Merlina of Bellingham, Washington.
10. "European Union Jump Starts Car-Free Day 2000," Environmental News Service, February 7, 2000.

11. Jeff Israely, "Italy's Traffic Headaches Given a Roman Holiday," *Boston Globe,* February 7, 2000.

12. "Europeans Leave Cars at Home," BBC News, September 22, 2000.

13. "Quirky 'Car-Free' Day in Colombian Capital," Reuters, February 25, 2000.

14. "Bicycle Use Plunges: The Struggle for Sustainability in China's Cities," *Sustainable Transport,* Fall 1999, p. 6.

15. "Auto Boom May Add to China's Pollution," *San Francisco Chronicle,* May 18, 2000.

16. From a contemporary Reclaim the Streets leaflet.

17. Reclaim the Streets tells its own history on the Web site www.gn.apc. org/rts/evol.htm.

18. Julia Guest, "A Green and Pleasant Land?" *E* magazine, May-June 1996.

19. Jane Holtz Kay, *Asphalt Nation: How the Automobile Took Over America and How We Can Take It Back* (New York: Crown Publishers, 1997), pp. 120–21.

20. Laird Harrison, "Depaving Paradise," *Audubon,* March-April 2000.

21. Information from the San Francisco Bicycle Coalition home page at www.sfbike.org.

22. Bob Schildgen, "Critical Mass," *Sierra,* September-October 2000.

23. "Berkeley Youth and Bikes Provide a Fresh Food Alternative," press release from Berkeley Youth Alternatives, March 22, 2000.

24. Jane Holtz Kay, *Asphalt Nation,* p. 128.

25. "Strategic Plan 1998–2003," Tri-Met, adapted April 22, 1998, p. 2.

Bibliography

Alvord, Katie. *Divorce Your Car!* Gabriola Island, B.C.: New Society Publishers, 2000.

Beatley, Timothy. *Green Urbanism: Learning from European Cities.* Washington, D.C.: Island Press, 2000.

Cartledge, Bryan, ed. *Transport and the Environment.* New York: Oxford University Press, 1996.

Cervero, Robert. *The Transit Metropolis: A Global Inquiry.* Washington, D.C.: Island Press, 1998.

Clarke, Arthur C. *Voices from the Sky: Previews of the Coming Space Age.* New York: Harper & Row, 1965.

Davis, Mike. *City of Quartz: Excavating the Future in Los Angeles.* New York: Vintage Books, 1992.

DeCicco, John, Jim Kliesch, and Martin Thomas. *ACEEE's Green Book: The Environmental Guide to Cars and Trucks.* Washington, D.C.: American Council for an Energy-Efficient Economy, 2000.

Doyle, Jack. *Taken for a Ride: Detroit's Big Three and the Politics of Pollution.* New York: Four Walls Eight Windows, 2000.

Durant, John. *Predictions.* New York: A. S. Barnes and Company, 1956.

Engwicht, David. *Reclaiming Our Cities and Towns: Better Living with Less Traffic.* Philadelphia: New Society Publishers, 1993.

Garreau, Joel. *Edge City: Life on the New Frontier.* New York: Doubleday, 1991.

Gordon, Deborah. *Steering a New Course: Transportation, Energy and the Environment.* Washington, D.C.: Island Press, 1991.

Hawken, Paul, Amory Lovins, and L. Hunter Lovins. *Natural Capitalism: Creating the Next Industrial Revolution.* New York: Little, Brown and Company, 1999.

Hertsgaard, Mark. *Earth Odyssey: Around the World in Search of Our Environmental Future.* New York: Broadway Books, 1998.

Hood, Clifton. *722 Miles: The Building of the Subways and How They Transformed New York.* New York: Simon & Schuster, 1993.

Kay, Jane Holtz. *Asphalt Nation: How the Automobile Took Over America and How We Can Take It Back.* New York: Crown Publishers, 1997.

Kennedy, Lawrence W. *Planning the City on the Hill.* Amherst: University of Massachusetts Press, 1992.

Kunstler, James Howard. *Home from Nowhere: Remaking Our Everyday World for the Twenty-first Century.* New York: Simon & Schuster, 1996.

Kurzweil, Ray. *The Age of Spiritual Machines.* New York: Viking, 1999.

Langdon, Phillip. *A Better Place to Live: Reshaping the American Suburb.* Amherst: University of Massachusetts Press, 1994.

Lewis, Tom. *Divided Highways: Building the Interstate Highways, Transforming American Life.* New York: Viking, 1997.

Newman, Peter, and Jeffrey Kenworthy. *Sustainability and Cities: Overcoming Automobile Dependence.* Washington, D.C.: Island Press, 1999.

Putnam, Robert D. *Bowling Alone: The Collapse and Revival of American Community.* New York: Simon & Schuster, 2000.

Raddle, Bruce. *The Merritt Parkway.* New Haven: Yale University Press, 1993.

Sperling, Daniel. *Future Drive: Electric Vehicles and Sustainable Transportation.* Washington, D.C.: Island Press, 1995.

Stover, John F. *The Life and Decline of the American Railroad.* New York: Oxford University Press, 1970.

Suarez, Ray. *The Old Neighborhood: What We Lost in the Great Suburban Migration: 1966–1999.* New York: Free Press, 1999.

Thompson, Gregory Lee. *The Passenger Train in the Motor Age.* Columbus: Ohio State University Press, 1993.

Index

JIM MOTAVALLI, a frequent flier, rail passenger, and ferryboat rider, is the editor of *E: The Environmental Magazine* and the author of *Forward Drive: The Race to Build "Clean" Cars for the Future* (Sierra Club Books). He is a columnist for the Cleveland *Plain Dealer*, Environmental Defense, and the Appalachian Mountain Club's *AMC Outdoors* magazine. His work has appeared in the *New York Times*, the *Boston Globe*, the *Hartford Courant*, *Sierra*, and many other publications. He lives in Fairfield, Connecticut, with his wife and two daughters and teaches at Fairfield University.